Youth, Unemployment and Schooling

EDITED BY

STEPHEN WALKER AND LEN BARTON

Open University Press

Milton Keynes : Philadelphia

Open University Press
Open University Educational Enterprises Limited
12 Cofferidge Close
Stony Stratford
Milton Keynes MK11 1BY, England

and

242 Cherry Street
Philadelphia, PA 19106, USA

First published 1986

British Library Cataloguing in Publication Data

Youth unemployment and schooling.
  1. Youth employment—Great Britain
  2. Vocational education—Great Britain
  I. Walker, Stephen, 1944– II. Barton, Len
  331.3′4′0941   HD6276.G7

ISBN 0-335-15228-7

ISBN 0-335-15227-9 Pbk

W 28296 / 20 . 2 86

Library of Congress Cataloging in Publication Data

  Main entry under title:
  Youth, unemployment and schooling.
  Includes index.
  1. Youth—employment—addresses, essays, lectures.
2. Unemployment—addresses, essays, lectures.
3. Vocational education—addresses, essays, lectures.
I. Walker, Stephen F. II. Barton, Len.
HD6270.Y677   1985   331.3′412042   85-28418

ISBN 0-335-15228-7

ISBN 0-335-15227-9 (pbk)

Text design by Clarke Williams
Typeset by Gilbert Composing Services, Leighton Buzzard, Beds.
Printed in Great Britain.

Contents

Acknowledgements

The chapters that appear in this collection are all versions of papers originally presented at the International Sociology of Education Conference held in Birmingham in January 1984. The Conference is supported by Carfax Publishing Company, of Oxford.

We are grateful for the encouragement and help of our publisher, John Skelton, and of Janet Cowsill in the preparation of the manuscript. Our thanks must also go to Sandra Walker and Joan Barton for their patience and support.

Contributors

Paul Atkinson Department of Sociology, University College, PO Box 78, Cardiff, CF1 1XL.

Len Barton Department of Education, Bristol Polytechnic, Redland Hill, Redland, Bristol BS6 6UZ.

Carol Buswell Faculty of Community and Social Studies, Newcastle-upon-Tyne Polytechnic, Northumberland Road, Newcastle-upon-Tyne NE1 8ST.

Roger Dale School of Education, Open University, Milton Keynes MK7 6AA.

Hilary Dickinson, Department of Sociology, Garnett College, Roehampton Lane, London SW15 4HR.

Michael Erben Department of Sociology, Garnett College, Roehampton Lane, London SW15 4HR.

Denis Gleeson Department of Education, University of Keele, Keele, Staffordshire ST5 5BG.

John Horne, Department of Sociology, North Staffordshire Polytechnic, Leek Road, Stoke-on-Trent ST4 2DF.

Knud Jensen, Royal Danish School of Educational Studies, Emdrupvej 101, 2450 Copenhagen NV, Denmark.

Roy Nash, Department of Education, Massey University, Private Bag, Palmerston North, New Zealand.

John Solomos, Centre for Research in Ethnic Relations, University of Warwick, Coventry CV4 7AL.

Stephen Walker, Department of Education, Newman College, Bartley Green, Birmingham B32 3NT.

Claire Wallace Department of Social Science, Plymouth Polytechnic, Drake Circus, Plymouth PL4 8AA.

Introduction

Living on the line is no joke. The fact that the various miseries of unemployment – the struggles to preserve dignity and identity, the battles to fend off the feelings of being trapped, isolated and discarded, the fights to make ends meet – are all becoming depressingly familiar parts of the everyday experience of more and more people in Britain today makes them no less shocking, no less saddening. But, if the immediate problems that surround the growth of mass unemployment are daunting, there is also a very real prospect that the long-term consequences of both the increase itself, and the various policies being mounted in reaction, will be even more profoundly disturbing and threatening. This is particularly true with respect to the organisation of schooling. The severe and complex problems for education that already exist as a result of the sharp and sustained growth in unemployment amongst school-leavers and young adults during the 1980s are difficult enough. But the deeper impact these trends might have on schooling and education in the future, and the impact of policies being adopted to confront present problems, might well be much worse.

   As we muddle through the successive crises for education directly or indirectly occasioned by the rise of and the reactions to mass youth unemployment, we have reached something of a turning-point. Our own crystal ball is no better than anyone else's. But, there is enough evidence already available about the effects of persistent youth unemployment to be able to predict that different responses to the problems will have radically different results, and that teachers, pupils and those concerned about education will have to reconsider carefully, the short- *and* the long-term implications of their present lines of action.

What can we learn, then, from our recent experience of having more and more school-leavers facing the prospect of no work at the end of their formal education? Two fairly obvious lessons, at least: that the problems arising will not gradually go away; and that the disruptions they cause hit educational processes at all levels–personal, institutional and even analytical, or conceptual.

Take the first lesson. For various reasons, it seems certain that mass youth unemployment is not a temporary phenomenon. First, with unemployment amongst school-leavers running at 30 per cent nationally and at over 50 per cent in some areas, as against an economic growth forecast of around 3 per cent, even the most optimistic would have to predict that fairly large numbers of school-leavers will be unable to find work during the next fifteen years. Couple this comparison with the fact that any of the modest economic growth in evidence at present is mainly confined to those industrial sectors that are not labour-intensive–and that, be it for reasons that we applaud or protest, the British economy remains non-competitive with rival economies–and the prospects become even gloomier. Given these conditions, in which unemployment in general seems likely to remain at a high level, young people and particularly certain sections of youth will continue to be forced into no work or into 'trash' work, especially if those determinants of job selection that allow employers to implement preference for older, more experienced and, *ergo*, 'more reliable' workers remain unchallenged. Perhaps most significantly, we must also question the extent to which there exists the political will, the political courage, to adopt policies aimed at changing the conditions that support mass unemployment if those policies represent any kind of threat to the interest of elite groups or of powerful voting blocks.

The second general understanding to be pulled out of recent experience is that the problems of mass youth unemployment, unlike other concerns, do not exert pressure on separate, identifiable parts of the education system but upon the system as a whole. A direct consequence of mass unemployment is that it drastically and dramatically reduces the ability of a large number of people to satisfy or to define basic material needs. The loss of access to the wage, however, is not only a question of monetary loss. It also involves a kind of escape from getting drawn into those social relations of production that are oppressive and exploitative. But the crucial price to be paid for this enforced salvation is another loss–a loss of access to the *social* power of the wage. In capitalist societies, it is difficult to preserve a distinction between the 'worth' of an individual, as conferred by their wage, and their identity. Of course, the wage provides purchasing power and the capacity to participate in competitive consumption. Access to the wage also carries access to a culture in which collective struggle over the wage and the conditions in which it is secured is a defining element. But the social power of the wage derives from its mediating power. It has gradually evolved to become the major mediator in the relentless drive for individuals to compare themselves against each other; it is used to articulate and to explore differences in rank and status, rights and 'worth'. To be out of work, and out of wage, means you are also outside of that crucial form of discourse that is the accepted framework for the expression of identity and for the assessment and comparison of individuals' social status, accomplishments and achievements. The consequences for education of a situation in which this kind of social exclusion from one of the dominant forms of identity formation, this loss of sociality itself, is the certain future for a large number of pupils are shattering.

On the personal level, the situation leads to a challenge to basic assumption about the *value* of being schooled. There has always been a group of pupils who assess their schooling as having little intrinsic worth. But a base-line in the logic used by teachers and school managers to counter this evaluation has been reference to the utilitarian defence that schooling mediates access to work and the wage, and referees the inequalities that surround the transition from education to adult status. It didn't really matter that such logic was viewed with suspicion by many teachers and more pupils. It was there. It provided a kind of ideological prop that could be used to fend off challenge and to obviate the need to provide further jusifications for schools or their provisions. Once this prop is removed, however, and mass youth unemployment makes the utilitarian logic look very thin, then both pupils and teachers are compelled to set out on a search for either a new logic or a new perspective of schooling. Furthermore, the search is made doubly difficult if compulsory schooling has to be defended or justified in terms that, for some, can have no reference to a social identity acquired through participation in the social discourse processes connected with the wage.

At the institutional level, this challenge has a knock-on effect. This is not just in terms of questions about the content of schooling, the efficacy or acceptability of assessment methods and the distribution of educational resources–important though these are. The challenge works upon the principles on which relationships in schools are based–principles through which individuals relate to the institution and to each other. A highly visible and certain loss of access by many pupils to the identity-forming experiences of waged work creates the conditions in which those pupils who feel that they are likely to be selected for unemployment begin a quest for a new source of identity-forming experience; i.e. it acts as a catalyst for cultural production. We can speculate that pupils will draw on many different aspects of their day-to-day lives to further this quest. They will work with their previous school experience but they will also be drawn to experience outside school, especially their contact with unemployed youth, in the sense that this is a search for social rather than educational identity.

The precise forms these solutions will take are impossible to predict. The pupils themselves will produce and develop their own solutions using whatever cultural artefacts they can find. But the problem for the principles on which relations between individuals and schools are established is this: teachers walk on a knife-edge as they decide upon the response they will make to the ideas and actions pupils produce in their necessary search for a different kind of identity-forming experience. The response has to strike an exact balance between accommodating pupil interest (and therefore winning a basis for the establishment of a working consensus in schools) on the one hand, and ensuring that the collectivising potential of newly-created pupil cultures is carefully controlled. The possible challenge to the *whole* institution, of having large numbers of pupils identifying collectively with an alternative ideological and cultural formation is the thing to be avoided. The institutional problem for schools, then, is to devise a principle through which it can be ensured that pupils *do* work together for the common good of schooling but *do not* work together for ends and interests that shatter the fragile compromise between teachers and pupils on which schools depend.

A similar kind of contradictory pressure is exerted by persistent and high youth unemployment on analyses of educational processes. The severity and urgency of the personal and institutional problems surrounding mass youth unemployment

4

have given rise to a dangerous trend is some analysis, especially that of some policy-makers, which involves partist rather than wholist conceptualisations. Recognising the explosive potential of having large numbers of the population suffering a crisis in social identity, some observers have been drawn into suggesting solutions that, interestingly, provide good examples of how ideology penetrates analysis and bad examples of educational research. For example, as Roberts comments in the introduction to his impressive *School Leavers and their Prospects* (1984),

> The return of mass youth unemployment has been accompanied by many diagnoses. Some blame young people themselves insofar as their attitudes, skills and qualifications are judged deficient by the standards set in modern industries. The second step in this argument is to criticize schools for failing to offer adequate vocational preparation. It says more about the distribution of ideological power than the real sources of young people's difficulties that unemployment has led to education and school-leavers being questioned more strenuously than the economy.

This kind of argument is much in evidence in the rhetoric of a broad range of current policy discussions; it is employed in official documentation about YTS and TVEI projects, in proposals about 'new' modes for public examinations like CPVE and the GCSE, and it creeps into the analysis of quite routine inspections and evaluations of how schools are working. What is objectionable about this argument is not just the return to a crude deficiency model that shifts blame for social problems away from the perpetrators and on to the victims, nor even the reactionary form of structuralism it acquires through presenting social problems as mechanical rather than fundamental failures. It is essentially flawed in that it represents the kind of social analysis that concentrates investigation on parts of a social system, on specific individuals or organisations, and thereby fails to explores the links between *how* people live and the social conditions *in which* they live, the linkages between social action and social structure. One of the most tangible lessons, for us, that can be learned from recent experience is that the existence of mass youth unemployment has served to expose, dramatically, the essential contradictions of schooling and of social life.

We have argued elsewhere (Walker and Barton 1983), of the necessity of using a notion of contradiction in attempts at understanding and explaining schooling. This view is based upon the recognition that a person's individuality is both realised and

5

restricted through participation in group life and that it is through this contradiction that social actions and social structures connect. Teachers, for example, can be viewed as the mediators of contradictory expectations, and distinction can be made between private and public ideologies, between official and unintended consequences and between situational and structural features of their lives.

The degree to which particular contradictions can be solved or balanced within the existing social formation has always been a point of serious concern for educational analysis. However, the nature and the extent of youth unemployment has contributed to a marked increase in the contradictory nature of schooling and in the disturbances caused by changes in the ideological mechanisms by which contradictions are managed or obscured. As we have suggested, tensions in the effectiveness of the legitimacy function of schooling have become increasingly apparent. Whereas, in the past, the credibility of schools was to be seen in the promised fulfilment of a job, unemployment has brought this seriously into question. As Roberts (1984) succinctly notes, 'the gap between winners and losers is all too visible'; and thus the justification for qualifications and the consequent motivation to succeed is applicable to fewer pupils, the majority adopting a realistic outlook in which such qualifications are seen to be irrelevant. Similarly, the legitimacy of the educational processes through which qualifications are distributed is also put in doubt.

Legitimation crisis in education is only one illustration of the effect of the rise in youth unemployment. The contributions in this book should be seen as more detailed explorations of the central points of this illustration that, first, mass youth unemployment has exposed and heightened the contradictions of schooling and, secondly, that responses to consequent increases in tension have to be evaluated in terms of the extent to which the cure is likely to be more serious than the disease.

Three specific contradictions receive detailed consideration in the chapters in this collection, although individual writers also introduce a wealth of other analytic and strategic concern about youth, unemployment and schooling. These contradictions are:

(1) those that surround the 'new' vocationalism in education, at the levels of both rhetoric and current policy;
(2) those expressed in inequalities of educational input, experience and outcome, particularly in the promise of equality

of educational opportunity for marginalised groups like black pupils and girls and the reality of discrimination; and

(3) those to do with the location of educational power with respect to the design and control of education.

We have used this interpretation of some of the unifying themes in the contributions that follow as a basis for ordering them.

The first four chapters in the book, by Horne, Dale, Gleeson and Buswell, are interrelated in the sense that they all probe some of the deeper implications of aspects of the new vocationalism in education, which forms part of the reaction to the problems for education of mass youth unemployment. An essential contradiction here is between vocationalism as a form of increased educational opportunity and vocationalism as a form of increased social control; in these first four chapters this contradiction is considered with respect to its history, its evidence in TVEI policy and its manifestation in post-school training programmes.

The next two chapters, those by Wallace and Solomos, focus on the ways in which anticipated and real experience of unemployment amongst school-leavers has compounded the contradictions that work upon girls and upon black youth, within and after schooling. Both papers demonstrate how an analysis of these issues about youth and unemployment provides insight into the more fundamentally contradictory nature of schooling and its social location.

The collection concludes with chapters by Atkinson *et al.*, Nash and Jensen, which all draw upon analysis of how problems to do with schooling, youth and work have been evidenced and approached in other countries: France, New Zealand and Denmark. These three papers share a concern with the tensions that exist between politicians and teachers, between educational administrators and practitioners, in terms of competing perspectives, interests and degrees of control.

In an important way, these last three chapters inform our understanding of one of the essential contradictions of schooling clearly exposed through recent experience: the tension between central and local interests, between social and individual control. A notable feature of the governmental response to mass youth unemployment in Britain has been the marked increase in authoritarian, central control of the education system–through the use of the Manpower Services Commission and through government intervention in resource allocation and curriculum design.

We believe, therefore, that the discussion in these last three papers of the deeper significance of changes in educational control is both timely and apposite. In fact, we would venture to suggest that a particular value of the whole of this collection is that it addresses a new danger in the politics of education. The danger is that a real consequence of the pressure on teachers, which arises from the strain of managing contradictions deepened by mass youth unemployment, is that they may be coerced, seduced or recruited into courses of action that isolate them from their fellows, increase their powerlessness and threaten their own interests and ambitions.

References

Roberts, K. (1984) *School Leavers and their Prospects*. Milton Keynes, Open University Press.

Walker, S. and Barton, L. (1983) *Gender, Class and Education*. Lewes, Falmer Press.

CHAPTER ONE

Continuity and Change in the State Regulation and Schooling of Unemployed Youth

John Horne

Introduction

This chapter emerges from two research interests that began as discrete but increasingly refuse to remain separate: the state management of unemployed young people in the twentieth century; and the social history of leisure and popular culture in Britain since 1900. The way that the unemployment of relatively large numbers of young working-class people is construed as a particular problem in periods of economic crisis has been remarked upon by Gareth and Teresa Rees. There is what they call an 'ideology of youth unemployment', which at times informs the actions and proposed remedies of an 'opinion-forming elite': 'the leadership of the major political parties, employers' organizations and trade unions, the civil servants and professionals, voluntary organizations and so forth' (Rees and Rees 1982: p. 27). The components of the ideology are the twin concerns of the *demoralisation* and the *employability* of workless youth. Indeed, as Teresa Rees has recently added, it is especially *male* youth unemployment that provokes greatest alarm:

> Time and time again, in the 1930s as well as the 1970s and 1980s, the 'opinion-forming elite' identify unemployed young men as being the threat to disorder. It is they who will, it is feared, start the revolution, become vandals and criminals, join extremist groups, start riots and so on. The adverse effects on girls are scarcely mentioned except in terms of promiscuity or prostitution (and even

the latter is to conform to social order rather than to challenge it).

(Rees 1984: p. 5)

This serves to remind us that the category 'youth', whilst used as a homogeneous term, can often result in the experience of white males being taken as the norm against which other youths' experiences are examined. As we shall see, the experience of unemployment is different for boys and girls, young men and young women.[1] Coupled with this concern for the 'enforced leisure' of young people there developed, especially in the 1930s, a debate over the 'problem of leisure' itself (see Durant 1938). As one commentator put it:

> It is the use of leisure time that is of such importance to the youth of today, for in the future this may be increased owing to the shortening of routine working hours and the increase of part-time work.

(Bell 1934: p. 77)

With regard to the social history of leisure in Britain, particularly in the inter-war period, it is still difficult to argue with Howkins and Lowerson's assessment that 'we probably know more about Victorian pubs, coffee rooms and clubs than we do about those of the 1920s and 1930s' (Howkins and Lowerson 1979: p. 57). Only a handful of studies recognise the complex and contested social relations of leisure and popular culture in Britain in the twentieth century (see Cook 1977, Lowerson 1980, Tomlinson 1983, for example). Leisure was seen as a social problem by certain commentators involved with youth in the 1930s, as it is seen again today (see Leaman 1984). Indeed it has been a great temptation when seeking to understand the connections, if any, between these responses in the crisis conditions of the 1930s to reflect upon the persistence of certain themes in the contemporary debates over youth, unemployment and schooling.

In an earlier paper, I wrote that 'there is much evidence for continuity between previous and present policy in the area of youth unemployment. Whilst YOP seems new its trial period was not in 1975 but between the wars, albeit in a more *ad hoc* fashion' (Horne 1983: p. 337). Here I want to subject my earlier hunch (for that is what is was essentially) about the Juvenile Instruction Centres of the 1930s to some qualifications and revisions. To a large degree I concur with the view of Philip Cohen:

> There *is* some very old wine being poured into new bottles at the

MSC. Nonetheless history does not repeat itself even if ideologies never cease to do just that. The dole schools of the 1930s do not have the same conditions of existence as the youth training schemes of the 1980s, and the contemporary forms of social-and-life-skilling have quite a different *raison d'etre* from that of the original Victorian version.

(Cohen 1984: p. 120)

It is still worth remarking, however, that the Manpower Services Commission-sponsored schemes and courses of the 1970s and 1980s do not offer a completely new 'paradigm' in the relationship between schooling and the youth labour market (for this argument see Baron *et al.* 1981). The 'recurring debate' over the proper relationship between education and industry in Britain has a long history, which has gone through several phases (for that phrase see Reeder 1981). At moments of crisis, ideas and implicit strategies and policies that at other times remain dormant perhaps take on a sense of urgency and come to dominate discussion in the fields of education and youth policy. As Reeder concludes, 'any society which feels threatened from without or enfeebled from within is likely to assert the value of useful knowledge and to stress the importance of the extrinsic purposes of education' (Reeder 1981: p. 200). To avoid charges of idealism one would then want to investigate specific moments and even local conditions. This I am currently doing by researching juvenile unemployment in the 1930s in and around the Potteries in North Staffordshire.

In the sections that follow I shall draw upon official and non-official commentaries of the inter-war period to detail both the intentions behind 'instruction centres' for the young unemployed and the nature of 'provided instruction'. Evidence concerning the responses to this will then be outlined. The major point of departure from my earlier essay is in my interpretation of the role of the 'dole school', an issue I shall take up in the conclusion.

The problem of 'enforced leisure' and the Instruction Centres

'Enforced leisure', as unemployment was often referred to in the 1930s, became increasingly supervised as the inter-war period progressed. In the case of unemployed 'juveniles' seven different arrangements for the provision of instruction for them were tried in the space of twelve years after 1918 (Bell 1934: pp. 1–9). In 1930 it became a statutory obligation of the Minister of Labour to promote

11

the establishment of 'Junior Instruction Centres' or classes and in the 1934 Unemployment Act juveniles were to be made to attend JICs as a condition for the receipt of dole money.

There is some debate over the exact extent and nature of youth unemployment in the 1920s and 1930s (see Garside 1977, Benjamin and Kochin 1979, Garside 1979). It is evident, none the less, that it has not been adopted as a dominant motif of the 1930s and as a result has been virtually ignored, not least by educational historians (see Bernbaum 1967). This is probably partly to do with the regional nature of inter-war unemployment. As the Ministry of Labour pointed out:

> In order to get a true picture of the unemployment position amongst juveniles, regard must therefore be paid to the duration of the periods of unemployment as much as to the numbers of juveniles unemployed.
>
> (Ministry of Labour 1935a: p. 10)

When this is done, the regional differences between Lancashire, South Wales and Scotland, all recording over 25 per cent 14–18-year-olds out of work for three months or more in 1933, and the Midlands (12.5 per cent) and the South East (7.3 per cent) are striking. At the end of 1934, 111 centres and 13 classes had been open in 94 towns in England and Wales with an aggregate attendance of 113,000 (Ministry of Labour 1935a: p. 16). By 1938, 157 centres were open, with 37 daily classes. The peak years were 1935 and 1936, with 188 and 187 centres open respectively. Although it is not clear how many of the recorded attendances were 're-enrolments' there are indications that the 1934 Act, making attendance compulsory for the receipt of dole, had some impact (see Burns 1941). Because of the variations in the impact it is necessary to study the local situation of specific areas. The *ad hoc* nature of the emergence of dole schools can be illustrated with reference to the Potteries (although other accounts exist; see, for example, Pope 1977, and for contemporary reports Jewkes and Winterbottom 1933, Meara 1936).

JICs were not established in the Potteries, North Staffordshire, until February 1928, even though in other parts of the country, including Wolverhampton (the nearest industrial town, thirty miles to the south), such places had been established immediately after the First World War. In Stoke-on-Trent the main effect of recession in the 1920s was unsystematic, short-time work. Up to 1928 therefore attempts to cope with the young unemployed were sporadic. In 1927, for example, in response to an invitation of the Controller of the Midland Division for 'Empire Settlement' (a rather global enterprise to get people to find work by moving elsewhere – even to the colonies!), the Juvenile Employment Committee for Stoke-on-Trent arranged with the manager of the Hippodrome, Stoke, for the film *Life in Australia* to be shown at several local 'picture palaces'. It is interesting to note that the response of the local populace was less than enthusiastic (Stoke Juvenile Employment Committee, 3rd Report, 1927):

> 'The film was much appreciated but in view of the fact that Stoke-on-Trent is an inland city emigration does not appear to appeal to its young people'(!).

In addition to this attempt to uproot 'Potters' (impossible at the best of times!) it was decided, 'with a view to showing a personal interest' in the young unemployed, to provide a series of 'Weekly Talks'. Held on Wednesday mornings in the Town Hall, Hanley, the talks were given by Councillors Timmis and Hollins (later to be MP), by Mr G. Taylor, a local headmaster and the Chief Executive Officer for Juvenile Employment and by Mr J. A. Thompson, on various subjects from 'The Conditions of Signing for Unemployment Insurance Benefit' and 'How to Apply for a Situation' to 'Weather Forecasts' and 'Engines – Ancient and Modern'. I have been unsuccessful, so far, in obtaining information on the response of young people to these lectures.

A year later, as unemployment amongst the young increased, it was decided to open 'Unemployment Centres' (as JICs were known until 1930). The centres opened on 6 February 1928 at Burslem (for boys) and Fenton (for girls), 'each class being in attendance for three hours a day on five days each week' (Stoke JEC, 4th Report, 1928). The instruction seems to have been concentrated on practical work and physical training. By December 1930 over 2,264 young people had been in attendance at these centres.

The next year (1931) saw the employment situation worsen further (there were 4,718 *fresh* insurance benefit claims from boys and girls) and as a result a new Junior Instruction Centre, The Elms, Shelton, was opened for giving instruction. The JEC 7th Annual Report (January 1932) notes that the centre was officially opened (as it appears so many were) by the Minister of Labour, Miss Margaret Bondfield MP, who gave an 'inspiring address'.

13

'Only the best is good enough for the unemployed'

The different local conditions, the intermittent attendances of the young and the resulting instability and insecurity of employment for the staff are some of the reasons why any attempt to generalise about the educational experience offered in the 'dole schools' is difficult. Nevertheless there appear to have been certain features of the 'illustrative, rather than exhaustive' curriculum outlined by the Ministry of Labour that were fairly widely accepted. The suggested activities included woodwork, metalwork, weaving and other miscellaneous handicrafts for boys, and home handicrafts, cookery, housewifery, laundry and home nursing for girls (Ministry of Labour 1935b: p. 32). In addition a degree of 'general educational teaching. English. Workshop arithmetic (primarily for boys). History and Civics. Drawing and painting. General Knowledge' (ibid.) was recommended. The emphasis was clearly upon practical work and general education rather than training for specific occupations. The aim in most JICs was the 'development of manual dexterity' rather than vocational training or particular job skills (Bell 1934). In many ways the curriculum suggested was a hybrid, reflecting both developing educational ideas and the sort of 'leisure-time' activities encouraged in youth clubs and societies. As the Ministry of Labour memorandum continued:

> a Junior Instruction Centre should not be conducted on the lines of an ordinary school, but should be inspired to a large extent by the club spirit, and the boys and girls in attendance should realise that the instruction they receive is something which will be likely to help them in securing employment and in making them better citizens.
>
> (Ministry of Labour 1935b: p. 23)

The increasing interest in developing such things as pen-friends, study visits, school trips and school-related clubs and societies in the Elementary schools in the 1920s and 1930s – reflecting the changes in thinking about the curriculum and what Bernbaum called 'the search for greater realism in teaching' – was paralleled by the recognition that a different form of pedagogy and control was required than in the school situation (Bernbaum 1967: p. 87).

Valentine Bell, author of the Carnegie Trust report on *Junior Instruction Centres and their Future*, had been head of the Battersea Voluntary Day Continuation School and involved in the National Association of Boys' Clubs where a mixture of informal methods, practical work and physical training was common. He believed that these methods were equally applicable to the young unemployed: 'The secret in the JICs is to start with the interests of the young folk and work up from them. Even the toughest of lads can display interest when a paint box is given to him' (Bell 1934: p. 55). Flexibility in pedagogy was necessary not only because of the floating student population, but also because it became clear to Bell that different 'types' of unemployed youth needed catering for:

Lads	(a)	Those who have had several jobs since leaving school and to whom unemployment appears to be a natural expectation . . .
	(b)	Those who have had continuous jobs for two or three years but have made no efforts to improve their education or qualifications . . .
	(c)	Those from homes where the influence is good and parental control is very effective . . .
Girls . . .		those who are noisy and boisterous and those who are mannered.

(Bell 1934: pp. 22, 23)

According to Bell it was the lads in group (b) who 'feel they have a grievance in being compelled to attend a JIC' and 'the girl who refuses, point-blank, to take off her coat' who might interfere most with the smooth running of a centre and thus required most skilful handling (Bell 1934: p. 23).

A further feature of provision was the curriculum differentiation between the sexes. It was considered preferable, wherever possible, to instruct boys and girls separately, in different subjects and for different futures. As Teresa Rees notes, 'for girls appropriate skills are ones that point to a life in the home or in domestic service' (Rees 1984: p. 8). Thus the Social-Darwinist-inspired anxiety about the 'physical deterioration' of the population at the turn of the century was sustained.[2] In the 1930s this was compounded by the middle-class concern about the 'servant problem'. Hence the 'training' offered for girls was aimed almost exclusively at preparation for domestic service. In a series of radio broadcasts called 'SOS', and reprinted in *The Listener*, the public-schoolmaster, writer and occasional broadcaster S. P. B. Mais made the following comment:

During my visit to Cleveland . . . I found the girls of this area quite willing, indeed anxious, to go into domestic service. . . . As I am myself employing one of these girls, I can vouch for their quality and capacity for work. The Council (Cleveland Training and

15

Employment Council) charge no fees, and have an arrangement by which these girls are conveyed to London for 12s.6d.

(The Listener, 1 March 1933: p. 325)

Paddy Scannell has made some interesting observations about Mais's mode of address, the positioning of his audience as middle-class like himself and the political context within which his radio series came on the BBC (see Scannell 1980). Whilst Mais is here talking about the policy of 'industrial transference'–another form of state policy towards the young unemployed in the inter-war years–the assumptions about appropriate training for un-employed, working-class girls is consistent with that informing the 'dole schools'. Indeed, Valentine Bell considered that 'the aim of every superintendent of a Girls' centre is to have a cookery, laundry and housewifery centre' (Bell 1934: p. 50). For many girls, however, while the cookery was popular 'Housewifery was not altogether liked. As one girl expressed it, "I have done 3 hours scrubbing before coming to the Centre" ' (ibid.: p. 51)–an important reminder that the experience of unemployment and unemployment schemes often serves to *reproduce*, rather than disrupt, the sexual division of labour (see Farish 1984 for an analysis of the Youth Training Scheme that illustrates this function in contemporary Britain).

A final common feature of the JICs was some kind of provision for physical training or gymnastics. The Ministry of Labour suggested that:

> Training should be given to the body as well as to the mind, and physical training and games should hold, therefore, a part of the curriculum of every course, though the course should not be allowed to develop merely into a place of amusement.

> (Ministry of Labour 1935b: p. 24)

The ambivalence of the Ministry's recommendation reflects a debate waged during the 1920s and 1930s over the social benefits of team games in clubs. The origins of the ideology of 'athleticism' have been well charted by J. A. Mangan (1981). The debate in the inter-war years was between those who sought to extend the values of loyalty, disciplined citizenship and obedience through team games and exercise and those who felt that such values were the preserve of public-schoolboys. Bell was of the opinion that there was nothing 'like field games to teach this type of lad the value of team spirit' (Bell 1934: p. 54). The Ministry was aware, however, that there was a 'type' who would gladly play games all day:

the importance of physical training and organised games as an instrument for the creation of alertness, initiative and energy should not be overlooked. It is possible through this medium to remove many undesirable habits, and to create that fresh outlook which is required in all walks of life and work. A word of warning is, however, necessary in this connection. There are boys who would be content to play football all day and everyday. . . . The centre aims at something higher than this. . . . the boys and girls who are there enrolled must be made to realise that it is not established entirely for their recreation and amusement. The object of the Centre is not only to arrest deterioration but also to move in a positive direction towards the cultivation of habits of industry and useful occupation.

(Ministry of Labour 1935b: p. 33)

In sum, 'while games and recreation should have a proper place in the activities of the Centre the time devoted to them should be strictly limited' (ibid.: p. 34). Here we can see what Peter McIntosh calls the 'utilitarian' view of physical training mixed with concern over its excesses (see McIntosh 1963: pp. 106–13, especially on inter-war debates in the House of Commons).

In examining the curriculum suggested, and in many areas adopted, it becomes clear that the provision of instruction for unemployed youth in the JICs involved an attempt to direct their leisure-time interests and forms of association towards a middle-class/'respectable'-working-class norm. It is interesting to note that in some centres the opportunity to engage in discussions and debates on issues such as unemployment, money and trade marked real advances on the topics and methods of conventional schooling and were attractive to attenders (Bell 1934: p. 100). S. P. B. Mais reported on the JICs in Liverpool and considered them to be exemplary. The principal of one told him, 'Only the best is good enough for the unemployed' (*The Listener*, 22 February 1933: p. 286). The JICs might have provided a 'liberal education' in some areas but, as will be shown below, a major response to these attempts to fill the days of 'enforced leisure' was the fatalism of the jobless.

'The boys were all right, they got woodwork': responses to the dole schools

R. H. Tawney, in a characteristically robust pamphlet, *Juvenile Unemployment and the Raising of the School-Leaving Age*

17

(Tawney 1934), made three main criticisms of the JICs. He felt the centres could not offset the 'demoralisation' that the young unemployed felt; the projected rising number of 14–18-year-olds (due to demographic factors) would increase the strain on an already 'creaky', insufficient and inefficient scheme; and thirdly, the influx of young workers when they found employment would add to pressures on the adult wage rates and thus lead to a spiral of depression. Tawney was certainly not alone in arguing for the raising of the school-leaving age as a more constructive answer to the 'problem' (cf. Jewkes and Winterbottom 1933). Such arguments gained ground in the 1930s, as we know (cf. Simon 1974). However, in the first half of the decade the problem of providing 'palliatives' most exercised the minds of the 'opinion-forming elite'.

The Ministry of Labour *Memorandum* (1935b) noted the likelihood that 'from time to time' difficulties would occur 'among boys and girls of widely different types who form most courses and many of whom attend the courses in the first place against their wishes' (p. 22). For persistent absenteeism, which I shall consider in a moment, there were two sanctions. The first was the forfeiture of benefit, for the day on which the 'offence' of non-attendance occurred. The second, and apparently more severe, was the possibility of fines being levied against the youth or the parent after consultation with the Minister of Labour himself! I have little evidence yet to show how these sanctions were used. However, one of my Potteries interviewees revealed the following incident:

> I found it really very boring. One day in an arithmetic class, the teacher said: 'And no one is to get this sum wrong deliberately.' Well, I was cheesed off with the whole thing, so I did. He called me out and sent me to the woodwork shop. Well, I'd never learnt any woodwork at school and I couldn't do much. I got fed up with not being treated with respect. The teacher wouldn't even let another lad show me how to 'square off' a piece of wood. I told him he wasn't being fair. He said, 'I'll stop thee dole.' I said, 'If thee'll stop me dole, I'll stop thee breath'! He reported me then, see! The day after, I got a letter from the dole office and I went along, had my dole stopped for the day for insubordination, and then went back. You had to, there was nothing else to do.

He continued:

> Because you were going down there, I got the impression that they thought you were dirt. And they could do just what they liked and

they could say just what they liked and they could threaten what
they liked. It felt like that to me. I didn't feel like standing for it. All
as I wanted from anyone, as young as I was, was respect and nothing
more. I respected them, I expected the same back. But they treated
me in a way I didn't like, I treated them with the same, contempt.
Which was natural.

(Bill)

There were some local outbreaks of opposition, for example in the
'little Moscow' of Nelson, in Lancashire. Pope (1977) notes that the
establishment of centres was delayed due to the left-wing make-up
of the local education committee. They objected to the element of
compulsion in the scheme. After 1934, however:

> Nelson's Juvenile Employment Committee, with the enthusiasm of
> the converted, described the centres as a 'valuable asset' to
> unemployed boys and girls, doing much 'to maintain the spirits of
> these young people'.

(pp. 29–31)

The labour movement was caught in the dilemma of whether to
'boycott' the JICs altogether or fully endorse and get involved with
them. John Gollan (1937) reported that at the 1936 Annual
Conference of Trades Councils held in London:

> after keen discussion the conference endorsed, by a majority, the
> point of view of the General Council, which . . . felt it could not
> oppose the principle of training schemes or transference but that the
> method and conditions under which these were effected required
> constant vigilance.

(p. 174)

Despite the many different architectures within which centres were
established, it is significant that such places were invariably
referred to as 'dole colleges' or 'dole schools' by those in receipt of
'provided instruction'. This label stuck not so much because of the
establishments within which instruction took place, nor necessarily because of the 'staff', but precisely because at a time when the
young working class were expecting work, they were directed into
hastily assembled 'continuation' centres and classes. G. Meara
(1936) explained the situation in South Wales:

> Many boys who attend the centres call it 'going to the Dole college';
> there is something half bitter, half proud in that description. The
> bitterness must be removed, the pride fostered. It can best be done by
> talking less of preventing deterioration and demoralisation and

19

more of educating boys and girls to make a more fitting contribution to the society of which they are part.

(p. 88)

In a recent article Rex Pope (1978) records that Inspectors and 'School' Attendance Officers were kept busy chasing up non-attenders. Many youths

> in the immediate post-First World War period . . . went without their out-of-work donation rather than, as they saw it, return to school. In the 1920s and early 1930s, voluntary attendance by those too young to draw benefit was almost always limited and occasional.
>
> (p. 17)

Moreover:

> Even though the 1934 Act introduced an obligation on all unemployed juveniles to attend Centres where provided, whether or not they were in receipt of benefit, absenteeism was often around 10%–20%.
>
> (p. 18)

In many cases the cause of absenteeism was to do with the accommodation of the centres. As Meara (1936) reveals:

> In some cases the centres are extremely badly housed. The Borgoed Centre for Boys, for instance, is a badly lighted and ventilated part of the Baptist Chapel below street level, in which the electric light has to be kept burning all day. Among the boys who attend it, it is known as 'The Dungeon'. In Neath the boys are accommodated in a part of an old workhouse, built in 1838, and there is a definite reluctance on the part of the parents to send their boys to what is called 'The Old Workhouse' or 'The Union'. This situation did not escape the attention of the Superintendent for Neath, who observed, 'The Advisory Committee have done their best to increase the numbers of non-claimants, but all their efforts have been in vain, and will be so, as long as we remain in the present buildings.'
>
> (p. 82)

That the problem of absenteeism persisted after compulsion was introduced in 1934 is surely an indication that the centres were recognised for the essentially custodial places that they were. Certainly this is borne out by some of the recorded statements of attenders. Jeremy Seabrook was told (Seabrook 1973): 'It was just a gimmick really, to keep us of the street' (p. 202). In interviews I have conducted with people in the Potteries there is a consistent reference to the compulsion of attendance:

Oh, we wanted work! But, you know, you just had to go to 'school' to get your dole money.

(Jack)

We had to do it [attend the dole school] or we didn't get no dole money. And then we had to sign on at Queen Street.

(Edna)

Another of my Stoke interviewees put it this way:

The boys were all right, they got woodwork and what-have-you, but us women had either got to do laundry or cooking – there was nothing else for us to do. It was very boring, I thought.

(Gladys)

With regard to physical training and games, Bell noted that 'all round, difficulty has been experienced in persuading the elder girl to take up gymnastics . . . lest they should spoil their clothes' (1934: p. 54). Apart from the reasonable disinclination to do gym in your everyday clothes, perhaps here is a sign of the distinction made on the part of the unemployed between one form of 'physical activity' and another – 'prescribed' – form.

It cannot be denied that some moments of centre activity were enjoyable. Pope remarks that it is best seen as 'fatalism amidst compulsion'. Jack, for example, remembers the woodwork classes with pleasure: 'You could make skittle tables, and if you were still there, if you'd made it by the time you'd finished at the dole school, you could have bought it.' No one, however, except local publicans, could actually afford to purchase the tables!

Some centres attempted to establish an 'old boys' network, but most attenders never returned, if they could avoid it. For example, out of an estimated total of 16,000 different enrolments at the Belfast Centre, the review of courses for unemployed juveniles in Northern Ireland received evidence from only one former pupil (Ministry of Labour (NI) 1938: p. 10). Often, as we have seen in South Wales, parents kept their children away. This was done not only because of the connotations of the centres with 'unfree' labour, but also if the children were expected, or forced, to do chores that they didn't do at home. One of my interviewees remembered an incident involving a singing lesson:

One morning, as we went there, 'she' said we'll all have a singing lesson. So we all stood there and we were singing 'Golden Slumbers, kiss your eyes'. Well, when you're 16 you felt daft, you know. So I said to my mate, 'Are you asleep yet?' And this teacher she said to me,

'That young woman thinks it's funny; she must come out in front of all the boys and girls, and sing the song herself!' I said, 'No way.' Anyway she says, 'You'll go in the laundry room.' Well, I'd never washed even a pocket handkerchief – my mother wouldn't allow me – she used to wash clothes herself. And she says, 'You can get those sheets out of the boiler.' So she gave me a boiler stick to get them out. And of course – I was only about four stone, so you can tell how thin I was – the sheets were too heavy for me. And the boiler stick hit me in my mouth. Of course I had a blistered mouth, didn't I? When I came home, my mother said, 'If that's the dole school, you're going no more – whether we live or starve!' [Author: So what happened, did you go back there?] Oh yes, I had to, otherwise couldn't get no dole if I didn't.

The following statement was made by the Lord Mayor of Newcastle-upon-Tyne in 1934:

> In this area there are thousands of young persons of both sexes who are now attaining the age of 20 without ever having done a day's work. They see no prospect of employment. . . . Instruction centres merely play with the problem. They do not teach a trade and at best merely help to keep these young folk physically fit.
>
> (Gollan 1937: p. 170)

The comment, is, I would argue, precisely correct. Instruction Centres were only 'playing' with the problem by attempting to create the atmosphere of a club or 'institute of leisure'. But such 'play' is consistent with the 'ideology of youth unemployment', which remains with us today: 'Unless you give jobless youth a shovel, sports or even a gun (under proper supervision), then indiscipline and lawlessness will result. They will pick up the bricks.' Despite the research evidence, of the 1930s and 1980s, which disputes this and shows instead fatalism, apathy and confusion amongst the majority of youth, such a chain of reasoning underlay the formation of the JICs in the 1930s (see Jahoda 1982: pp. 50–52).

Summary

In their paper cited earlier, Gareth and Teresa Rees made the comment about dole school attenders that 'there is certainly no evidence to suggest that they found getting a job any easier, a factor which probably contributed to the centre's unpopularity' (Rees and Rees 1982: p. 20). Whilst some Ministry of Labour memoranda suggested at the time that the Instruction Centres would have a beneficial impact on employment prospects, none of the people I have interviewed would recognise the dole schools as having any such function. If never entirely the 'institute of leisure' that some commentators advocated, dole schools were places where one neither learnt a trade nor trained for a specific job. Whilst they had differing degrees of success in different parts of the country they must generally be conceived of as attempting to provide a form of 'club' for unemployed youth. 'Success' then would not be gauged in terms of re-employment – in most cases this could occur only when local industrial and labour market conditions picked up – but rather in terms of how well the 'prescribed fun' was endured by and cultivated in the young attenders. JICs, in other words, attempted to intervene into the *culture* of working-class youth.

The intentions behind the JICs of the 1930s closely resembled those of the voluntary-based youth organisations that sprang up between 1880 and 1910. As M. Blach wrote, the idea underpinning them was that

> children needed to receive a sense of group identity, group loyalty and group pride above and beyond the peaky gang, and well above the divisive 'working-class' identification. The clubs were to act to promote loyalty from the sub-groups to local institution, thus to society and to nation.
>
> (Blanch 1979: p. 105)

Serving a similar function to the 'ideology of athleticism' in the Victorian and Edwardian public schools (see Mangan 1981) the ethos of the dole school reveals a continuation of nineteenth- and early twentieth-century concerns over the prevention of 'deterioration' (both physical and moral) and the need to promote habits of 'discipline and self-respect' (see Ministry of Labour 1935b: p. 22).

Conclusions

I am aware that in an earlier article I may have overstressed the similarities between the JICs of the 1930s and the MSC schemes of the 1970s and 1980s. At the level of ideology, and in particular the 'ideology of youth unemployment', there are undoubted parallels between the two periods. The problem of unemployment is once again being discussed in terms of 'employability' (the work habits,

23

skills, etc. of young people) and moral harm (the demoralisation'
and attack upon the 'work ethic' for young men, and the sexuality
of young women). The ideology provides the framework within
which discussions proceed about the 'problem' and leads to the
proposal of individualistic and moralistic solutions, rather than
intervention into the labour market or the creation, through
Enterprise Boards, of real jobs (see for example GLC Economic
Policy Group 1983). The debate over schooling has been marked,
as in the 1930s, by a strong attempt to tie the education system
firmly to the fluctuating needs of industry and hence capital (see
Reeder 1981: p. 186). Finally the *ad hoc* 'muddling through' of the
British state in times of economic crisis and restructuring is
common to both moments. But here the similarities end and as
Cohen (1984) has suggested it becomes necessary to be clear about
the differing 'conditions of existence' of the schemes and the
specific inflexion given to the ideology of youth unemployment in
the two periods.

What is new about the situation in the 1980s? The composition
of the young work-force: 50 per cent 16–19-year-old blacks
unemployed; about a quarter of all 16–19-year-olds unemployed;
and the vigour of the MSC in extending the schooling, i.e.
dependency, age to 19 with the effect of depressing young people's
wages and removing half a million people from the unemployment register; these are obvious features of contemporary reality.
Despite the MSC schemes there are still 1,261,300 people under 25
unemployed, and over a quarter of them have been without a job
for twelve months or more (*Employment Gazette* 93 (5), May 1985).
As in the 1930s, there are regional and local variations in the
impact of unemployment: 39.4 per cent in Strabane, 23.9 per cent
in Cardigan, 25.8 per cent in South Tyneside, compared with 5.1
per cent in Winchester and Eastleigh, and 6.3 per cent in Aylesbury
and Wycombe (ibid.: pp. 21–3). However, in terms of the
consequences for youth, the restructuring of the 'transition from
school to work' and the relationship between education and the
'needs of industry' in the 1980s is far more widely felt and
profound. Not only the political terrain, but also the way in which
the ideal 'worker–citizen–consumer' is being constructed via the
MSC emphasis on 'social and life skills' is radically different from
the 1930s (see Cohen 1984: pp. 119–26 especially).

There is a connection between the forms of instruction provided
for the young unemployed and other agencies concerned with
youth in the two periods. However, in the 1930s shifting

educational ideologies and attitudes combined with the experiences of youth workers influenced the curricula and activities of the dole schools in a 'liberal–humanist' educational direction, as shown in the concern for new 'topics' and methods. In the 1970s and especially the 1980s it is the MSC-inspired emphasis on 'social and life skills' and 'work socialisation' in schemes for the young unemployed that is permeating the wider schooling system. The direction of the flow of influence has been reversed. In the 1930s the concern with skills, discipline and work habits was evident, but not so tightly bound as in the present day. A full account of the precise way in which this relationship develops and emerges has still to be written. It might be possible, for example, to trace the way in which members of the 'opinion-forming elite' embody some of the constituent elements of the dominant ideology in education (see Dale 1983 for an attempt at this). Further research that cross-cuts the conventional specialist boundaries of the sociology of youth, the history of education and training, policy and cultural studies would be necessary to provide the full story.

Schemes introduced for the instruction and management of the young unemployed provide the state agencies involved with much information (through the development of means of surveillance of a population that was barely known before) that can be useful in assessing the possibilities and boundaries of intervention after the 'crisis' has passed. In his later work Michel Foucault looked at the development of the 'disciplinary society' that involved the increasing monitoring of the population by state agencies (Foucault 1977: pp. 264ff.). He argued that by the establishment of what he calls 'mechanisms of normalisation' state agencies concerned with particular 'problems' were not so much likely to 'solve' them but to gain knowledge, hence a form of power, over them. In 1938, for example, the Ministry of Labour report on Northern Ireland discussed the phrase 'unemployed juveniles': 'The two words embrace a great variety of types of boys and girls between the ages of 14 and 18, differing widely in ability, knowledge, physique, tastes and experience of the world.' The report continues:

> Rule-of-thumb methods of classification are out of place for many juveniles, and worst of all for young men and women who have had varied experience of the world. Time spent upon investigating by private discussion the personal needs and prospects of each juvenile can seldom, in our view, be time wasted.
>
> (Ministry of Labour (NI) 1938: p. 28)

25

Here might be found the origin of profiling!

Just as developments in 'techniques of surveillance' and 'mechanisms of normalisation' occur, so too does resistance to state initiatives. It is increasingly becoming clear that young people learn much about employment from experiences in the juvenile labour market and from older friends in the local community (see Finn 1984 and Jamieson and Lightfoot 1981). Schools and the YTS schemes are therefore not the only channels of information about the 'world of work' or providers of the experience of 'work-socialisation'. The attempt to shape the hearts and minds of youth into totally obedient, compliant and flexible workers is still fraught with contradictions for the state, as it was in the 1930s.

Notes

1 A point discussed by Christine Griffin at the Westhill Conference in a paper entitled, 'Young Women's Experience of Unemployment'. Despite considering myself conscious of 'gender-blind' categories in sociology, in an earlier article I often referred to 'youth' when I really knew only about 'male youth' (Horne 1983).
2 Again thanks to Westhill Conference delegates who referred me to turn-of-the-century discussions about the 'Schoolgirls' curriculum (for example Carol Dyhouse 1977).

References

Baron, S. *et al.* (1981) *Unpopular Education.* London, Hutchinson.

Bell, V. (1934) *Junior Instruction Centres and their Future.* Edinburgh, T. & A. Constable.

Benjamin, D. K. and Kochin, L. A. (1979) 'What Went Right with Juvenile Unemployment Policy between the Wars: A Comment'. *Economic History Review.* XXXII (4), November.

Bernbaum, G. (1967) *Social Change and the Schools: 1918–1944.* London, Routledge & Kegan Paul.

Blanch, M. (1979) 'Imperialism, Nationalism and Organized Youth', in J. Clarke *et al.* (eds.), *Working-Class Culture: Studies, History and Theory.* London, Hutchinson.

Burns, E. M. (1941) *British Unemployment Programs: 1920–1938.* New York, SSRC.

Cohen, P. (1984) 'Against the New Vocationalism', in I. Bates *et al.*, *Schooling for the Dole?* London, Macmillan.

Cook, D. (1977) 'The Battle for Kinder Scout'. *Marxism Today*, August.

Dale, R. (1983) 'Thatcherism and Education', in J. Ahier and M. Flude (eds.), *Contemporary Education Policy*. London, Croom Helm.

Durant, H. (1938) *The Problem of Leisure*. London, Routledge.

Dyhouse, C. (1977) 'Good Wives and Little Mothers: Social Anxieties and the Schoolgirl's Curriculum, 1890–1920'. *Oxford Review of Education* 3 (1).

Farish, M. (1984) *The Youth Training Scheme: A Critical Response*. London, Polytechnic of the South Bank.

Finn, D. (1984) 'Leaving School and Growing Up: Work Experience in the Juvenile Labour Market' in I. Bates *et al., Schooling for the Dole?* London, Macmillan.

Foucault, M. (1977) *Discipline and Punish: The Birth of the Prison*. London, Allen Lane.

Garside, W. R. (1977) 'Juvenile Unemployment and Public Policy between the Wars'. *Economic History Review* XXX (2), May.

(1979) 'Juvenile Unemployment between the Wars: a rejoinder'. *Economic History Review* XXXII (4), November.

Gollan, J. (1937) *Youth in British Industry*. London, Gollancz.

GLC Economic Policy Group (1983) *Jobs for Change*. London, GLC.

Horne, J. (1983) 'Youth Unemployment Programmes: a Historical Account of the Development of "Dole Colleges" ' in D. Gleeson (ed.), *Youth Training and the Search for Work*. London, Routledge & Kegan Paul.

Howkins, A. and Lowerson, J. (1979). *Trends in Leisure, 1919–1939*, London, SSRC/Sports Council Panel.

Jahoda, M. (1982) *Employment and Unemployment*. Cambridge University Press.

Jamieson, I. and Lightfoot, M. (1981) 'Learning about work'. *Educational Analysis* 2: pp. 37–51.

Jewkes, J. and Winterbottom, A. (1933) 'The New Sports Ideology'. *Youth in Society* 90: pp. 16–18.

Jewkes, J. and Winterbottom, A. (1933) *Juvenile Unemployment*.

Leaman, O. (1984) 'The New Sports Ideology' Youth in Society 90: pp. 16–18.

Lowerson, J. (1980) 'Battles for the Countryside', in F. Gloversmith (ed.), *Class, Culture and Social Change*. Sussex, Harvester.

McIntosh, P. C. (1963) *Sport and Society*. London, C. & A. Walts.

Mais, S. P. B. (1933a) 'Liveliness on the Educational Front'. *The Listener*, 22 February 1933: pp. 285–7.

(1933b) 'The Women's Side of the Unemployment Programme'. *The Listener*, 1 March 1933: p. 325–6.

Mangan, J. A. (1981) *Athleticism in Victorian and Edwardian Public Schools*. Cambridge University Press.

Meara, G. (1936) *Juvenile Unemployment in South Wales*. Cardiff University Press.

Ministry of Labour (1935a) *Report on Juvenile Employment for the Year*

1934. London, HMSO.

(1935b) *Memorandum on the Establishment and Conduct of Courses of Instruction for Unemployed Boys and Girls.* London, HMSO.

Ministry of Labour (NI) (1938) *The Instruction of Unemployed Juveniles.* Belfast, HMSO.

Pope, R. (1977) ' "Dole Schools". The North-East Lancashire Experience, 1930–1939'. *Journal of Educational Administration and History* IX (2), July.

(1978) 'Education and the Young Unemployed: a Pre-War Experiment'. *Journal of Further and Higher Education* 2 (2), Summer.

Reeder, D. (1981) 'A Recurring Debate: Education and Industry', in R. Dale *et al.* (eds.), *Education and the State, Volume 1: Schooling and the National Interest.* Lewes/Milton Keynes, Falmer/Open University Press.

Rees, G. and Rees, T. L. (1982) 'Juvenile Unemployment and the State between the Wars', in T. L. Rees and P. Atkinson (eds.), *Youth Unemployment and State Intervention.* London, Routledge & Kegan Paul.

Rees, T. L. (1984) 'Reproducing Gender Inequality in the Labour Force: the Role of the State'. Paper No. 84/27e, *Proceedings of the Standing Conference on the Sociology of Further Education.* Blagdon, Coombe Lodge.

Scannell, P. (1980) 'Broadcasting and the Politics of Unemployment 1930–1935'. *Media, Culture and Society* 2: pp. 15–28.

Seabrook, J. (1973) *City Close Up.* London, Allen Lane.

Simon, B. (1974) *The Politics of Educational Reform.* London, Lawrence & Wishart.

Stoke-on-Trent Juvenile Employment Committee (1927, 1928, 1932 *Annual Reports.*

Tawney, R. H. (1934) *The School Leaving Age and Juvenile Unemployment.* London, Workers Educational Association.

Tomlinson, A. (1983) 'Good Times, Bad Times and the Politics of Leisure: Working-Class Culture in the 1930s in a Small Northern English Working-Class Community'. Paper delivered to a conference on *Working-Class Cultures, Sport and Leisure.* Kingston, Ontario, Queen's University. March.

Acknowledgements

I would like to acknowledge the helpful and constructive comments of three anonymous external referees on the earlier conference paper version of this chapter.

CHAPTER TWO

Examining the Gift-Horse's Teeth: a Tentative Analysis of TVEI

Roger Dale

When I was beginning to think how I might put this chapter together, the most difficult problem I faced was the title. The difficulty derived from the way that the introduction of the Technical and Vocational Education Initiative (TVEI) had been throughout the two years since it was announced, and the year since the original fourteen schemes had got under way, such a controversial issue that the very title of an article discussing it could easily betray the author's attitude towards it. Some people involved in TVEI saw it as a gift-horse, that could not possibly be rejected but should be welcomed as a means of introducing a long-delayed restructuring of the educational experiences of students between 14 and 18 years old. Support for this view appears to have increased since the first scheme started in September 1983, to the point where the *Education Guardian*, scarcely the place one would have expected to find great support for the Initiative, was discussing TVEI as if it were the accepted model for secondary education, and as if it was resources rather than reservations about it that prevented many more local authorities and schools putting on TVEI-type courses (*Guardian*, 23 October 1984).

At the time of its announcement, TVEI's critics heavily outnumbered its supporters, and that may well still be the case. From the start there have been continuing expressions of hostility and anxiety about the possible divisiveness of TVEI, its use as a means of reintroducing selection and its possible narrowing effect on the curriculum. From this point of view TVEI is not so much a gift-horse as a Trojan Horse.

The difficulty presented by these two opposed views of TVEI is compounded by the fact that, because of the very wide variation in TVEI schemes in different local authorities and schools, it is possible for both sides to find evidence in the practice of TVEI to bear out their worst fears or most optimistic hopes of what it might achieve. However, it should not be assumed that the existence of widely differing practices under TVEI means that that common label should be regarded as a deception or even as misleading. As I shall show below, the structure, ideology and management of TVEI ensure that there are both common elements in all schemes and limits to what can be done in its name and with its resources. The way forward in understanding TVEI, then, does not lie in outlining a case for or against it and backing it up with evidence that it would be fairly easy to find in at least some of the nearly four hundred schools and colleges currently involved in the scheme. Nor does it lie in bandying around the evidence of different kinds of practice, nor yet in seeking to establish that one set of practices is authentic and another aberrant.

Given the great variation in TVEI practice within an identifiable common structure, understanding TVEI involves examining how and how far its origins, aims, structure and ideology affect and are affected by the existing patterns of educational practice in the local authorities and schools involved in the scheme. In this chapter I shall be focussing on the structure and ideology of TVEI and on its effect in schools.

It is not possible to consider those topics without some prior understanding of the origins and aims of TVEI. I have discussed these at greater length elsewhere (Dale 1985), and the following paragraphs draw heavily on that article. In an announcement that came like a bolt from the blue to all the interested parties (the DES, LEAs, teacher organisation, even the MSC) the Prime Minister told the House of Commons on 12 November 1982:

> in response to growing concern about existing arrangements for technical and vocational education for young people expressed over many years, not least by the National Economic Development Council . . . [she had asked] the chairman of the Manpower Services Commission together with the Secretaries of State for Education and Science, for Employment, and for Wales, to develop a pilot scheme to start by September 1983, for new institutional arrangements for technical and vocational education for 14–18-year-olds, within existing financial resources, and, where possible, in

association with local authorities.

Though the announcement was greeted with almost universal hostility, agreement was quite rapidly reached, and local authorities were asked to bid for inclusion in a pilot programme whose objectives were to

> widen and enrich the curriculum in a way that will help young people prepare for the world of work, and to develop skills and interests, including creative abilities, that will help them to lead a fuller life and to be able to contribute more to the life of the community . . .

and to help students 'learn to learn'.

Fourteen local authorities were chosen to take part in the pilot scheme, which started in September 1983. All the projects were drawn up to match guidelines that framed TVEI as follows:

> a pilot scheme; within the education system; for young people of both sexes; across the ability range; voluntary. Each project must provide a full-time programme; offer a progressive four-year course combining general with technical and vocational education; commence at 14 years; be broadly based; include planned work experience; lead to nationally recognised qualifications. Each project and the initiative as a whole must be carefully monitored and evaluated. The purpose of the scheme is to explore and test ways of organising and managing readily replicable programmes of technical and vocational education for young people across the ability range.

(MSC 1983)

A central feature of the scheme is that these authorities then signed contracts with the MSC for the delivery of the project outlined in their application. Their projects were all drawn up to match the guidelines but they differed considerably from each other in philosophy, numbers of schools involved (though most schemes included between five and eight schools and colleges of further education) and the number of pupils to be involved (though funding was based on an assumption of five annual cohorts of 250 pupils per authority).

Each local project has a specially appointed co-ordinator, and is responsible to a local steering group made up of representatives of both sides of industry, education interests, voluntary organisations and so on. The steering groups report to the TVEI Unit in the MSC and to the local authority.

This skeletal outline of how TVEI was set up tells us nothing of why it was set up in that way, or indeed why it was thought necessary to introduce it at all. We can discover the answer to those questions only by looking into its origins, into the construction and diagnosis of the problem to which TVEI was presented as a solution. By looking into the problem it was created to solve, we can also appreciate the broad limitations and constraints, opportunities and predispositions, built into TVEI.

The construction of the problem TVEI was to solve has two main elements, both of which had been central features of discussions about the future of secondary education since the previous Prime Minister, James Callaghan's, Ruskin College speech in 1976. On the one hand, the content and orientation of schooling had to be changed. On the other, the process of changing schooling itself needed to be changed. The argument that the secondary school curriculum over emphasised the 'academic' at the expense of the 'technical and vocational', and that schools have to be geared more closely to the needs of industry, goes back much further than James Callaghan (see, for example, Reeder 1979, Esland and Cathcart 1981).   The knowledge, skills and attitudes that young people were taught in school were all inappropriate both for the great majority of them and for what Britain and its economy required. Young people were typically leaving secondary education ignorant, if not contemptuous, of the economic basis of the nation's wealth, the way the country makes its living. As well as being ill-disposed towards industry, what they had been taught in school fitted them ill for the knowledge and skill requirements of the modern economy.

This construction and diagnosis of the problem – or even the crisis – in education had, as I have suggested, been a particularly prominent feature of educational discussion for some years before TVEI came on the scene. Yet despite the pervasiveness of the diagnosis, little had changed by way of a response. The existing means of bringing about educational change had had little effect. It was also clear that even if it were possible to remove the 'academic bias' of secondary education, it would not automatically revert to some pristine, 'economy-friendly' condition; a positive alternative was required. This alternative, heavily implicit in the Great Debate, and explicit before and after it, remains 'vocational education'.

Vocational education is, however, a very slippery and ambiguous concept, largely because it is defined in opposition, or contrast, to what it is hoped it will supplant. Thus vocational education is called on in the Great Debate and Green Paper to save a system with an inappropriate curriculum bias, low standards, and insufficient and ineffective links with industry. It comes to be associated with at least three distinct purposes: making pupils able to get jobs, making them better performers in jobs, and making them more aware of the world of work, and the workings of the economy that awaits them.

Vocational education, then, becomes almost a 'slogan system', with an apparent surface appeal for a wide range of different constituences who are each able to invest it with the capacity to meet their own needs or fit in with their own interests. In so far as TVEI incorporates the ambiguities inherent in the notion of vocational education, its implications for those taking part in it are connotative rather than denotative, permitting if not encouraging a wide range of different interpretations.

However, the range of possible variation is not unlimited, and the nature and effects of the limits to interpretations of TVEI will be discussed in the remainder of this paper. The parameters that local TVEI schemes have to operate within derive not only from its origins and ambitions, already briefly mentioned, but also from the structure and the ideology of the initiative. Once drawn up, these local and school schemes are subject to new variations as they are put into practice in the context of existing schools and colleges.

Central to the structure of the initiative is the contractural relationship betwen the local authorities involved and the MSC. In this structure, local education authorities are

(a) contradictually responsible *for*
(b) the development and delivery of agreed and approved curricula and syllabuses
(c) leading to agreed and approved qualifications
(d) for a named cohort of pupils representing the full ability range and
(e) with steps taken to overcome gender stereotyping of subjects
(f) making accountable use of resources (human and instructional) bought with TVEI money, and
(g) accepting certain requirements (the provision of work experience and residential education, and the development of records of achievement)
(h) *to* a local steering committee that reports to both the LEA and the TVEI Unit in the MSC.

The contracts are monitored in four main ways, which it will be worthwhile to describe very briefly. The most direct means is the annual planning dialogue that takes place between representatives of local TVEI schemes and representatives of the TVEI Unit. These planning dialogues consider both existing progress and, in some detail, curricular and expenditure plans for the following year. On the basis of the planning dialogue the TVEI Unit sends a response to the LEA, which can range from full support for the next year's proposals to requests for more or less major changes.

A second level of TVEI schemes' accountability is to the local steering group, which is made up of a fairly loosely defined mixture of representatives of both sides of industry, voluntary organisations, teacher professional organisations, local politicians and so on. The expectation of the steering group appears to be that it will advise on how best to implement each local scheme, bearing in mind such factors as local labour markets and local education policy and provision. In practice, they seem to operate rather differently from each other. In some schemes they are taken very seriously, with each participating school having a steering committee that reports to the LEA steering committee; while at the other extreme, some steering committees meet relatively infrequently and do little actual 'steering'. Where steering is done, it could be in the direction of seeking either to minimise or to maximise the impact of TVEI on existing educational provision; steering committes might seek to identify and follow closely the educational requirements of local industry, or they might seek to retain control of the scheme tightly within the schools. It is impossible, therefore, to establish a priori the intensity and the purpose of the policing of the contract carried out by the steering committee.

The third means of monitoring the implementation of the contract is the requirement on LEAs to submit regular financial and non-financial returns to the TVEI Unit. The financial returns relate to all TVEI-related spending and may be backed up by close auditing. One set of non-financial returns concern TVEI pupils and teachers. They entail the provision of detailed information about all the pupils identified as TVEI pupils, their full timetables and so on. The same kind of information is required in respect of all these teaching TVEI, not just those whose appointments were funded with TVEI money.

The other non-financial return consists of a 'curriculum database' for which TVEI schools supply information on the whole timetable of their fourth and fifth years. This information covers matters like the subject of each lesson, the make-up of the pupil group (gender, TVEI/non-TVEI, ability) and the teacher's main teaching subject.

This kind of quantitative accountability audit of the schemes is supplemented by the monitoring activities of the TVEI Unit Advisers. These are a small group of experienced educationists, carrying out broadly HMI-like activities, but with rather greater capacity to intervene in the scheme and to negotiate its development than is typically available to HMI. The advisers each cover a number of TVEI schemes. They are the first point of contact with the TVEI Unit for the schemes they oversee. They carry out support and advisory work on the ground as well as some more strictly monitoring activities. It is typically with and through the TVEI Unit advisers that LEAs initiate and negotiate changes in their contract–not surprisingly, given the haste with which the scheme was set up, a fairly common occurrence.

In addition to those accountability, audit and monitoring activities there is an extensive programme of evaluation of TVEI. Two major national evaluations (both intended to be formative) are funded by TVEI, one basically quantitative to be carried out by the NFER, the other basically qualitative, to be carried out by Leeds University. Besides the national evaluations, each of the second-round TVEI authorities (for details of the various 'rounds' of TVEI, see Dale 1985) was required to set aside at least 1 per cent of its funding for independent external evaluation, and by now most of the original fourteen first-round authorities, too, have set some form of local evaluation in train. These local evaluations differ from each other in their aims and methods, and in the resources available to them; they report to local steering committees and through them to the LEA and the TVEI Unit in the MSC. One other body with an interest in TVEI is HMI. Groups of HMI went into each of the first-round authorities in 1984, and it is planned that they will carry out similar or even more intensive exercises with second-round authorities early in 1985.

Given all these accountability, audit, monitoring and evaluation exercises, it is hardly surprising that some schools fear being 'evaluated to death' and half-jokingly suggest that they will soon be spending more time completing evaluation returns for all the interested parties than they will on making TVEI work. This may be slightly exaggerated, but undoubtedly the concentrated focus on TVEI does have very important implications for the schools involved. The overall effect is to ensure that TVEI is taken very seriously by the schools, though only a small minority of their pupils may be involved. The need to account for what happens in TVEI in very much more precise detail than is required of them by any other body, and over a much wider range of topics – for instance, teachers in receipt of TVEI allowances may be required to demonstrate what they do in justification of those allowances – almost inevitably gives TVEI a far greater prominence within the school than other less closely observed programmes that might involve many more staff and pupils.

One other feature of the structure of TVEI that affects its reception and the effectiveness of its implementation is the fact that it operates 'at the margins' of the school. That is to say, everything that TVEI brings to a school is additional; it cannot be used for the funding of the school's other activities. However, TVEI funding does not cover the cost of all the education received even by TVEI pupils. For the majority of their time in school, most TVEI pupils are being taught by 'non-TVEI' teachers, using 'non-TVEI' equipment. Furthermore, TVEI funding is much more secure, at least for the five years for which it has so far been committed, than most of the other funding available to the school. It is, for instance, not dependent on local authorities' decisions about the level and allocation of funding available to schools. Whether these are influenced by falling rolls or declining rate income the result over recent years has been to cut the number of teachers in secondary schools. This, of course, means that the TVEI-funded areas are likely to grow in proportional strength over the five years of the project, as the only areas immune from the cuts. All of this suggests that TVEI's operation at the margins of the school, like the intensity of it monitoring, provides it with disproportionately greater influence than might be assumed from the level of funding and the number of pupils involved.

The structure of TVEI, then, provides a framework that has at least a potential for control over the direction and detail of each local scheme, and ensures that at the level of the school TVEI is both prominent and likely to be influential. It does not, though, tell us how the structure is used in practice, how closely (and how) it is related to the guidelines for TVEI. Nor, of course, do the level and intensity of monitoring reveal its purpose; but two of the purposes of the monitoring must be to provide a basis for replicating the scheme, through the identification of good and bad practice, for instance, and to control the use of resources provided. Hence, in order to understand TVEI in action, we have to try to locate the criteria for identifying good and bad practice, and for deciding what are appropriate uses of the resources.

At this point, the analysis becomes particularly tentative, but I want to suggest that there is a broad ideology in which those criteria are rooted. This ideology is related not only to the TVEI guidelines, but also to a view of a broad set of educational practices through which they might best be achieved. This view, which also takes seriously both the injunction that TVEI is about helping young people 'learn to learn', and the argument about the effectiveness of 'learning by doing', assumes that the guidelines will not best be achieved through the normal patterns and processes of secondary schooling.

Any label for this ideology is bound to be misleading, but in the hope that it is more than compensatingly enlightening, I will refer to it as the 'new FE' ideology, since it has been developed theoretically especially by the Further Education Unit and in practice through the experience of various vocational preparation courses for unemployed young people, under the auspices of the MSC, in colleges of further education. Perhaps its most complete expression as far as schools are concerned is in the proposals for the Certificate of Pre-Vocational Education, which are clearly influenced by it. However, before going on to describe what seems to me the most salient characteristics I must emphasise that neither is the ideology explicitly formulated in TVEI, nor are all those involved in TVEI equally enthusiastic about it (some are very committed, others much more sceptical), nor are all its component parts equally appropriate in TVEI. On the other hand, it has had some impact in TVEI schools where teachers talk about having to learn a new language, and where they refer increasingly less self-consciously to things like 'occupational training families' or 'generic skills' that had previously not been so common in their vocabulary. The medium through which this broad ideology is often made especially evident in TVEI schools is the development of profiling. This merits an article in itself, but both the desirability and the practicability of confining pupils' profiles to being records of achievement and nothing more, and containing their ramifications into practically all other areas of school life, are matters of extensive debate in many TVEI schools.

The key features of this 'new FE' pedagogy can be listed quite briefly. They include a model of curriculum organisation that, putting it extremely simply, stresses the extrinsic rather than

37

intrinsic value and importance of education. It is based on the teaching of courses with specific skill and/or knowledge targets to which traditional 'subjects' contribute, rather than being themselves both the purpose and the medium of teaching and organisation. Another aspect of this is an emphasis on the teaching of skills as well as, or rather than, the teaching of a particular content. In terms of pedagogy, too, the emphasis is on the instrumental value of education for students. This places the students at the centre of their own learning and sees them negotiating their own curriculum on the basis of their strengths, preferences and intentions, rather than fitting them to the demands of the timetable. The process of learning also places students and their motivation at the centre of things, with an emphasis on problem-solving and experiential learning rather than more abstract and academic processes. The student is similarly placed at the centre of the assessment process, where there is a preference for criterion rather than norm referencing, and where the crucial feature of profiling enables students both to contribute to their own record of achievement and to make use of it as a basis for negotiating their own curriculum.

This is a condensed and abstract account of a complex and far from coherent or complete set of concepts and practices, but it does, I hope, catch the central thrust of TVEI ideology, in so far as that can be said to exist. In essence, that ideology represents a major challenge to the professional and academic interests that have been the dominant influence on the secondary school curriculum and of the educational experiences of most young people in school. It seeks to move the centre of gravity away from the academic, rooted in the university-controlled GCE domination of the secondary curriculum, to the vocational. It is a means of working through the practical curricular, pedagogic and assessment implications of that attempted shift from the expressive to the instrumental, the intrinsic to the extrinsic. The nature of the intended shift, and an idea of how far it has progressed already, is well caught in the following quotation from two leading exponents of 'progressive' comprehensive education:

> In the past the comprehensive school appeared to gear itself to meet its main challenge from the pro-grammar-school lobby, in terms of the performance of a minority of its pupils in the Ordinary and Advanced Certificates of Education. Now schools are being questioned about their failure to equip pupils with sufficient skills to adapt to current uncertainties attached to adult life.

(Galton and Moon 1983:p.5)

The TVEI effect

Both the structure and the ideology of TVEI constrain the breadth of possible interpretations of the TVEI guidelines. They do not do this in a denotative way, however, and the scope for possible interpretations of the guidelines remains wide. The most important effect of the structure and ideology is that they make treating TVEI as merely a piece of curriculum reform, in the narrow sense of changing the subjects taught to a particular group of students, extremely difficult. Conceving of, and delivering, an acceptable interpretation of TVEI almost necessarily involves a combination of factors. Critical differences between TVEI schemes come not only from their emphasising different aspects of the guidelines - such as subject development, profiling or work experience - but from the particular combination of those aspects in each school. This combination is a key component of what I will call the 'TVEI effect', and its precise formulation is shaped by the reaction to, and interpretation of, the TVEI guidelines, and the resources available in the changing context of each school.

The TVEI effect, what TVEI means within any school, is not produced only by each school's interpretation and combination of the set guidelines, however. It is also a function of the *salience* of the scheme within the school. This is made up of a number of factors, which will be discussed below. Like the combination of TVEI guidelines adopted within a school, the salience of TVEI results from the reaction of the headteacher and staff to the introduction of the scheme in the context of a particular school at a particular point in its history. The combination of TVEI guidelines and the scheme's salience within a school are mutually influential, whether mutually supportive or mutually hostile, and their relationship, together with the effect on the scheme of any changes in what is going on in the major part of the school, gives the TVEI effect its internal dynamic and determines the nature of the school's response to external factors.

In this final section of this chapter, then, I first of all consider something of the range of variation in the interpretation of some of the guidelines. I then go on to look at the idea of the salience of TVEI in the school, and finish by suggesting some of the key conditions within schools under which the guidelines are interpreted and the salience determined.

Most obviously, introducing TVEI into a school might be expected to involve some change in what is taught, either through the introduction of new subjects to the curriculum or in the modification of existing subjects. There is, however, considerable variation in the extent of change in what is taught, from the introduction of a whole new slate of 'TVEI subjects' that did not previously exist in the school, to the use of TVEI resources to teach existing, and unmodified, syllabuses more effectively. It is important to recognise that the degree of subject change brought about by TVEI is not the only nor necessarily the most important index of its effect on schools. Though we would be right in assuming that it will typically be a central component of the TVEI effect, it is possible to conceive of a potent TVEI effect being achieved in a school with little modification of pre-TVEI syllabuses.

A key 'non-subject' aspect of the TVEI is profiling. Though the guidelines speak only of 'records of achievement', in the great majority of TVEI schemes that requirement is met by something called 'profiling'. The possible variations of practice under that heading are very wide. Some schemes have adapted 'off the shelf' existing forms of profiling, while others have devised their own, often at great cost in teachers' time and effort. A variety of possible uses of pupils' profiles exists. They can be summative or formative, for teacher use only or available to parents and students too, and so on; but the major distinction in their contribution to the TVEI effect is between those (relatively few) schemes where that contribution is substantive, where profiling is a key organising axis of the whole scheme, and those where it is limited to a more or less important service function.

The contribution of work experience to the TVEI effect can be appreciated in a rather similar way, in that its extent and nature vary with the degree to which the two periods of work experience that students must undergo in the course of the four-year scheme are integrated into the scheme as a whole, or treated as quite separate part of it. It is possible for the curriculum as a whole and the period of work experience to be organised in full recognition of the mutual benefit they could provide; or it is possible for the organisation of work experience to be seen as just another chore entailed by taking the TVEI money and using it for things that are really important. The reaction to, and integration of, work experience can, indeed, stand for the perceived place and importance of 'links with industry' as a whole within TVEI schemes.

Residential education's contribution to the TVEI effect, too, varies with the nature and extent of its integration into the scheme as a whole. This applies to both of the two main forms it appears to have taken: the 'outward-bound' form, where the 'adventure and self-reliance' medium is a more central part of the message than the actual context in which it takes place; and the 'curriculum enrichment' form, where students are brought into contact with aspects of their subjects that lie outside the ability of the school to provide.

Besides the guidelines contained in the contract there are some other necessary accompaniments of bringing TVEI into a school, which may be important components of the TVEI effect. One of these, which has already been mentioned, is the prominence of the scheme in the school. Another very important one, which it is easy to take for granted, is the need for schools to spend in a relatively short time relatively large sums of money, (though the precise amount of money available for spending by schools and the precise degree of control they have over that spending vary). This presents both technical and political difficulties. The technical difficulties arise as much as anything from schools' sheer inexperience of disposing of large sums of money in a short time in the most appropriate way. This inexperience, together with the short time-scale, may indeed lead to a conservatism in spending the money, i.e. a tendency to spend it on somewhat more advanced equipment for teaching essentially the same content. More time for deliberation, and the consideration of alternatives, may have led in some cases to rather more 'radical' uses of the money.

The political problems associated with the distribution of the extra funds may also tend to push it into a similarly conservative direction. Any distribution, whether it is of equipment or additional salary points, is likely to be perceived as threatening by one or other subject departments or groups of staff within a school, and again there is some pressure towards changing as little as possible, 'doing more of the same' or introducing initiatives that cross the whole curriculum.

The magnification of the TVEI impact in the school through monitoring and marginality clearly enhances its prominence. This relates to what I have called the 'salience' of TVEI in the school. This contributes a great deal to the TVEI effect. It is made up of three components: indentity, integration and compass. Identity refers both to the amount and to the nature of what is known about the scheme within the school. The public identity of a school's TVEI scheme can be found in the way the scheme is

41

publicised to the staff and to the pupils and_parents. It appears perhaps most clearly in the way TVEI is 'marketed' to pupils and parents. Is it separately identified in the options booklets? Is there a preferred target audience implicit in the way the scheme is described (and especially in the subjects it is possible to take alongside TVEI)? How far is its technical and vocational nature stressed, and especially its 'job-getting' potential? The clarity, popularity and divisiveness of the TVEI identity within a school are rooted in part in the kind of public face presented. They are also rooted in the less public aspect of TVEI in practice, which itself derives from the kind of changes entailed by the way the school interprets and combines the guidelines.

Together with its identity, the extent of its integration into the school as a whole determines the 'profile' of TVEI in the school. It is possible, for instance, for TVEI pupils, their parents and those who teach them not to be aware of their TVEI status. The degree of integration of TVEI into the school is associated with the degree of separateness of the TVEI group(s). This is a function of the number of hours they spend being taught as a separate group, the number of teachers teaching them, whether or not they are a group for non-TVEI purposes – especially whether they are a distinct registration group – and whether or not they have their own accommodation. The extent of TVEI's integration into a school is associated not only with the degree of isolation of those directly involved in it. It is also determined by the spread of information about it among those teachers not directly involved, whether they are made aware only of what they 'need' to know for the smooth operation of the scheme – which in many cases will be nothing – or of the broader details and ramifications of the scheme as a whole as it develops.

What I am calling its 'compass', the degree to which it penetrates and affects the workings of the rest of the school, is another part of its salience, but it is not directly linked to the height of profile. The compass of TVEI in a school comes about through a combination of articulation and infection. Articulation refers to the changes necessarily implied for the rest of the school by TVEI; for instance, in the timetable, or the need to construct viable classes in particular subjects. Infection refers to the 'voluntary' reactions in the rest of the school to TVEI. These can be either positive – as might occur, for instance, in a decision to profile whole year groups and not just the TVEI effect, the combination of the guidelines and its salience, departments teaching 'core' subjects to accommodate any changes in approach implied by the introduction of TVEI; such as, for instance, a shift from English to 'communications', or Mathematics to 'numeracy'.

It is crucial to realise that the form taken by both components of the TVEI effect, the combination of the guidelines and its salience, emerges, and continues to change, through a complex process of negotiation between what was before TVEI and what might emerge as a result of it. These negotiations, explicit and implicit, between head and staff, co-ordinator and departments, members of the same department and so on, do not take place in a neutral arena. That arena is defined and marked by the history of previous negotiations, which are unique to each school. TVEI both heightens the importance of some facets of that history, and brings new aspects of it into play, as well as filtering the effect of external events into and on the negotiations. Among the especially prominent conditions of negotiation over TVEI are:

(1) The generally low level of morale within the teaching profession, following some years of declining funds, falling roles and apparent decreasing public esteem. This meant a warm welcome for almost anything that promised extra funding and the possibility of professional development.

(2) Considerable resistance among both the leadership and the rank and file of the teaching profession to a narrowly defined 'vocational education' – the preparation of factory fodder – and to anything that threatened the principles of comprehensive education.

(3) The heightening of this resistance through the apparent attribution to teachers of blame for national decline in the debates that prefigured TVEI, where teachers appeared as scapegoats, as part of the problem rather than part of the solution.

(4) The existence of a growing pressure towards some kind of differential reward for different performance in the payment of teachers.

(5) The possibility that some subjects might disappear from the curriculum with declining staffing levels.

(6) Apprehension over the effects of the entry of the MSC into the area of further education.

(7) A heightened awareness of competition between secondary schools, possibly involving their very survival, as a result of falling rolls.

43

Not all the factors apply in all cases. More importantly, they do not all carry equal weight. For instance, the need for extra funds in most cases outweighed any reservations about TVEI. It did not, though, remove those reservations, and a common pattern of acceptance of TVEI into a school is to attempt to do it with minimum infringement of those reservations. But that is only one form of response, albeit fairly typical. The main point is that whatever the orientation towards TVEI, however significant the various conditions of negotiation may be, TVEI is never merely imposed on schools. It is always accepted on certain implicit or explicit conditions based largely on the existing history, ideology, structure and location of the school, to produce a TVEI effect unique to that school.

Conclusion

I have argued here that although TVEI varies immensely across authorities and schools, it does not vary infinitely. The variations are constrained by the origins of the initiative, the problems it was created to solve. These led to it taking on a particular broad structure and ideology, both of which allowed a very wide range of local variation. The nature and extent of that variation are shaped in the schools into their unique TVEI effect by their own history and the conditions under which TVEI was accepted into the schools. In the end, although it may be changed or even transformed by TVEI, the surest guide to understanding TVEI in a school is what the school was like before.

References

Dale, Roger (1985) 'The Background and Inception of the Technical and Vocational Education Initiative', in Roger Dale (ed.), *Education, Training and Employment: Towards a 'New Vocationalism'?* Oxford, Pergamon.

Esland, Geoff and Cathcart, Heather (1981) *Education and the Corporate Economy: Course E353 Unit 2.* Milton Keynes, Open University Press.

Galton, Maurice and Moon, Bob (eds.) (1983) *Changing Schools, Changing Curriculum.* London, Harper & Row.

Manpower Services Commission (1984). TVEI Operating Manual.

Reeder, David (1979) 'A Recurring Debate: Education and Industry', in G. Bernbaum (ed.), *Schooling in Decline.* London, Macmillan: pp. 115-48.

Acknowledgements

I would like to thank Hugh Carr-Archer, Gaynor Cohen, Simon Sandberg, Pat Sikes, Mike Taylor and Gordon Vincent for the valuable comments and suggestions they made on an earlier version of this chapter.

CHAPTER THREE

Further Education, Free Enterprise and the Curriculum

Denis Gleeson

Background

Despite the interest shown by sociologists of education in the relationship between schooling and capitalism in the mid-1970s, this interest has been short-lived. In recent years recession and rising youth unemployment have ironically undermined sociological accounts of the ways in which schools reproduce the preconditions of capitalism. Not only has the collapse of work seriously undermined traditional conceptions of schooling, but it has also made it increasingly more difficult to talk, in any straightforward sense, about 'correspondence' between school and work (Bowles and Gintis 1976). Rather less interest is now taken in the ways in which capitalist relations find their expression in the curricular arrangements of schooling, and more in the effects of political and economic change on the macro-context of state education policy (Ahier and Flude 1983).

There are perhaps compelling reasons why this should be the case. At one level unemployment, demographic change and cuts in public expenditure have radically altered the conventional relationship between school and work, thereby extending the period during which the young enter adulthood and capitalism itself. At another, recent attempts to reshape LEA budgets to make them more receptive to government training initiatives have ensured the central place of the state in structuring national priorities at the local level (MSC 1981, White Papers 1981 and

1984). Perhaps not surprisingly, keener interest is now taken in the shape of state education and training policy and the ways it is seen to regulate the activities of unemployed youth. To date the focus of that interest has centred on various structural functions associated with training; that is, how it:

- reduces the level of youth and adult wages;
- encourages employers to train rather than employ;
- reduces the significance of apprenticeship;
- enacts employer definitions of worker status;
- hands employees over to employers for positive vetting.

(ILP 1983, LRS 1983, NTG 1983)

It is not my intention here to undermine the importance of such a perspective. In many respects it identifies the dominant social control 'function' of training and the way in which the 'new' vocationalism exploits young people. Moreover, it also draws attention to the regulative aspects of training policy and its close association with contemporary conservative political and economic thinking. The weakness of the approach is, however, that it does not adequately explain the ways in which such political and economic thinking finds its expression in the curricular arrangements that support training policy. As a consequence we know little about how the various 'functions' described by this perspective are realised (or not as the case may be) within the complex social relations of further education and training practice. It is to this neglected aspect of the relationship between curriculum and policy that this chapter is addressed.

Introduction

Until recently the further education activities of 16—19-year-olds remained a neglected area of sociological enquiry; FE's voluntaristic and entrepreneurial character perhaps reflecting the low status image traditionally associated with technical education. With a few notable exceptions (Venables 1967, Robinson 1968, Tipton 1973) research in the sociology of education has tended to focus on schooling with little or no attention paid to the activities of industrial trainers. However, the legacy of youth unemployment and the rise of the MSC have ensured that the debate about FE and training is unlikely to remain unchanged. Once considered an educational backwater, FE has today entered the forefront of educational debate. In the two decades following publication of the Crowther Report (1959) much has happened to the non-advanced FE sector, not least to the expansion and diversification of its links with industry, student intake and curricular arrangements. Since then, however, the degree of decentralised development has been increasingly brought under control by centralist measures designed to incorporate FE within the wider context of state training policy (White Paper 1984).

During a period in which government has reduced support for publicly owned industry and pursued an aggressive policy of privatisation, training policy remains a conspicuous exception. As spending on the 'New Training Initiative' (MSC 1981) tops £4.5 billion in 1986, a watershed in training policy has been reached, whereby the state has now taken over responsibility of training from employers (Ryan 1984). At a time when the efficiency of state enterprise is viewed with considerable scepticism it is ironic that government policy should effectively nationalise training, thereby removing it from the private sector and placing it in the hands of the Civil Service. It should be recognised, however, that training policy does not simply represent a response to unemployment but is also designed to alter relations in the work-place in favour of employers (Fairley and Grahl 1983). From this viewpoint, training has a closer relationship with private enterprise than might first appear; it also represents an important political mechanism through which labour is made ready and available for work. This matter will be taken up later.

For present purposes what remains less than clear is the part FE is likely to play within the more centralised arrangements of training. At the moment FE is at the crossroads between its voluntaristic tradition and the newer compulsory elements that have come to challenge it. If in 1968 the non-advanced sector of FE could be described as 'unchartered territory' (Robinson 1968), this sector has now taken on a more systematic appearance. Paradoxically, the rise of youth unemployment has not only initiated far reaching reforms, but it has also bred fresh life into many of Crowther's original proposals, notably in relation to the extension of FE 'for all'. If, however, Crowther's ghost would appear to be alive and well, considerable ambiguity exists about how far FE and training represent an 'alternative route' or 'second chance' for those students traditionally denied access to their ranks, but now included through MSC provision. This chapter considers two interrelated aspects of this problem. The first concerns changing patterns of student participation in FE and the structuring of youth opportunities in the labour market via various types of curricular experience, notably 'basic skills' and 'generic skills' training. The second concerns the ways in which political and economic policy find their expression in the curriculum and organisation of FE, thereby shaping the wider social relations between FE, industry and the state. At the outset it is perhaps important to say something about recent developments in FE and training and its incorporation within more centralised forms of control.

Continuity and change in FE and training

Despite the recent controversy surrounding the way in which the MSC 'bought its way' into FE (Moos 1984), its entry has been achieved relatively easily. If, at one level, this can simply be explained in terms of cash inputs, at another, many educationlists, trade unionists and others welcomed MSC intervention as a progressive means of extending training provision to school-leavers traditionally denied access to its ranks. Rising youth unemployment and the slow response of the DES in the mid-1970s prompted some commentators to view MSC overtures in a reformist light (Hayes 1983, Watts 1983). Moreover, attempts to initiate training measures such as YOP served only to illustrate the inadequacies of existing training provision and to legitimate the further extension of mass training as a good thing. However, at this time pragmatism and reformism also combined to enable colleges to maintain levels of student intake threatened by the collapse of local labour markets. In this respect LEAs and colleges were not 'innocent' parties in the market-place negotiations that took place in the late 1970s, wherein the flexibility of the points system allowed cash and provision to change hands.

Thus the way in which private enterprise finds its expression in the arrangements of further education is not a new phenomenon. Indeed, the ethos of contemporary FE is rooted in its voluntaristic and entrepreneurial traditions, which have for long been associated with the fortunes of the local labour market. Unlike mass schooling, FE has taken a highly individualistic path, its survival depending very much on the patronage of local industry, and the ability of individual colleges to attract greater student numbers. As Tipton (1973) has noted, the points system alone has ensured that many colleges remain in a perpetual state of flux, since they are constantly called upon to redefine their courses to attract new customers. This has ensured not only that the colleges operate on the basis of market forces, but that they also seek to manipulate the points system to ensure expansion and growth. Consequently the emerging pattern of FE provision since the post-war period has been patchy and has come to depend on a points system firmly anchored to the production forecasts of local industry. Perhaps not surprisingly the development of those staple forms of provision that fall within the compass of FE have traditionally tended to be both parochial and chauvinistic, catering mainly for the needs of young male apprentice workers.

With the decline in demand for industrial craft work (manu-facturing, shipbuilding, steel and so forth) in the 1960s and 1970s, FE was compelled to compensate for its loss in student intake by recruiting from a flourishing tertiary and service sector. The erratic pattern of industrial and corporate development in the 1960s, strange as it may now seem, led to demand for 'new' types of trained labour and new courses; in business and management studies, technician education, secretarial, social work, nursing, GCE studies and so forth. Thus as a result of entrepreneurial expansion many colleges became less tied to the fortunes of local manufacturing industry, particularly in the South-east, and could recruit from a wider intake of full- and part-time students than hitherto. Yet despite the progressive appearance of FE at this time, and claims that it offered a genuine 'second chance' of social mobility for working-class youth (Cantor and Roberts 1974, Bristow 1976), the vast majority of school-leavers remained outside FE and training. According to Hordley and Lee (1970) the main beneficiaries of FE at this time were the middle class, who were more likely to adopt FE as a 'second chance' (or even as a 'second choice' – Raffe 1979) route into employment or higher education.

Thus from arguments so far it would seem that the forces that impelled expansion of FE in the 1960s and 1970s correspond more closely to shifts in the occupational structure than to any clearly thought out policy of FE and training. Consequently, it is not difficult to discern the motives underlying the diversification of FE at this time, which led to the shelving of many low status courses and the upgrading of others. Neither is it surprising that regional and other labour market conditions acted to heighten competition between the colleges, resulting in the proliferation of new courses, which ironically rendered the FE system less open and less comprehensive than it might at first appear. It was not until the late 1970s and the early 1980s with the establishment of YOP, and later YTS, that FE was able to tap the unemployed and unemployable market made available to it via MSC funds (Gleeson and Mardle 1980). As on previous occasions the stimulus to broaden the FE training base arose in relation to dramatic changes in the youth labour market: in this case its almost total collapse. It is this space that the Department of Employment and its major agent the MSC has sought to exploit in recent years and that has, somewhat paradoxically, opened up new avenues of training reform.

Since Crowther the overall failure to establish a coherent policy for 16–19s has enabled the MSC to make political capital out of existing inadequacies of provision, while at the same time manipulating the entrepreneurial legacy of FE to its own advantage. Not only has this secured the state's management of school-to-work transition as a permanent feature of social policy, but it has also redefined the relationship between FE and the labour market it once served. If such state intervention has enhanced the corporate image of FE, by redefining its curriculum towards national rather than local objectives, (Moos 1984), it has also drawn attention to the failure of the DES, LEAs and colleges to provide post-school FE and training to the majority of school-leavers. Although in its earliest days the Conservative government was suspicious, even hostile, towards an expensive quango such as the MSC, it has since recognised the MSC's ideological and tactical significance. Thus, under the aegis of enlightened reform, following on the Great Education Debate (1976–9), the Conservative government, via the MSC, has established direct control over non-advanced FE and training and achieved a tighter grip over both the transition and transmission points between school and work. By this method central government has gained access to the education system and its resources, and encroached on decision-making territory previously occupied by the DES, LEAs and unions. This is epitomised in the recent switch in resources from the rate support grant to the MSC, in order to fund the takeover of 25 per cent of non-advanced FE work. Clearly such practice represents a distinct break with established social democratic thinking that, until the late 1970s, characterised policy and decision-making processes in education.

If, however, the MSC is seen to have taken the initiative by extending provision to a sector of school-leavers previously

51

excluded from training policy, it remains far from clear what benefit they derive from their 'new' experience. While patterns of participation in FE and training by class, race and gender have altered in recent years, evidence suggests that the position of young people in the labour market has changed very little (Dex 1983, Raffe 1983, Lee and Wrench 1984). Moreover, close inspection of student participation in various types of courses suggests that there exists a close interplay between those divisions found in the labour market and those found within FE and training itself (Gleeson 1983). Perhaps not surprisingly, as training opportunities have expanded in recent years, the existence of tripartite divisions have become more apparent. Though certainly less select in intake than in the past FE now directs its courses to three broadly defined yet distinct target groups. Elsewhere (Gleeson 1983) I have described these as:

- the traditional though now declining male *craft* apprentice intake (now including female craft skills: typing, child care, beauty therapy, hairdressing, cookery and so forth);
- The *academic/technical* intake of the late 1960s and 1970s: including business, management and technician studies, secretarial, nursing and social work studies, GCE studies etc;
- the *tertiary modern intake:* the unemployed and unemployable of the 1980s; the curriculum of which is largely given over to generic skills training, work experience and 'life skills' training.

Though in practice far less discrete, such broad divisions indicate something of the patchwork nature of FE and training provision at the present time. Hence, tripartism, crude device as it may appear here, broadly reflects and delineates various changes in the youth labour market and the kind of opportunities (or not as the case may be) open to young people. Noticeably the forms of curricular knowledge associated with the different routes not only separate off various categories of student, but they also confirm their status in the labour market hierarchy. At the level of teaching, administrative and curricular relations, for example, these distinctions are made manifest in a number of covert ways. Assessment of the academic/technical students' higher calibre is reflected both in the ways teachers perceive the commitment and motivation of such students (Gleeson 1980, Avis 1981) and in terms of the physical resources allocated to them. As the so-called high status element of the curriculum has grown, a tendency now exists to categorise increasing numbers of FE conscripts as 'less able', and the courses they undertake as 'Mickey Mouse'. This is noticeably the case in relation to YTS and other related low level courses associated with 'remedial training' (Atkinson and Rees 1982). In the specific case of female participation in nursing, child care and other gender-specific courses, this assumes an even more questionable dimension; here vocational training represents little more than a reinforcement of gender roles and an apprenticeship in home crafts (Blunden 1983, Gibb 1983). Elsewhere, evidence regarding black youth on YTS courses indicates that they are consistently more likely to be allocated to schemes offering inferior opportunities of subsequent employment (Fenton 1984, Lee and Wrench 1984). The 'Catch-22' for black youth is that no matter which route they take, and no matter what their level of qualifications in comparison with whites, they suffer disproportionate discrimination in the job market (Brown 1984). This view would seem to confirm the conclusions of a recent report, which indicates that

> if you had the misfortune to be born in the 1960s, and are therefore seeking your first job in the early 1980s, it does help enormously to be born the right sex and right colour, and into a family with the right occupational connections.
>
> (Lee and Wrench 1984)

While it would be misleading to exaggerate the sort of tripartite divisions so far described, there is little doubt that state training policy for the unemployed has simply added another dimension to the existing fragmented pattern of post-school provision. Cuts in education budgets and the sequestration of rate support funds in favour of the MSC have, moreover, increased the pressure to treat the unemployed as a distinct rather than an integrated group within the broader context of FE and training. There is at present enormous pressure on the colleges and LEAs to respond to the training requirements laid down by the MSC; many face the prospect that if they are unwilling to 'service' MSC requirements the MSC will simply look elsewhere and utilise the private sector to satisfy its 'off-the-job' requirements. The problem has been affected further by changing regional and demographic factors, which have intensified competition between schools, colleges and MSC for a statistically declining cohort of 16-year-olds. As the following diagram indicates, the direction of 16-year-old leavers remains as confused as ever, with noticeable divisions opening up between YTS, non-YTS and full-time provision.

53

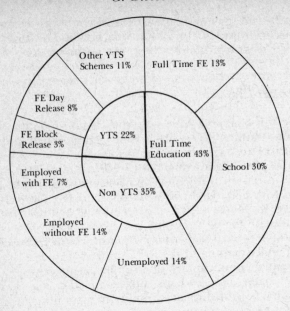

Figure 3.1 *Educational and economic activity of English 16-year-olds,
1983–4*

Source: The Times Educational Supplement, 7 December 1984.

In the absence of any comprehensive policy to deal with such a
fragmented situation, a two-tier system of provision has arisen
almost by default: one half administered and controlled by the DES
and LEAs, incorporating academic, technical and occupationally
related forms of education and training; and the other administered and controlled by the MSC, incorporating 'on-the-job' and
'off-the-job' forms of training. Despite resistance on the part of the
colleges to such a division there are clear indications that many
LEAs have surrendered a sizeable proportion of non-advanced FE
work to the MSC, and that others, stripped of cash, are soon likely
to follow. The danger is that a significant section of non-advanced
FE will simply become the 'dumping ground' for increasing
numbers of dissident and disaffected young people (Moos 1984).
One consequence of this administrative separation is that it
reinforces arbitrary divisions between education and training, and

marginalises the unemployed as a separate category with their own particular institutions, curriculum, teachers and so forth. It is to this aspect of the discussion that I now wish to turn.

Vocational literacy

So far in this chapter I have sought to demonstrate the ways in which state training policy has reinforced rather than challenged various tripartite divisions within further education and training. It has also been argued that the rise of vocationalism marks a response to certain ideological imperatives, and should not be confused with making young workers or industry more efficient. According to Moore (1983) the vocational 'realism' currently associated with the new training paradigm conceals its inherent irrationality; its purpose is seen as blocking a coherent social and political understanding of the world of work. To date, however, the curricular implications of this argument have not been seriously taken up. Perhaps understandably the dominant emphasis has been on the macro conditions of training; the ways in which training represents a substitute for employment, a mechanism for regulating youth labour markets and so forth. Yet despite evidence indicating that training creates a pool of low wage workers, it is the ideological arguments in favour of how private enterprise *ought* to work that are important for understanding the essential curricular ingredients of the new vocationalism. The kinds of argument that, for example, support generic skills training do not find their expression in work practice, but in an idealised conception of how industrial relations ought to function under free market conditions. The ideological significance of skills training is that it projects the learner as a flexible entity, capable of being employed or re-employed in a variety of different jobs within the same occupational training family. Essentially there are two problems with this notion of training for competency in OTFs. In the first place there is no clear evidence what transferable skills are, how they are transmitted and how they are transferred (Jones 1984). Secondly, OTFs assume a causal connection to exist between work and the curriculum: the assumption being that one can unambigiously work backwards from work to the type of training required for the performance of that work. Elsewhere in further education, developments in business, management and tecnician education reflect this causal mode of curriculum design. Such a

model suggests that once synchronisation between technical education and work is achieved, the educational system will simply
provide the type and commodity required by the labour market.

It is within this idealisation of the links between work and
education that contemporary training policy is located; its aim is
to reduce worker dependence on outmoded skills and to ensure the
adaptability of the worker in the face of changing economic
circumstances. Consequently, a major selling point of transferable
skills training to employers is not the level of technical skills it
imparts but the *type* of labour it provides. In this respect youth
training takes on a different meaning from that traditionally
associated with training for a specific job. Here the concept of
socialised labour trained for *anything* is perhaps a more accurate
assessment. Thus, despite the apparent vocational realism
employed in this approach no discernible links exist between the
content of training provided and the actual content of work
available. This is most marked in the area of 'self-starting', an
element designed to introduce entrepreneurship into the curriculum. Whether intended or not, attempts to prepare trainees to earn
a living or make out in non-work situations (by 'starting your own
business' or by 'preparing for self-employment') pre-set young
people to think of themselves *outside* rather than within the
mainstream of society. From this perspective it is not vocational
realism but vocational idealism that has come to challenge
contemporary educational practice (Esland and Cathcart 1984).

If the spirit of individualism evident in such an approach bears
the imprint of radical conservative thinking, it should not be
confused with attempts to increase the efficiency of industry or to
enhance the freedom of the individual. Rather, it is the uncertainty
of the young's employment prospects that legitimates the
construction of 'skills training' and allows the state to 'protect'
youth from the inimical influence of unemployment. Perhaps not
surprisingly within the context of communication and life skills
training, 'standing on one's own feet' is not concerned with the
individual acting on society, or of him/her struggling against the
forces that entrap him/her. Essentially, the life management
approach to 'SLS' training emphasises individual *adaptation* and
survival; society as such is not thrown open to question other than
in the narrowest of terms.

Consider, for example, the MSC's view of the skills trainers are
asked to evaluate under the heading 'The world outside
employment':

The World Outside Employment

	Yes Not Yet	with Help	Yes
The importance of keeping clean			
How to use a bank or building society			
How to plan money			
About any staff discounts, the social club, etc.			
How to be loyal to the work-place			
What people expect of each other away from work			
How to apply for a job			
How to use the telephone			

(MSC 1984)

What is perhaps most revealing here is the preface that describes the check-list as 'a variety of skills and knowledge which when understood can assist a young person to develop within the community as a whole'. Elsewhere in the same notes of guidance, 'personal effectiveness' is measured in terms of the trainees' ability to 'talk to strangers', 'be polite and helpful', 'behave in the right way', and so forth (MSC 1984). In this respect the curriculum supporting such basic skills represents little more than a crude attempt at colonising everyday life (Atkinson 1984), linked with filling in forms, opening accounts and generally 'being good'. Not only does this kind of presumptive approach fail to get to grips with the very real educational and learning difficulties that affect young people, but it also conveys an implicit assessment of their position and worth in society. One consequence of this is that trainees are made more aware of what mainstream society expects of them, in terms of attitude, behaviour, motivation and so forth, but which as *outsiders* is nevertheless beyond their reach.

Under these circumstances youth training represents little more than a particular form of mass vocational literacy that shifts responsibility for the reproduction of workers back on to themselves. Training the unemployed not only enables them to 'stand on their own two feet' (after all, we trained them) but also seeks to handle the perceived workers' reproduction deficiences, i.e. their lack of basic skills. By making workers more responsible for their own destinies – epitomised in the terms 'on your bike'

G. Gleeson

(Norman Tebbitt 1983) and 'taking your skills with you' (Hayes 1983) – in this way no recriminations can be made against employers or the state, since it is the market that is the deciding factor. In this respect training policy simply replicates nineteenth-century liberal economic thinking: the point being to have an unlimited elastic supply of labour the quality of which is not *that* important (Broady 1981). The paradox of training is that the demand side is presently being manufactured by the state, via the MSC and its managing agents, and cheap labour 'sold back' to employers as a going concern. As the following newspaper advertisement, sandwiched between second-hand cars and situations vacant, indicates, YTS labour can be 'conveniently' marketed and packaged like any other product.

> Work Experience Places Wanted – No Cost to Employers. School-leavers who have been professionally trained in typing and other secretarial subjects by Sight and Sound are available for work experience with Central London employers under the Youth Training Scheme. No cost to employers, no paperwork. Please ring our YTS Liaison Officer for full details.
>
> (London *Evening Standard*, 25 October 1983)

While there is, of course, no clear evidence that basic skills training has any direct effect on young people's attitudes, it is perhaps what gets left out of the curriculum that is important: notably the absence of any general and political education. Yet recent attempts to keep politics out of training (Morrison 1983) have ironically only drawn attention to this neglected area. Peter Morrison's now famous proclamation that 'I am totally convinced that the youth training scheme is all about the world of work, and I don't want it to get a bad name if politics got involved' *(The Times Educational Supplement,* 23 September 1983) has, if anything, increased public suspicion of the MSC's political ambitions in redefining curricular priorities in this area. Despite attempts to play down the censorship of political education in YTS there can be little doubt, as the following communique from the MSC to managing agents makes clear, that politics has little to do with learning about British industry:

> Managing agents should note that their agreement with the Commission requires that the training programme be run in a 'manner acceptable to the Commission'. A key requirement will be that it is not involved in any activity of a political nature or any activity likely to bring the Commission into public controversy or

discredit. If this requirement is not met it could result in the immediate closure of a programme.

(MSC 1983)

It would seem from such remarks that the debate about 'teacher accountability' has shifted in a direction unforeseen by the DES in the immediate years following Jim Callaghan's Ruskin College speech (1976). Despite the problem of how to teach trainees about work without reference to the wider structures of society, such directives convey a political message regarding the MSC's view of training, and its own standing with employers. Perhaps this explains why the MSC has chosen to opt for 'guidance and counselling' as a more acceptable means of fostering in young people those skills that will enable them to adopt 'the right role at work' (MSC 1983). Closer inspection of the meaning of this phrase indicates that 'acceptance of authority', 'taking orders' and 'work skills' represent the most significant core elements of the skills involved (MSC 1977, 1982). Quoting from MSC guidelines, Seale (1983), for example, detects a 'semi-punitive' approach to counselling:

"4.2   The role of the counsellor
He/she must be aware of
4.2.1 any change in work performance against the trainee's
       norm
4.2.2 signs of alienation in matters of time-keeping,
       discipline etc., and
4.2.3 any unsatisfactory relationships
Any of the above must be seen as a need for counselling."
(MSC guidelines quoted in Seale, 1983)

Here counselling is seen by Seale as little more than a mechanism for policing the individual's motivation towards work, and providing essential information for inclusion in his/her personal profile. No less remarkable is the MSC's appraisal of the skills essential to what it terms 'a satisfactory private life' (MSC 1977, 1982), wherein the skills of 'making friends', 'resisting provocation' and 'making conversation' represent the extent of MSC thinking on the subject.

That this is all there is to life, or that such limited conceptions eschew political involvement, reflects a particular ideological position presenting training as a neutral mechanism necessitated by individual rather than structural constraints. From this position questions regarding how industry is organised and

59

managed, how wealth is accumulated, how wages, skills and allowances are legitimated and sustained, can be conveniently edited out of training as politically extraneous. The political effect, however, is to separate off the study of work from the society that surrounds it, thereby reducing the entire framework of industrial matters to a narrow set of technical propositions. As a consequence, 'learning about British industry' and 'entering the world of work' become little more than euphemisms for learning about one's place. It is within this overall structure that trainees' political horizons are controlled and their broader vision of the issues and possibilities surrounding them severely restricted.

Beyond critiques?

It could be argued that the issues to which this chapter are addressed are simply political and economic in nature, the solutions to which cannot be conceived of in terms of education and training alone. Having said this, however, the discussion of possible alternatives does not automatically follow on. It is also the case, for example, that the problem cannot be explained in terms of the truism 'there ain't no jobs', crucial as this may be. One of the ironies of MSC policy is that it has drawn attention to long-standing issues in the relationship between school and work, which predate the rapid increase in unemployment in the late 1970s. Prior to this time little sociological interest was taken in the fate of young workers entering dead-end jobs, the majority of whom had little or no access to further education or training. If the research literature and official documents in this period focussed on topics such as 'occupational choice' and 'career opportunities', the reality open to many young people was that of low paid and unskilled work. Thus simply to demand a return to the full employment conditions of the 1960s, even if that were possible, ignores the limiting effects of various types of work on young people's long-term social opportunities. As Roberts (1984) has recently argued, popular as a mass extension of unskilled or semi-skilled work might appear at the present time, it would not alleviate the problem of low pay, boredom and chronic job changing; neither would it clarify what the relationship should be between education, training and work. The problem at the moment is that chronic job changing has been replaced by chronic scheme changing (Raffe 1983) without any fundamental appraisal being made of the nature of work itself.

According to Tipton (1983) there is a basic flaw in much of the current thinking about how to improve the quality of training; its terms are that no questions are asked about the quality of work, its structure, design, organisation and so forth. At present extending training for existing forms of monotonous and humdrum work is likely to increase conflict and tension between trainees, teachers and employers as expectations are frustrated. To date the nature of work has been taken as given by educationists and others and, as a consequence, few attempts exist to combine policies for training with policies for work design. Moreover, trade unions and employers have shown little interest in the need for workers to participate in well designed jobs or even reduce working hours. Yet, as Tipton (1983) argues, training *is* for jobs. The likelihood is that little will be achieved on this front until a legal duty is placed on employers to consult with unions on all training issues, and the right to education and training is placed on the collective bargaining agenda. Despite the obvious pitfalls, only by re-defining and restructuring work patterns does it offer the possibility that 'training for work' may take on a broader meaning than the present narrow vocationalism allows. Little will happen on this front until trade unions are more actively involved in industrial democracy (Bullock 1977) and government and industry legally obliged to co-operate in matters regarding work design, training and the further education of all workers. Without such co-operation it is unlikely that training provision in its present form will inspire much confidence or public support.

This, however, is likely to pale into insignificance if both an educational policy and an enlightened funding programme for 16–18-year-olds are not found to address the present patchwork nature of non-advanced FE provision. At the root of the problem is a totally inadequate system of financial provision for students in this age group; at the moment their lack of political muscle renders them prey to parental dependence, discretionary grants or the MSC's 'shilling'. While the sitation of such students is unlikely to stir so much as a back-bench revolt, the sheer size of the problem suggests that jerry-built training will, in the long term, not succeed. Given that increasing numbers of school-leavers are unlikely to enter the labour market much before 18 or 19, the arguments for building a comprehensive education and training system are compelling (TUC/Labour Party 1984); not least because the ground rules of schooling have significantly changed.

Regional, demographic, occupational and other factors have

not only altered the structural relationship between school and work; they have also called into question present makeshift arrangements for regulating young people's entry to the labour market. To date there has been no concerted attempt to develop a co-ordinated education and training policy for the 16–19 age group as a whole. Instead we have witnessed a succession of critiques of standards in education and the assumed failure of teachers to direct pupils towards more vocationally relevant subjects. Meanwhile the traditional examination system has remained untouched other than in terms of tinkering with the GCE/CSE system and introducing an array of 16, 17 and other pre-vocational reforms. As such the 'new' vocationalism has followed a separate path from mainstream schooling and has done little to challenge entrenched assumptions regarding high status knowledge in the curriculum and its close asociation with the examination system and the labour market hierarchy. In this respect the dominant emphasis on theoretical, abstract and scientific knowledge has gone largely unquestioned by the MSC. For the so-called disadvantaged, however, the dominant pedagogic experience has been extended and remains firmly anchored within practical, relevant and vocational knowledge: a form of control traditionally associated with ensuring the lower orders' obligation to the system and their awareness of its dominant moral codes.

Perhaps the major weakness of contemporary training policy is that it neither specifies specific skills training nor provides an adequate general education. Thus, under present conditions, the young lose out both ways; on the one hand, they do not gain marketable or recognised skills and, on the other, they do not acquire knowledge and understanding, however broadly defined, that allow them critical insight into the political or economic workings of society. Perhaps not surprisingly, the expansion of vocational training has resulted in inferior general education, without the employment prospects of young people altering much one way or the other. One effect of YTS, and also TVEI, is that it forces young people to settle on vocational training and employment issues too early on. Despite the publicity given to core areas and transferable skills training, early specialisaton narrows the options open to young people later on in life. Consequently, without a broadly based general education it is most unlikely that students will be able to utilise forms of training that they have not been educated to absorb.

Unpopular as the demand for general education may be at

present, the indications are that employers, educationists and others do not recognise the relevance of contemporary "skills training," which is not seen to embody the general indicators of competence required to gain access to the job market. It is perhaps time to recognise that experimentation with generic skills training has been a failure, and that the sacrifice of general education for a gain in vocationalism has not been worth the trade (Jackson 1981). The perfunctory time accorded to either learning technical 'know-how' or acquiring general knowledge suggests that students are getting neither education nor training. The irony, as Willis (1984) has pointed out, is that working-class youth who know much about work, and are prepared to put up with its most boring and exploited forms, should have basic work skills pushed down their throats from a very early age. Moreover, the fact that so few workers eventually end up in trades for which they were trained suggests that training without general education has, anyway, little vocational relevance. The likelihood is that a broadly based education, which combines learning about work alongside the study of society, including options drawn from the arts, sciences, humanities, social sciences and so forth, will in the long run have more public support and perhaps possess greater vocational relevance. This is not to advocate resurrecting piecemeal injections of liberal studies or political education, which in the 1960s and 1970s, were driven like a wedge into the curriculum to offset the worst effects of over-specialisation. What is called for at the present time is a balanced curriculum that integrates a broad range of theoretical and practical skills and seeks to break down existing tripartite divisions. Bringing education back in will not be an easy task, not least because the terms and conditions of conventional liberal humanist education have changed. As Tipton (1983) has argued, if educationists and teachers feel understandably squeamish about becoming involved in 'narrow' training, then the solution is to reconstitute the debate surrounding the relationship between education, training and work. Perhaps the major starting point here is to define vocational education and training more broadly, to emphasise youth's active involvement in rather than separation from mainstream society, and to treat their needs as seriously as those of employers. As one commentator has recently noted, it is not dole schools or work experience that the young unemployed require now but 'schools and' (in a well known phrase) 'really useful education and rewarding, unexploitative work' (Horne 1983).

If, in the short term, jobs are not available to 16–18-year-olds they should not be fobbed off with 'cottage industry' employment (handyman repairs, gardening, delivering, housework, helping the aged and so forth) or compensated for their loss with remedial schemes that do little more than infantilise them and make them even more dependent on the state. It is this aspect rather than unemployment itself that perhaps constitutes the present 'crisis', and poses as much an education as an economic problem. The obvious need at present is to consider programmes for education and training alongside a programme for jobs. Education and training without the possibility of employment as a foreseeable goal is not only politically unacceptable but also likely to cast doubt, no matter what the quality, on various types of training provided (Roberts 1984). What is required now are *policies* that do not simply delay entry into work or provide employers with cheap labour (this only exacerbates unemployment) but offer young people systematic career development, training and opportunities for full-time skilled work (Casson 1979). It is as a contribution to this aspect of the present debate about education and training that this chapter is addressed.

Note

A modified version of this chapter first appeared in the Open University Course unit *Policy Making in Education E333* (see Dale 1985).

References

Ahier, J. and Flude, M. (1983) *Contemporary Education Policy*. London, Croom Helm.

Atkinson, P. (1984) 'Interruption and Reproduction: the Classification and Framing of Work and Education'. Paper presented at the SSRC/CEDEFOP Conference on *The Transition between School and Work*. Berlin January 1984.

Atkinson, P. and Rees, T. (eds.) (1982) *Youth Unemployment and State Intervention*. London, Routledge & Kegan Paul.

Avis, J. (1981), 'Social and Technical Relations: the Case of Further Education.' *British Journal of Sociology of Education* 2 (2).

Bates, I. *et al.* (1984) *Schooling for the Dole*. London, Macmillan.

Baxter, J.L. and McCormick (1984) 'Seventy Per Cent of our Future: the Education, Training and Employment of Young People'. National Westminster Bank *Quarterly Review*. Autumn.

Blunden, G. (1983), 'Typing in the Tech', in D. Gleeson (ed.), *Youth Training and the Search for Work*. London, Routledge & Kegan Paul.

Bowles, S. and Gintis, H. (1976) *Schooling in Capitalist America*. London, Routledge & Kegan Paul.

Bristow, A.J. (1976) *Inside the College of Further Education*. London, HMSO.

Broady, D. (1981) 'Critique of the Economy of Education'. *Economy and Industrial Democracy* (2).

Brown, C. (1984) *Black and White Britain*. London, Policy Studies Institute.

Bullock Committee (1971) *Report of the Committee of Inquiry on Industrial Democracy*. London, HMSO.

Cantor, L. and Roberts, I. (1974) *Further Education in England and Wales*. London, Routledge & Kegan Paul.

Casson, M. (1979) *Youth Unemployment*. London, Macmillan.

Crowther Report (1959) *15–18*. London, Central Advisory Council for Education HMSO.

Dale, R. (1985) *Education and Employers' Needs: Towards a New Vocationalism*. Oxford, Pergamon.

Dex, S. (1983) 'Second Chances? Further Education, Ethnic Minorities and Labour Markets', in Gleeson (1983).

Esland, G. and Cathcart, H. (1984) 'The Compliant Creature Worker' Paper presented at the SSRC/CEDEFOP Conference on *The Transition between School and Work*. Berlin January 1984.

Fairley, J. and Grahl, J. (1983) 'Conservative Training Policy and the Alternatives'. *Socialist and Economic Review* Autumn.

Fenton, I. *et al.* (1984) *Ethnic Minorities and the YTS*. Sheffield, MSC.

Gibb, V. (1983) 'The Recreation and Perpetuation of the Secretarial Myth', in Gleeson (1983)l

Gleeson, D. (1980) 'Streaming at Work and College'. *Sociological Review*. November.

 (ed.) (1983) *Youth Training and the Search for Work*. London, Routledge & Kegan Paul.

Gleeson, D. and Mardle, G. (1980) *Further Education or Training?* London, Routledge & Kegan Paul.

Hayes, C. (1983) 'Taking your Skills with You'. *The Times Educational Supplement*, 20 May 1983.

Hordley, I. and Lee, D.J. (1970) 'The Alternative Route: Social Change and Opportunity in Technical Education'. *Sociology* 4.

Horne, J. (1983) 'Youth Unemployment Programmes, an Historical Account of the Development of Dole Colleges', in Gleeson (1983).

ILP (1983) *The Tories' Poisoned Apple*. Independent Labour Publications.

Jackson, P. (1981) 'Secondary Schooling for the Poor'. *Daedalus* 4. Fall.

Jones, P. (1984) *What Opportunities for Youth?* Occasional paper No. 4.

65

London, Youthaid.

Lee, G. and Wrench, J. (1984) '16-18: the Crisis of the School Leaver'. *Universities Quarterly*. Autumn.

LRS (1983) *Youth Training: A Negotiators' Guide*. London, Labour Rsearch Department.

Moore, R. (1983) 'Further Education, Pedagogy and Production', in Gleeson (1983).

Moos, M. (1983) 'How Far further for Further Education?'. *Youth Policy* 2 (1).

Morrison, P. (1983). Report of a BBC Radio 4 interview by M. Jackson, 'Forces Rally against Political Ban' *The Times Educational Supplement*, 23 September 1983.

MSC (1977) *Instructional Guide to Social and Life Skills*. London, MSC.
  (1981) *A New Training Initiative: Task Group Report*. London, MSC.
  (1982) *Guidelines on Content and Standards in YTS*. London, MSC.
  (1983) *A Handbook for Managing Agents in YTS*. London, MSC.
  (1984) *Notes on Guidance. Occupational Training Families* (Bowyer and Sanzeri). London, MSC. June.

NTG (1983) *Training and the State: Responses to the MSC*. Manchester, Network Training Group.

Raffe, D. (1979) 'The Alternative Route Reconsidered'. *Sociology* 13.
  (1983) 'Education and Unemployment', in Gleeson (1983).

Roberts, K. (1984) *School-leavers and their Prospects*. Milton Keynes, Open University Press.

Robinson, E. (1968) *The New Polytechnics*. Harmondsworth, Penguin.

Ryan, P. (1984) 'The New Training Initiative after Two Years'. *Lloyds Bank Review* 152. April.

Seale, C. (1983) *FEU and MSC: Two Curricular Philosophies and their Implications for YTS*. Unpublished mimeo. London Garnett College of Higher Education.

Tipton, B. (1973) *Conflict and Change in a Technical College*. London, Hutchinson.
  (1983) 'The Quality of Training and the Design of Work', in Gleeson (1983).

TUC/Labour Party (1984) *A Plan for Training*. London TUC/Labour Party Liaison Committee.

Venables, E. (1967) *The Young Worker at College: A Study of a Local Tech*. London, Faber. *The Times Educational Supplement*.

Watts, A. (1983) 'Schools and the YTS'. *The Times Educational Supplement* 13 May 1983.

White Paper (1981). London, HMSO.
  (1984) *Training for Jobs*. London, HMSO.

Willis, P. (1984) 'Conclusion: Theory and Practice', in Bates *et al*. (1984).

CHAPTER FOUR

Employment Processes and Youth Training

Carol Buswell

Youth training schemes have been introduced at a time of unemployment, occupational restructuring and sub-regional differences that are more marked now than at any time since the structural shifts of the 1930s. Concerns that many, if not most, of the young people on such schemes will not acquire paid employment and that, in any case, government schemes have themselves begun to undermine youth wages and such permanent jobs as did exist, have focussed our attention on the *labour market* context of this policy. Discussion has also centred on the nature of the training and the relationship of this to such jobs as may be available to young workers – many of which require no 'training' or 'skill' in any accepted sense of these terms – and this debate hinges round the nature of the *labour process* in contemporary society. But since the labour market and the labour process tend to be studied by writers with different theoretical perspectives and interests the connections between the two are often under-emphasised.

Least powerful groups, including young workers and women, occupy the lower echelons of the segmented labour market. Recession and occupational restructuring have, in addition, altered the balance and amount of employment available; and because occupations are 'typed' and seen as the preserve of particular social groups more powerful groups may be displacing the weaker ones within the sectors of employment currently available. If this is the case, there will be changes in the labour process particularly with regard to the social relations of work and youth training schemes, should be seen in this context.

Occupations themselves are characterised by internal labour markets. Evidence suggests that those inhabited by young people are now relatively closed enabling little, if any, elevation through the hierarchy; and the assumptions within schemes about the knowledge and skills that such workers 'require' should be examined in relation to these internal labour markets. If there is a disjunction between the training and the job it is becoming obscured by the shifting definition of 'skill', which has now come to include aspects of an individual which are crucial in the social relations of work which, it is argued, is the central site of change. New technology, too, an important element of some of the tertiary occupations for which young people are being trained, is introduced with regard to the existing social relations of employment; and the possible renegotiation of these social relations becomes a crucial factor enabling or inhibiting the protection of particular areas of employment for particular groups of workers.

In this context the education and training of young people assumes importance in several ways. By teaching the use of what are, currently, new technologies and processes the training may serve to elevate the actual *experience* of work for the individuals involved and it may contribute to the 'typing', or retyping, of such occupations and processes, which has ramifications far beyond education. The training may also be important in reinforcing or changing the actual or potential social relations between groups and this is the facet that crucially affects the opportunities of particular groups within the population. This chapter will attempt to suggest some connections between employment markets and processes with special reference to youth and gender in order to illustrate the setting within which youth training schemes are operating.

The labour market

The important characteristic of the labour market in general is that it is sectoral and segmented. Industry shifts are part of a trend towards an international economy, which, within Britain, is creating a diverse structure where differences between workers in different sector and localities are probably increasing (Fothergill and Gudgin 1982). Some writers conceptualise this as a 'dual economy' with a corporate sector dominated by large corporations with a high capital-to-labour ratio, large-scale production and stable growth; and a competitive sector of small, mainly local, firms with a low capital-to-labour ratio, low productivity and characterised by low wages and instability (Cawson 1982). Within and across this sectoral division are segmented labour markets usually defined as containing 'primary' and 'secondary' jobs, the features of the latter being few prospects, unstable employment and occupied by members of 'marginal' groups – blacks, women, the old, the young and the handicapped. The existence of a segmented labour force with different labour market statuses may also, as Craig *et al.* (1982) suggest, create the situation where jobs are classified not by their content but according to the position of the workers who normally undertake the work and some groups have social characteristics which place them in the position of having to accept these jobs. Offe and Hinricks (1977), in discussing this secondary labour market in Germany, argue that cultural and institutional norms assume that these marginal groups have alternate means of subsistence outside the labour market and these cultural assumptions become of crucial importance when considering the structural position of youth and the processes that contribute to the maintenance of this position.

Young people's position in the secondary labour market has made them vulnerable to unemployment. In 1979 the rate for young people was three times as high as that of adults in the United Kingdom; teenage rates were higher than those of young workers and the rate for teenage girls was highest of all (OECD 1980). Recession and strucutural changes have had the greatest impact on the sectors where there is the highest concentration of first-time workers (Rees and Gregory 1981) and young people have bitter first-hand experience of this in their job-seeking attempts. But it should be remembered that youth, like adult, unemployment is not distributed evenly across localities. In some places it is worse than in the 1930s, e.g. in Newcastle the Juvenile Employment Service recorded 877 vacancies in the first quarter of 1934 compared with 206 for the same period in 1984. The unemployment of young people in the city represents 20 per cent of the total and there are now about half as many vacancies as in the 1960s for the same number of school-leavers (Grant 1984).

Whatever the official MSC line of YTS being 'training' and not directly part of job-seeking, the schemes are, in fact, presented as a way obtaining a better chance of a job. The MSC booklet aimed at young people states: 'YTS offers broad training to help you get off to a good start in working life'; it will 'help you to be more attractive to employers' and give you 'a certificate to show what you can do, which will be useful when you are applying for a job afterwards'. In the booklet aimed at parents, the MSC maintains:

> If your child does decide to leave school at 16, the YTS will offer a good start to working life. Whether or not they are offered jobs by the employer, they will have learnt similar things which will be useful in this or other jobs or for doing further training.

The OECD (1980) identified the 'weak structural position of youth' as one of the reasons for youth unemployment. To counter this weak position it recommended policies which 'prepared people for work, remedial education, job creation and differential wages'. With its human capital perspective the Organisation considered that the 'investment' that these policies would entail would eventually lead to social and economic 'returns'.

But youth is not a homogeneous group. It comes classed, raced, regioned and gendered and with respect to this latter category the position of women in the labour market is also important. In 1977 more than half of all women in paid employment were in three service industries and a quarter were in manufacturing – the growth in numbers having been accommodated in the growth of the areas of employment they had traditionally inhabited (Buswell 1983). In 1981 women comprised over 70 per cent of the labour force in clerical, catering and service jobs (EOC 1981) and within these occupations gender segregation is high; 63 per cent of women work only with other women doing the same or similar kinds of job and 81 per cent of men work only with other men (Martin and Robers 1984). This extremely marked gender division takes on crucial significance for men as well as women in the current occupational restructuring. In the North-east, for example, although women are faring worse in terms of employment relative to the country as a whole, the jobs that have become available, with the decline of primary and some secondary industries, are in new industries where the jobs are low paid, unskilled, short-term, poorly unionised and often part-time – i.e. geared to a female work-force while the male work-force is simultaneously being displaced (Pimlott 1981). So policies designed for young people as though the labour markets are the same for them regardless of their gender, race or region might be misconceived anyway. It has been pointed out, for example, that adult and continuing education might be more appropriate for girls, given their likely futures, than teenage schemes designed to facilitate male employment patterns (Roberts 1984).

The labour market acts as a series of social filters between 'skill' and the wider economy and class structure; and, of course, 'skill' has been used as an exclusionary mechanism by more powerful workers over weaker ones which helps to maintain the labour market segmentation. Credentials also play an important role in mediating between groups and the occupational structure, but, as has been pointed out, increasing credentials might be used for recruitment to the labour market and may be totally unrelated to that which is required in the labour process (Berg 1970). This might lead to the assumption that school qualifications will figure more highly in the future, but the opposite may be the case. Training officers, the new gatekeepers, come from diverse bakcgrounds and are likely to have more in common with employers than with teachers and careers officers. One managing agent, for example, in its leaflet describing its scheme to young people states: 'YTS presents an opportunity for trainees to prove their ability to firms. Trainees who have not done well at school can work hard in their YTS and "begin again".'

Ashton *et al.* (1982), in identifying different selection strategies of employers, found that the strategy of using qualifications as a preliminary sorter – after which non-academic criteria are used – was the most widespread mechanism for clerical, sales and skilled manual jobs; of the non-academic criteria used, 'attitude to work' and 'self-presentation' were seen to be the most important. Training schemes are an attempt both to minimise the importance of the 'academic' and to reassess young people on different criteria. Thus it would not be surprising if, having attained a place, performance on the scheme then comes to outweigh original school qualifications. The present system is described by Roberts (1984) as a 'vicious 16 plus more devisive than the 11 ever was' whereby the academic elite bypasses the depressed youth labour markets, and the prospects of the rest depend more on luck and employers' whims than attainments.

The labour process

With regard to the labour process Braverman's (1974) application

71

of Marx's theory led him to conclude that there would be a tendency to widespread de-skilling through new forms of technology and the application of scientific management principles to complex labour processes such as clerical work. As the evidence for the alternative post-industrial society thesis is far from satisfactory – in the sense that writers such as Bell (1974) conclude that the 'knowledge society' will require more skill and education and yet fail to examine the nature and content of the growing occupations – most attention has been directed towards refining and working within the broad de-skilling framework by attempting to investigate empirically the possible tendencies towards de-skilling through the fragmentation of tasks, hierarchical organisation and management control (e.g. Wood 1982). It is within this perspective that the increase in credentialism and training is seen to be sometimes unrelated to the nature of the occupation to which qualifications and training give access. So access to the labour market requires qualifications or 'expertise' that are not actually a requirement of the labour process.

Braverman himself argued against confusing skill with dexterity, and it has been pointed out (Thompson 1983) that in the nineteenth century industrialists and economists talked of the introduction of machinery as elevating the intellect and doing away with the monotony of toil; which parallels some references today with regard to automation, where the assumption is that a reduction of physical labour equates with an increase in skill. In other words, there is an emphasis on the context rather than the nature of the work. But the context also includes the control mechanisms and some writers assume that 'direct control' of workers is a strategy that is only now a characteristic of peripheral industries and workers (e.g. Friedman 1977). It is argued that, rather than de-skilling, there is a process of semi-skilling based on a demand for workers with 'responsible autonomy' to enable them to do simplified routine tasks without constant supervision, and which will allow them willingly to subject themselves to costly machines (Frith 1980). But this is contested by Hill (1981), for example, who sees the long-run tendency towards direct control among central groups of both workers and industries. The tendency to think of all employment as being industrial or in large-scale organisations is reflected in this debate and the labelling of certain occupations, organisations and workers as 'peripheral' allows them to be discounted in the analysis. It is much more likely that 'responsible autonomy' is the main strategy in certain employment settings and 'direct control' in others.

This emphasis on certain sectors of employment is also a weakness in Braverman's argument, where the central place given to craft-work obscures the fact that, even in the past, a larger proportion of the (male) population was engaged in activities such as mining and transport (Thompson 1983). Even with regard to craft-workers it is hard to know, at this juncture, the actual range of mental activities and control that characterised their work. Pahl (1984), indeed, sees Braverman as one of the writers who postulates a 'golden age' of work, which follows on from a romantic tradition: 'as with similar myths referring to past times, the precise period that is held up for approval is always some time before a given author is writing' (p. 2). The social construction of skill, as an exclusionary mechanism, which helped to create and maintain the segmented labour market to the detriment of weaker groups, is also not an adequate part of the analysis; for, as Beechey (1982) points out, 'skill can refer to complex competencies which are developed within a particular set of social relations of production' (p. 63). So the issue hinges on the basis on which jobs and skills are constructed and whether 'criteria by which workers are differentiated and jobs defined are relatively independent of the real or "technical" skill content of jobs' (Wood 1982: p. 81).

What are the processes by which some jobs are defined as men's, women's or young people's work and is this independent of the changing nature of such jobs? It is within the context of this debate that conceptions and definitions of 'skill' *vis-a-vis* youth training by the various bodies involved in this policy attain importance in relation to the nature of the job for which training is being given. Some of the craft unions have had some influence in maintaining YTS training as the foundation year for the old apprenticeship courses and in maintaining an allowance above the YTS level. Most of the Construction Industry Training Board schemes are currently the old apprenticeship courses and they were allowed to counter the 'philosophy of YTS' by training for specific jobs in return for providing more than twenty thousand YTS places. Although the craft system serves some purposes for employers – as a form of control through family and local recruitment, the ability of skilled workers to earn money in their own time and to be employed by firms on a freelance basis – they also have an increasing need for more general (and cheaper) workers. The introduction of a YTS course in 'labouring' in parallel with the craft course is an indication of the restructuring of that sector of

C. Buswell

employment where definitions of 'specific' and 'generic' skills are being renegotiated.

The Manpower Services Commission has itself been accused of denuding the concept of skill of any meaning that it might have had by applying it to such things as answering the telephone. What has happened is that the MSC has rejected any industrial (or sociological) definitions of skill and has adopted, instead, a psychological perspective, which is interesting in the light of the increased use of psychological and behavioural concepts in education generally. In her study of 'skills' that were used for 1,000 typical jobs that young people might enter in London, Townsend (1982), in her report to the MSC states:

> The psychological definition of skill is wider [than the industrial one] and concerned with all the factors which go to make up a competent, expert, rapid and accurate performance.

In the light of this definition she maintains that interpersonal skills affect success at work and that knowledge is part of mental skill. To use a definition of skill which includes social and behavioural as well as mental attributes makes it possible to assess a person on all these dimensions, giving as much weight to features of personality, appearance and speech as to aptitude and knowledge. The development of 'profiling' as the form of assessment then becomes obvious. The psychometric approach also allows skills to be conceptualised as separate individual properties held in distinct quantities regardless of the context. For example, in a sample 'profile' the MSC circulates, there are four levels for each of the eleven skills listed; the lowest level, under 'problem-solving', is defined as 'the ability to reliably follow routine procedures only with guidance'; and the highest level maintains that a student can 'independently derive, implement and evaluate solutions to a variety of types of problems'(!). This fine grading of aptitude and behaviour along many dimensions also suggests fine distinctions in the occupational slots for which this assessment might be relevant.

Internal labour markets

Given that the range of jobs for young people within the segmented labour market is limited, complex computations of assumed abilities would indicate an assumption that *within* each

74

occupational category there are opportunities for differential performances ranging from the very basic to the most complex. Yet much recent empirical work on occupations suggests that many internal labour markets are becoming polarised in terms of function between the routine and more skilled workers, that this process is most marked in occupations that are subject to automation, technical change or a change in the capital-to-labour costs and that the new processes are tending to equalise types of work through the homogenisation of tasks rather than creating complex distinctions. Thus, developments in the labour process are not congruent with the difficulties of actually entering the labour market. Raymond Williams (1983) sees this development as the 'crisis of employment which will dominate future generations'. In the manufacturing sector this process is most clearly seen where some young people, for example, may be trained in joinery skills and actually be working in furniture factories where the main tasks of the majority of workers are stacking and machine-feeding and where only a few of the skilled workers assemble the objects, the rest of the workforce being managerial, administrative or clerical.

Hill (1981) describes how computerisation has produced a two-tier structure in banks and finance companies polarised into senior management and clerical workers. In this instance the computer itself checks and controls work, a function that used to be carried out by senior clerks and middle management; the co-ordination of work processes is now carried out inside the computer. Crompton *et al.* (1982) maintain that, with regard to clerical work, the impact of electronic data processing has been greatest in the banking and insurance sectors but that the impact is less in other sectors, for example local authority offices. They found the clerical labour force in such offices to be more heterogeneous, with a range of work from rule-bound, repetitive jobs – data entry, etc. – to jobs requiring considerable discretion and responsibility; but they noted a predominance of young, less qualified, women in the computer operation tasks with very few prospects of achieving the other kinds of work. In other words, the evidence suggests internal labour markets differentiated by relatively polarised tasks where *individuals* are located and where the possibilities of movement are now much slimmer than in the past as intermediate supervisory functions have been removed. Young people themselves, however, often conceive of *jobs* being at the bottom of a hierarchy, rather than individuals, and still think in terms of the possibility of 'working my way up' as though internal labour markets are finely graded hierarchies.

Young people who respond in this way may be reflecting the fact that the internal labour markets in small local firms and in the service sector may not be as polarised as the research on large-scale manufacturing and office sectors suggest. In hairdressing, for example, the ladder of apprentice, stylist and owner/manager is one that is, theoretically, available for all to climb and is represented in even the smallest salon. Similarly, small offices in local firms are more likely to have limited technology rather than whole computerised systems; but this is the sector of the labour market characterised by low pay, insecurity and instability being on the margins of the corporate network. Evidence suggests that in the Northern region large firms are now the main provider of current employment (HMSO 1983) almost 80 per cent of employment in manufacturing in the region is in establishments owned by companies with headquarters outside the North (Marshall 1978). So there may well be discrepancies between the young people's experience of work in their placements, with whichever employer will take them, and the future site of any real jobs.

The structure of internal labour markets, however, describes a relationship between the differential allocation of jobs and the related distribution of earnings and takes on crucial significance if considered in conjunction with the external labour market. It has been suggested, for example, that the erosion of skills at the wider level may weaken the bargaining position of certain workers, who may retaliate by attempting to control internal labour markets to the detriment of weaker groups of employees (Thompson 1983). In this sense control of internal labour markets can act as a counterweight to skill degradation and, if this is the case, would disadvantage the least powerful groups even more. Although these attempts to control internal labour markets have been related to wider de-skilling, in a recession the jobs that workers occupy may increasingly be the only ones available to them; it then perhaps becomes a question of attempting to manipulate that market as the only possibility at all. With regard to factory automation, for example, Game and Pringle's Australian study (1984) shows how men are now, in some instances, doing jobs that previously would have been done by women and they are able to be 'redefined' as male jobs because the jobs done by women have got worse – the women being concentrated in a fewer number of jobs in the labour-intensive sectors of factories which are the likely sites of future automation.

In the context of youth employment and training therefore, the assumption that there are complex intersections of occupational slots for differentially 'able' workers is not necessarily congruent with the labour market positions actually available. Yet the other assumption within the training schemes and MSC rhetoric, that there are transferable skills is, in fact, a recognition of the homogeneity of tasks across different occupations. These occupations are, however, within the same segment of the labour market.

Social relations

Technology and automation are sometimes seen as the *cause* of de-skilling and task polarisation, but Braverman himself recognised that machinery is used only in conjunction with, and as a supplement to, other methods of control. 'It has become fashionable,' he states, 'to attribute to machinery the powers over humanity which in fact arise from human social relations' (1974:p. 229) and Marx (1976) himself argued that technology provides a manifestation of other social relations. There is, therefore, an interactive process whereby technology will have an effect on the relations between workers, but such innovations will be partly a reflection of social relations *prior* to their implementation. The social relations, in this instance, obviously do not have to be inside production to be relevant as the social relations of gender, age and race outside the work-place are crucially inter-related to those inside. But the process of 'fetishism' whereby social relations involving people are represented as relations between 'things' is the process whereby technology is seen as an external and unalterable force.

It has been argued that social relations *form* and shape technical relations (Gorz 1976), so that existing technical relations cannot be thought of outside the social relations in which they are embedded. So social relations set the limits within which technical relations develop but are obviously not simply reducible to those in the sense that the relative weighting of technical and social relations is variable.

An example of the inter-relationship between technology and social relations is Crompton and Reid's (1982) research on clerical workers. Electronic data processing, they maintain, extended and transformed the trends *already* begun with the subdivision of

77

clerical labour and the previous use of mechanical forms of calculation and information processing. Thus, a clerk involved in 'batch processing' whose work relies on the performance of the computer and whose job parallels conveyor belt activities is simply a more refined version of the subdivision and mechanisation of labour that had begun well before the introduction of computers – which is one of the reasons that accounts for the high preponderance of women in this type of clerical work, where a female labour force of 21 per cent in 1911 rose to one of 70 per cent by 1966. The job, as presently constituted, represents a large stratum of routine workers with high labour turnover for activities that do not require extensive training. In other words, some routine tasks such as tabulating have been eliminated, but others, such as keying data into terminals, have been created by the introduction of computerised technology. Webster (1984), too, in her study of word processing and the secretarial function found a division between secretaries and typists. The former had very few of their skills and activities removed by the introduction of word processors,but the latter had jobs that were fragmented and de-skilled, not by the application of new technology, but by the prior division of labour upon which the technology was overlaid.

The argument that new technology, whilst displacing some jobs, creates others and that parallel to de-skilling there is a process of re-skilling, is countered (Rees and Gregory 1981) by the argument that whilst the computer did create a new industry and new occupations the microprocessor has developed from an existing industry and is more flexible and cheaper, which poses a threat to future employment. The process is officially documented. The Central Policy Review Staff document (1978) said with reference to public services: 'In 1977 the number of staff engaged in computer operations was about 14 thousand and the number "freed" by computers was several times that figure.' As Jones (1982) points out, 'computers are *intended* to displace labour' and Rees and Gregory (1981) maintain that the jobs that will primarily be lost are those presently occupied by young workers. The argument that students and pupils learn, in any education and training, social as well as technical relations is well known. Indeed, Gleeson and Mardle (1980) contend that employers support outdated college courses not because of the skills they impart but because of the work habits and forms of social relations into which they initiate students. Avis (1981) concludes that as the need for technical skills and knowledge is reduced so there is a correspondingly increased emphasis on the learning of social relations. With regard to the social relations between groups of workers, Gleeson's (1980) research illustrates, in the process of further education, a reinforcement of the social hierarchies between different types of workers, in his study between craft and technical workers.

Although the social relations of manufacturing and pre-dominantly male occupations may well be understood and described, at least with regard to the recent past, apart from studies of clerical workers relatively little is known about the social relations of work in many female service occupations. The training that young people may be given, in these instances, may or may not be congruent with the actuality of developments in the labour process in these spheres.

MacDonald (1980), however, sees the social relations within education not simply as a preparation for class obedience but also in preparing women for a subordinate role to men:

> The work of the school facilities the maintenance, *in the long run*, of the work force and the social relations of production through the transmission of a set of gender relations, its association with division between domestic and waged labour and all the contradictions this entails.
>
> (p. 32)

Social relations become of central importance when one considers the ways in which, and the sites for, the introduction of automation and micro-electronic processes and some of the divisions are already institutionalised in YTS. Game and Pringle's research (1984) suggests that the differences between men's and women's work are conceptualised as dichotomies which are given meaning in different contexts – for example, heavy/light, dirty/clean, mobile/immobile; it is therefore of more than passing interest to note that the use of the MSC's 'occupational training families' serves to reinforce these traditional dichotomies which give meaning to segregated gender labour markets.

One example of this is that jobs in distribution will tend to locate trainee shop assistants on 'retailing' courses and trainee warehouse workers on 'transport' courses. The extent to which warehouses either have become, or are likely to become, a site for extreme automation makes this work potentially less heavy than many other jobs; but the typing of it as allied to 'heavy' occupations such as transport (i.e. lorries) allows males to see it in their terms and may also prevent it from being automated as rapidly as shop work if technology is introduced to displace the most marginal workers first – in this instance girls as opposed to boys. Yet inasmuch as shop and warehouse work are two of the sectors in which young people have traditionally found employment, it may be that the marginality of youth, in general, may serve to make both areas vulnerable.

Gender divisions penetrate the youth category in so many ways that it is often a complex process dividing the strands of 'marginality', especially in relation to adult categories. For example on some YTS courses aimed predominantly at males it is sometimes suggested that things like 'sport' and 'weight training' be added to the curriculum to aid the tasks that these young people are, stereotypically, thought to need at work. But if many male jobs are less physically arduous than previously the inclusion of physical activities within training may militate against boys who could actually do the jobs. Yet the 'appearance' and 'clothes' that are requirements of many female occupations are expected to be provided privately at girls' own expense and in their own time. Indeed, some hairdressing, clerical and retailing students are expected to dress in the style and uniform of the organisation where they do their work placement, which may cause them economic hardship; whereas the 'protective' clothing of manual occupations is usually provided. The exact balance of 'youth' versus, and in addition to, 'gender' as a form of marginality will obviously vary contextually.

In various ways, however, external social relations appear embedded in training for occupations where these social relations help to determine the shape of labour processes. In the past the mental/manual divide has merited attention; and yet, as has been shown (Willis 1977), the dichotomy has meaning – for men – within a patriarchal framework and becomes conceptualised as work 'fit' for either men or women paralleling the gender-segregated work-force within occupations and has importance in terms of authority relations of men over women. In a changing occupational context the preservation of masculine skills becomes the issue of resistance. This has been seen (Phillips and Taylor 1980) in terms of the creation of more 'inferior' workers as the way in which men disguise the fact that their own jobs have become routinised or de-skilled. It has been illustrated (Game and Pringle 1984) in terms of men taking over machine-minding, which then serves to dichotomise jobs into technical/non-technical: men being able to represent the power of machines as their own power, symbolising masculinity and in contrast with the non-technical jobs and lack of 'expertise' of women within the same occupation or organisation.

Tertiary occupations

Many of the occupations in which women predominate have different dimensions from male employment and the social relations of one segment cannot be assumed from looking at the other. The work tasks in most 'servicing' occupations hinge round meeting people's needs rather than producing a particular quantity of goods. Thus, servicing workers have another set of social relations in which they must engage, between worker and client/customer, often on a one-to-one basis. Murgatroyd (1982) maintains that the concept of 'deferential dialectic' that has been supplied to marriage (Bell and Newby 1979) is a characteristic of the social relations of this kind of employment, and it takes on special significance when the workers are women and becomes a hidden job content whereby the assumed nurturant aptitudes of women slide into notions of servicing and become translated into specific occupational terms. If this is the case and if it is these occupations that can now provide some employment whilst traditional male occupations are declining, in order for men to enter these occupations some of the tasks may need to be 'defeminised' and the social relations renegotiated. The paradox of any movement in this direction – for men to displace women in service sector jobs – is that in future, as adults, their households will need more than this male wage which will be less than the wage in traditional male occupations and yet the traditional jobs for adult women might have disappeared.

In some instances changes in the labour process have already minimised the 'servicing' aspects of certain jobs. For example, in retailing shop assistants now have little opportunity to 'assist' customers as personalised selling has been replaced by advertising, which is done by specialists, meaning that less knowledge and expertise are needed in the shop and much of the labour has been taken over by unpaid shoppers (Game and Pringle 1984). Also in retailing there has been a noticeable shift from full-time to part-time and casual employment which, paradoxically, means that with regard to the labour process the social relations of selling may be less feminised but the shift to predominantly part-time work of the level of the labour market – estimated at 60 per cent of the work-force in 'sales' (Martin and Roberts 1984)–still makes it a 'female' occupation for the majority. As Robinson and Wallace (1984) point out in a Department of Employment report:

> Uneven labour requirements in the expanding service industries provide an obvious incentive for the increasing utilisation of female part-time labour. In the private sector the upward trend of female part-time employment has for some years been reinforced by organisational and operational changes, including the concentration of ownership and control, the creation of larger units, extension of trading hours and innovations in the preparation and presentation of goods and services–most notably in banking, retail distribution, hotels and catering and in the expanding leisure industries . . .
>
> Employers are less likely to hire labour in excess of their requirements when workers can be engaged virtually by the hour. In these labour-intensive industries the ability to control wage costs through the employment of part-time labour represents an important factor in determining the pace at which such developments take place.
>
> (p. 46)

The position of young people in this sector of employment has been the cause for concern. Bluestone (1981), for example, in an American context points out that over half the work-force in retailing was under 25, but he concludes that retailing has 'lost its ability to provide regular employment for all but a handful of skilled managers' (p. 95). The industry is, therefore, not particularly suitable for those seeking permanent employment. With regard to Britain, Davies (1982) maintains that during the present recession not only has the number of retailing jobs been reduced but there have been fewer young people employed than in the earlier period, as employers are now showing a marked preference for mature workers, whether part-time or full-time. His conclusion is that

> in the longer term the introduction of new technological innovations both within and outside retailing might have catastrophic repercussions on the work practice of employees and there could be a marked shrinkage in the labour force.
>
> (p. 163)

It is interesting, in this context, to note the large number of YTS retailing and distribution courses for an area of work that is predominantly casualised, where the casual work-force is made up of married women and young–the latter, of course, largely employed in gender-segregated work, with boys stacking and carrying and girls operating tills. The fact that courses are being 'bought and sold' has something to do with the amount and kind of provision offered regardless of the labour market.

Some private managing agents are not offering clerical courses, which are 'too expensive', but are offering only retailing ones. It could be argued that the courses that are 'too expensive' are the ones where young people learn some skill and the 'cheaper' courses are for jobs that, under fuller employment conditions, people have traditionally entered without training. It might also be noted that girls predominate in these fields and it is their skills–albeit stereotyped and subject to future automation–that might be cut. But as has been shown (Blunden 1983), with regard to the history of secretarial provision in further education, the nature and amount of the service provided are an important variable influencing the levels of take-up and attainment.

With regard to office work the introduction of electronic processing may be a way of simultaneously minimising the personal social relations and defeminising the task through the use of 'equipment'. Old technologies were incompatible with traditional ideas of femininity, but new technologies are not associated with such machismo factors as weight, grease or noise. However, men's relationship to technology is proprietorial. Cockburn (1983) maintains that electronics is inheriting its masculinity from the mechanical technology that preceded it and so the electronics that forms the basis of many clerical jobs will take over the mantle of the old mechanical machinery of production. Shifts in the terminology used in training courses give some indication of what might be occurring; typing has become 'keyboarding' and introduced as a preparation for computer use for both boys and girls, but it does allow boys to see it as a means to a 'technical' end.

The nurturant aspects of more personalised service occupations can be minimised by emphasising the 'professional' rather than the 'service' ethic. In hairdressing, for example, this is facilitated by the fact that the occupation is divided into two clear sectors: large salons, often owned and managed by men, often with unisex facilities and an emphasis on the 'expertise' of the stylists; and the small 'shampoo and set' trade, usually owned and managed by returning-to-work women employing two or three other women and with a local clientele.

Whether, and how, occupations 'change their gender' and the

renegotiation of social relations within work are aspects of the labour process that take on increased significance in times of structural labour market change. The weakening of gender boundaries within the family and within education has been seen as part of a process of transmitting a new set of gender relations more appropriate to corporate capitalism (MacDonald 1980), but this, of course, is not achieved without struggle and conflict. The extent to which girls (and teachers) will resist computerised tasks becoming defined as masculine and where the line comes to be drawn remains to be seen. One of the differences between young people themselves and employers/training officers/managing agents seems to centre on the significance accorded to interpersonal and social relations at work, which are seen by the latter group as characterised by various kinds of work/professional ethics and the workers' knowledge of their obligations. In the past young people were defined as 'irresponsible' because of frequent job changing and 'lacking in commitment'; presently this seems to take the form of work placement changing, which is defined as 'trivial' when youngsters dislike particular work settings and refuse to stay. Young people themselves often seem prepared to change work placements until they find somewhere amenable to them[1]‡[1]which usually seems to indicate more concern with the interpersonal and social relations than with the status of the organisation and the 'quality' of the training it purports to provide.

The 'de-skilled' and 'degraded' aspects of the labour process may, in some instances, not be experienced as such by workers themselves and the *experience* of work is crucially important. As Gorz (1977) graphically pointed out, for technical workers their possession of theoretical knowledge is what distinguishes them from others, and the assumed possession of knowledge can counteract work degradation even if there is a disjunction between its possession and use. In this sense, persuading young people that they have valued and necessary knowledge *may* be a counteracting tendency to actual developments in employment. The use of gadgets, for example computers or word processors, instead of pen and paper might also serve the same function. The expectation would be, however, that this would be the case only for the first generation of users; after the gadgets have become commonplace, the effect might not be marked. It should be remembered that many young people are presently being introduced to these machines during youth training, whereas the growth of computing and word processing in schools, especially with TVEI, will produce future groups of young people to whom these are familiar. So training schemes are likely to be more successful at the beginning of this policy, in encouraging students to assume they have acquired new and valued skills and knowledge, than they are likely to be in the future.

The educational element of youth training

Where young people are doing the thirteen weeks 'off the job' outside educational institutions it would not be surprising if the content were geared more to the 'practical' than the 'cognitive' in the sense of creating an 'off-the-job' environment as close to the 'on-the-job' as possible. But this may be tendency in colleges as well. It has to be remembered that colleges are, for the first time, in direct competition with private agencies; firms are informed, through the CBI for example, about the alternatives:

> Private sector training organisations can also help employers to provide high quality and relevant off-the-job training under YTS. One example is Sight and Sound Education Ltd. All Sight and Sound's courses are fully programmed and offer a common standard of excellence wherever training is given. They are available throughout the year, are highly intensive and aim to provide marketable skills in the shortest possible time.
>
> (CBI 1983)

But market competition is not the only, or even the main, reason for this emphasis, since prior to YTS it was argued that the conflation of education and training has been a significant feature of all curriculum innovations at 16-plus (Avis 1981). Moore (1983) has described this feature of further education as a repetition of an 'adaptive transformation' that occurred in schools some ten years ago in response to similar pressures and problems, i.e. incorporating individuals into the educational context by the inclusion of knowledge from 'everyday life', which is based on the assumption that theoretical knowledge is irrelevant to their needs.

A college environment cannot hope to replicate a work environment for people who experience the real thing for the rest of the time. As has been pointed out (Dickinson and Erben 1983), if a simulated task bears little relationship to the real task, what students might actually be learning is a set of attitudes which accepts the validity of the real tasks and/or the idea that routine tasks are more difficult than they are – which becomes an important consideration when seen in conjunction with changes in the labour process.

Conclusion

A discussion of both the labour market and the labour process for young people who may obtain employment is important if one accepts that people on YTS may well comprise the future pool from which such workers are selected, even though this will by no means be all of them. The chances of obtaining work will partly depend on the particular scheme, its mode and sponsor and on the relationship of these to the local labour market. A hierarchy of schemes is clearly developing whereby some Mode A schemes – run by employers or groups of employers – are likely to comprise the recruitment field for jobs within these firms. Prior to YTS only the more 'respectable' sections of the working class were the principal beneficiaries of further education (Lee 1975); Sammons's (1983) study of craft and commercial students found that a majority had a father in skilled work and it would seem that many Mode A schemes are drawing the same population.

The areas of employment available to young people are the ones characterised by the polarisation of tasks without the intermediate supervisory positions that made some elevation through the hierarchy possible, for some, in the past. Young people are in a weak position in this context, but the position of girls and women is particularly likely to deteriorate if new technology comes to be defined as 'male' and if the 'servicing' aspects of some tertiary occupations are renegotiated to become 'expertise'.

Current changes in the labour market are often debated as though full employment has historically been the norm. Evidence over the last two hundred years, however, makes this a dubious proposition. What has changed is what Pahl (1984) describes as the 'unprecedented cultural dependence on *one* form of work', and a failure to recognise that, other work, in the past, has had importance in confirming and creating social identity. The dependence on paid employment for a fair standard of living and decreasing opportunities to operate on the margins of the corporate economy are also, obviously, distinctive modern features. What is also different is the fact that much technical innovation in the past complemented labour and extended some of its capacity, whereas the new forms of technology have the potential to be labour-displacing in a permanent sense. Gorz (1982), for example, quotes a report of the German firm Siemens, which estimated that 72 per cent of the jobs in public services could be 'formalised' and 28 per cent automated by the end of this decade; in retailing, 25 per cent of the jobs could be completely eliminated. This sort of estimate means, in effect, that as technology revolutionises information-based employment this type of work could contract, and not expand, leading either to increased unemployment or to the creation of new types of non-technology-based employment.

Without indulging in futurology it is clear that the MSC programmes are congruent with some present changes in, for example, the recognition of generic 'skills' i.e. a homogeneity of work tasks across occupations and with a recognition that personal characteristics and interpersonal skills may be as important as knowledge and aptitude. In other ways the schemes may be perpetuating traditional social relations which may be subjected to renegotiation and change in the employment context. In terms, though, of the 'education' that is offered as part of these programmes some serious considerations may emerge. When attendance on the schemes is a matter of course for *all* young people who do not aim to go into higher education and who do not obtain employment, the majority of this age group will be involved; so there may well be a tendency towards a movement away – in terms of off-the-job content – from the kinds of learning not only that many young people could cope with but that which they would, in fact, accept.

A move in this direction can be questioned at the pragmatic, let alone any other, level. The underlying assumption behind the development of vocationally relevant courses is that the employment chances of students depend primarily on the content and quality of the education and training. But, as has been shown (Raffe 1984), students' chances of finding employment depend primarily on the structure of the labour market. If the *content* of the courses is less relevant than official rhetoric suggests it means, in effect, that the content can be changed in any direction without affecting future employment chances. The extent to which the content can be changed away from a 'training' direction, however, depends on the degree of relative autonomy of further education vis-a-vis other structures and institutions. Relative autonomy changes over time and some writers (e.g. Moos 1983) argue that

87

MSC control over the content of syllabuses has led to a decline in autonomy. But Lee (1983) suggests that the various external parties with an interest in further education make conflicting and mutually contradictory demands, which permit it to have autonomy of a kind and there might then be fewer, rather than more, restrictions over its operation with each increase in the number of external bodies. The immediate point is that external bodies often have a view about what is required and groups who might offer an alternative have never interested themselves much in education outside schools.

This now becomes a crucial issue because as the schemes come to include the majority of young people they will be dealing with a huge and diverse population and the nature of what those young people are offered should generate as much debate as the school curriculum has in the past. The question of the responsibility of colleges to their communities and regions should also be raised (Lee 1975). National schemes based on some idea of a national labour market are simply inadequate in certain sub-regional contexts. But the difficulties of relating courses to local labour markets are compounded by the rapid change in such markets and wide variations in what constitutes the 'local' market in terms of geographical factors not only of size but also such factors as ease and expectations regarding travel-to-work patterns. If, too, paid employment plays, in the future, a different role – because of its partial collapse for certain groups and/or because the nature of the work cannot elicit the industrial work ethic – then continuing education which offers other values, emphases and possibilities will be much more 'relevant' than minimal and short-term employment requirements that might presently be sold under that rubric.

References

Ashton, D. N., Maguire, M. J. and Garland, V. (1982) *Youth in the Labour Market*. Research Paper No. 34. London, Department of Employment. March.

Avis, J. (1981) 'Social and Technical Relations: the Case of Further Education'. *British Journal of Sociology of Education* (2): pp. 145–61.

Barker, D. L. and Allen, S. (1979) *Dependence and Exploitation in Work and Marriage*. London, Longman.

Barton, L., Meighan, R. and Walker, S. (eds.) (1980) *Schooling, Ideology and the Curriculum*. Lewes, Falmer Press.

Beechey, V. (1982) 'The Sexual Division of Labour and the Labour
   Process: a Critical Assessment of Braverman', in Wood (1982).
Bell, C. and Newby, H. (1979) 'Husbands and Wives: the Dynamics of the
   Deferential Dialectic', in Barker and Allen (1979).
Bell, D. (1974) *The Coming of Post-Industrial Society*. London,
   Heinemann.
Berg, I. (1970) *Education and Jobs: The Great Training Robbery*.
   Harmondsworth, Penguin.
Bluestone, B. *et al.* (1981) *The Retail Revolution*, Boston, Mass., Auburn
   House.
Blunden, G. (1983) 'Typing in the Tech: Domesticity, Ideology and
   Women's Place in Further Education', Gleeson (1983).
Braverman, H. (1974) *Labor and Monopoly Capital*. New York, Monthly
   Review Press.
Buswell, C. (1983) 'Women, Work and Education'. *Social Policy and
   Administration* 17 (3): pp. 220–31.
Cawson, A. (1982) *Corporatism and Welfare*. London, Heinemann.
CBI (1983) 'The CBI's Role in the Delivery of the Youth Training
   Scheme'. *CBI Education and Training Bulletin* 13 (2): pp. 1–4.
Central Policy Review Staff (1978) *Social and Economic Implications of
   Micro Electronics*. London, CPRS.
Cockburn, C. (1983) *Brothers: Male Dominance and Technological
   Change*. London, Pluto.
Cole, M. and Skelton, B. (1980) *Blind Alley: Youth in a Crisis of Capital*.
   Ormskirk, Hesketh.
Craig, C. *et al.* (1982) *Labour Market Structure, Industrial Organisation
   and Low Pay*. Cambridge University Press.
Crompton, R., Jones, G. and Reid, S. (1982) 'Contemporary Clerical
   Work: Case Study of Local Government', in West (ed. 1982).
Crompton, R. and Reid, S. (1982) 'The De-skilling of Clerical Work' in
   Wood (1982).
Davies, R. L. (1982) 'Retailing', in Pacione (1982).
Dickinson, H. and Erben, M. (1983) 'The "Technicisation" of Morality
   and Culture', in Gleeson (1983).
EOC (1981) *Sixth Annual Report*. Manchester, Equal Opportunities
Fothergill, S. and Gudgin, G. (1982) *Unequal Growth*. London,
   Heinemann.
Friedman, A. (1977) *The Anatomy of Work*.
Frith, S. (1980) 'Education, Training and the Labour Process', in Cole and
   Skelton (1980).
Game, A. and Pringle, R. (1984) *Gender at Work*. London, Pluto.
Gleeson, D. (1980) 'Streaming at Work and Colleges'. *Sociological Review*
   28 (4): pp. 745–61.
   (ed.) (1983) *Youth Training and the Search for Work*. London,
   Routledge & Kegan Paul.
Gleeson, D. and Mardle, G. (1980) *Further Education or Training?*

C. Buswell

A Case Study in the Theory and Practice of Day Release. London, Routledge & Kegan Paul.

Gorz, A. (1976) 'Technology, Technicians and Class Struggle', in A. Gorz (ed.), *The Division of Labour*. Brighton, Harvester.

  (1977) 'Technical Intelligence and the Capitalist Division of Labour', in Young and Whitty (1977).

Grant, O. (1984) Paper given at Durham University. March.

Hill, S. (1981) *Competition and Control at Work*, London, Heinemann.

HMSO (1983) Business Monitor Series PA1063. London.

Jones, B. (1982) *Sleepers Wake! Technology and the Future of Work*. Brighton, Wheatsheaf.

Lee, D. J. (1975) 'Neglected Territory: the Regional Factor in Further Education', in Van Der Eyken and Kaneti Barry (1975).

  (1983) 'Social Policy and Institutional Autonomy in Further Education' in Gleeson (1983).

MacDonald, M. (1980) 'Schooling and the Reproduction of Class and Gender Relations' in Barton, Meighan and Walker (1980).

Marshall, J. N. (1978) *Corporate Organisation and Regional Office Employment*. Discussion Paper No. 20. University of Newcastle, Centre for Urban and Regional Development Studies.

Martin, J. and Roberts, C. (1984) *Women and Employment*. London, DoE/OPCS.

Marx, K. (1976) *Capital, Volume 1*. Harmondsworth, Penguin.

Moore, R. (1983) 'Further Education, Pedagogy and Production', in Gleeson (1983).

Moos, M. (1983) 'The Training Myth: a Critique of the Government's Response to Youth Unemployment and its Impact on Further Education', in Gleeson (1983).

Murgatroyd, L. (1982) 'Gender and Occupational Stratification'. *Sociological Review*. November: pp. 574–602.

OECD (1980) *Youth Unemployment: Causes and Consequences*. Paris, OECD.

Offe, C. and Hinricks, K. (1977), quoted in R. Kreckel (1980), 'Unequal Opportunity and Labour Market Segmentation'. *Sociology* 14 (4), November: pp. 525–50.

Pacione, M. (1982) *Progress in Urban Geography*. Beckenham, Croom Helm.

Pahl, R. E. (1984) *Divisions of Labour*. Oxford, Blackwell.

Phillips, A. and Taylor, B. (1980) 'Sex and Skill'. *Feminist Review* 6: pp. 79–88.

Pimlott, B. (1981) 'The North-east: back to the 1930s?'. *Political Quarterly*: pp. 51–63.

Raffe, D. (ed.) (1984) *Fourteen to Eighteen*. Aberdeen University Press.

Rees, T. and Gregory, D. (1981) 'Youth Employment and Unemployment: A Decade of Decline'. *Educational Analysis* 3 (2): pp. 7–24.

Roberts, K. (1984) *School Leavers and their Prospects*. Milton Keynes,

Open University Press.

Robinson, O. and Wallace, J. (1984) *Part-time Employment and Sex Discrimination Legislation in Great Britain*. Research Paper No. 43. London, Department of Employment.

Sammons, P. (1983) 'Patterns of Participation in Vocational Further Education: A Study of School-leavers in Inner London', in Gleeson (1983).

Thompson, P. (1983) *The Nature of Work*. London, Macmillan.

Townsend, C. (1982) *Skills Needed for Young People's Jobs, Volume 1*. Manpower Services Commission, University of Sussex, Institute of Manpower Studies.

Van Der Eyken, W. and Kaneti Barry, S. M. (eds.) (1975) *Learning and Earning: Aspects of Day-Release in Further Education*. Windsor, NFER.

Webster, J. (1984) 'Word Processing and the Secretarial Labour Process'. Unpublished paper given to BSA Conference, Bradford. April.

West, J. (ed.) (1982) *Work, Women and the Labour Market*. London, Routledge & Kegan Paul.

Williams, R. (1983) *Towards 2000*. London, Chatto & Windus.

Willis, P. (1977) *Learning to Labour*. Aldershot, Saxon House.

Wood, S. (ed.) (1982) *The Degradation of Work?* London, Hutchinson.

Young, M. and Whitty, G. (eds.) (1977) *Society, State and Schooling*. Lewes, Falmer Press.

CHAPTER FIVE

From Girls and Boys to Women and Men: the Social Reproduction of Gender Roles in the Transition from School to (Un)employment

Claire Wallace

> Yes, because I want, like everyone else, I want everything in life. I don't want to get married to a girl and 'ave nothing behind me. You know, I want something behind me before I get married. 'Cos it's no use getting married and you're on the dole, you ain't working or anything like that, I mean you've got nothing to look forward to. I'd sooner 'ave a job behind me, the money behind me, before I get married anyway.
>
> (Unemployed man aged 18)

C.W.: 'What do you want to do?'

> Not just stay on this island and get married and have a husband and a baby and get out to work; dinner on the table and 'What did you do today?' That's terribly boring. I want to do something different. Do something with my life. Families are boring altogether. You know it's 'my family's better than yours, my baby's better 'n yours'. I live next door to a young family and it's all hassle all the time. The young girl up the road, she's got two children and she's worrying all the time about how she can pay the bills, because her husband's not living with her.
>
> (Employed girl aged 17)

Until very recently it has been assumed that male school-leavers will become full-time workers for most of their active lives, and that female school-leavers will combine periods of employment with domestic labour. The process by which this takes place through schooling and after has been termed social and cultural reproduction.[1] Sociologists have shown how gender and class

divisions in the labour market, the family and the education system
have all been reproduced in parallel in the course of the transition
to adulthood. But what happens to the growing numbers of young
people in Britain whose only prospects are unemployment? We
could hypothesise that an interruption on one plane of the process
would have implications for transitions and transmissions on
other planes.

With these considerations in mind, I conducted a longitudinal
survey of young people on the Isle of Sheppey in Kent, where
unemployment had always been around twice the national
average. A cohort of 153 young people, 50 per cent males and 50 per
cent females, were interviewed, firstly when they were 16 in 1979,
then two-thirds were followed up in 1980. In 1984, eighty-four of
these were interviewed for a third time when they were 21. This
third survey constituted a 15 per cent sample of the population of
that age. Respondents were asked about their experiences and
expectations of work, unemployment and the transition to
marriage and parenthood. In this way I was able to compare
responses at 16 with those after five years in the labour market.[2]
These three surveys were supplemented by participant observation
and conversations with young people at home, at school and in
their places of recreation, so that both survey and more
ethnographic forms of data collection could be combined.[3] There
has been much commentary in recent years about the so-called
'problem' of the young unemployed people during this period of
transition. I wanted to find out how they themselves saw the issues.
These years, between 1979 and 1984, were also times of escalating
unemployment. This cohort of school-leavers were therefore
amongst the first generation to enter adulthood without full
employment.[4]

The surveys, tape-recorded interviews and detailed notes taken
whilst 'in the field' form the basis of the material to be presented
here. Firstly, however, it is necessary to consider social and cultural
reproduction more generally and ways in which it might be
reformulated. This has been based upon what I shall term a
'traditional' model of class and gender relations, one based upon
an assumption of full employment.

The traditional model of social reproduction

Rapidly rising youth unemployment is a relatively recent

phenomenon. Having climbed throughout the 1970s, unemployment has more than doubled since 1979. Most accounts of youth are based upon their role in an era of expansion when unemployment of the levels we are presently experiencing was unforeseen and unexpected. Consequently, the traditional model of social reproduction focussed attention upon the transition from school to *work* (Carter 1966, Ashton and Field 1976, Willis 1977). In this model, groups of youth were reproduced through the education system so that they broadly fitted divisions between middle and working class, rough and respectable, short-term and long-term careers and so on. The 'problem' to be explained, then, was how young people came to accept these roles, or in the words of Paul Willis:

> The difficult thing to explain about how middle class kids get middle class jobs is why others let them. The difficult thing to explain about how working class kids get working class jobs is why they let themselves.
>
> (Willis 1977: p. 1)

Willis also drew attention to the relationships between sexuality, employment and youth cultures. For example, he describes the functions of the wage packet and the valorisation of low status manual labour as a way of demonstrating masculinity; and Brake (1980) describes youth cultures in terms of their representation of masculinity:

> From the analysis of working class youth sub-cultures it can be seen that what emerges are several focal concerns which seem to be present in most of them. The most important is masculinity, and as I have suggested, these are predominantly masculinist cultures, offering forms of masculine identity.
>
> (Brake 1980: p. 82)

Thus, in the traditional literature, social relations were reproduced through different varieties of male labour. Although a number of different models were produced (Althusser 1971, Bourdieu and Passeron 1977, Bowles and Gintis 1976), and several noted the complex and paradoxical nature of this reproduction, they were all either implicitly or explicitly andro-centric (MacDonald 1980).

Accounts of youth subcultures have been similarly gender-biased until recently, offering accounts of how male youth came to terms with their class position[5] (Hall and Jefferson 1975, Mungham and Pearson 1976). The neglect of the domestic dimension resulted in female youth being rendered 'invisible'

(McRobbie and Garber 1976).

The traditional models assumed that young women would be seeking employment immediately upon leaving school, but that their ultimate destiny is as wives and mothers, thus lowering their commitment to school and to employment. However, they also assumed that the economic and social subordination of women is based upon the fact that the persons to whom they are housewives will be male workers in full-time employment. Traditional assumptions about feminine roles therefore imply traditional assumptions about masculine roles and vice versa.

During the 1970s aspects of this traditional model was challenged by feminists. They attempted to compensate for andro-centrism by concentrating upon the experience of girls in education and employment (McRobbie 1978, Deem 1980, Spender and Sarah 1980). In doing so, they indicated the importance of the domestic sphere in determining the social and cultural repro-duction of female school-leavers and its role in socialisation into gender roles. Some argued that feminine youth cultures, the family and the labour market all reinforced one another to circumscribe the kinds of expectation that girls had:

> Girls are still schooled with the marriage market in mind, although this may not be acknowledged consciously. This inevitability in their lives provinced as much excuse within the school, as for the girls themselves, for their ultimate under-achievement. The belief that girls find their deepest and truest satisfaction in a husband and children is ever prevalent (and many of the Ealing girls endorse this); despite discussions about sexual equality and women's increasing presence in the workforce. It shows the power of the market of romanticism portrayed in magazines, but also shows the investment in the care and needs of people that is perfectly understandable in the light of women's working history and their alternatives.
>
> (Sharpe 1976: p. 130)

Because of this expectation, it is argued, teenage girls are heavily preoccupied with romantic love and catching the right man (McRobbie 1978, Sarsby 1983).

Others, however, have emphasised the contradictions inherent in the process of socially reproducing young women as both wage labourers and domestic workers. For example such pressures operate differently upon middle-class girls – who are educated for 'careers' – and working-class girls, who are given a more domestically oriented curriculum at school, despite the fact that they are likely to spend much of their lives in employment. This is reflected in women's own perception of their status. As Anna Pollert has observed in her study of women in a tobacco factory:

> Working class women face a double, yet interconnecting of contradictions: those of class and those of sex . . . they both accepted and rejected their inferior position, they were both at once satisfied and dissatisfied, they lived in unresolved conflict.

(Pollert 1981: p. 87)

Such contradictory pressures and the problematical nature of female social reproduction lead girls to use their femininity as a form of resistance at school (Anyon 1983, Davies 1983, Griffin 1985), or even to resist feminine roles themselves (Gaskell 1983). In general, however, accounts of male youth have emphasised their resistance to hegemonic ideologies, using masculinity as a weapon – as in Willis's study; whilst studies of female youth have tended to emphasise their subordination to patriarchal, as well as class, oppression. Thus, the 'problem' to be explained in the reproduction of femininity is the way in which future domestic roles come to dominate every other aspect of women's experience.

In general, then, accounts of male youth have concentrated upon their social reproduction in the 'public' sphere of school and the labour market, whilst accounts of female youth have shown how this is crucially related to the social reproduction of the 'private' sphere of the home. We do not know to what extent the private sphere affects masculine expectations. Thus concepts derived from feminist discourse could be usefully applied more widely.

In the context of rising unemployment research has indicated that there may be a growing *disjunction* between school and work, or a fracture in the 'traditional' process of social reproduction. Young people, it is argued, are unemployed because they are unemployable (OECD 1977). Although some have dismissed this conclusion as a form of political scapegoating (Youthaid 1981), others have argued perhaps young people are now less inclined to accept 'shit jobs' at 'slave wages' and that the mismatch therefore deserves some attention (Pryce 1979, Roberts, Noble and Duggan 1981, 1982a, 1982b, 1982c).

Discussion of *unemployment* has been likewise gender-biased. For males, it appears, unemployment is unambiguously disastrous, resulting in the loss of status, income and identity; whilst for females, it is argued, there is the possibility of alternative domestic roles (Donovan and Oddy 1982, Jahoda 1982).[6] However, the discussion of young women's unemployment suffers from lack of theoretical clarity, since there is some uncertainty as to whether teenage female unemployment should be treated in any different way to male unemployment or to that of adult females.[7] On the one hand, the emphasis upon girls' domestic careers has obscured an appreciation of their position as workers, but on the other hand, the designation of youth as a general category has tended to obscure the differences between genders. Thus the conflation of female unemployment with domestic labour has tended to obscure our understanding of employment amongst women (Marshall 1984).

I have indicated ways in which the traditional models of social reproduction are predicated upon full employment. The more recent rise in male unemployment means that traditional models may be becoming increasingly unrealisable for both genders. The 'problem' to be explained now is how traditional expectations based upon an era of full employment come to be readjusted to fit new circumstances.

An alternative conceptual framework

For analytical purposes I shall make distinction between three dimensions liking the public and private spheres. First, there is the *material* relationship between gender and employment roles. Young women generally have lower wages and fewer prospects than male youth. For these reasons, working-class girls can seldom afford to live away from the natal home, unless they move into the home of a spouse (Leonard 1980). For young men, on the other hand, higher wages have reinforced their sexual dominance, ensuring a greater consumer capacity and greater access to adult life outside the home.

Second, there are *social* expectations transmitted through the school, the family and the ideology of romance and so on, which portray young men as masterful and financially advantaged and young women as dependent and subordinate (Sharpe 1976, McRobbie 1981, Sarsby 1983). Finally, there are *symbolic* codes that define appropriate behaviour and provide the criteria for classifying the social world according to 'refined' and 'vulgar', 'rough' and 'respectable', 'good' and 'bad' and so on.[8] Girls who trespass across these symbolic boundaries become contaminated by

97

being labelled as promiscuous or deviant (Shacklady Smith 1978, Wilson 1978). Conversely, young men who trespass across symbolic boundaries are labelled as effeminate or 'poofters' (Willis 1977, Brake 1980, Connell 1983). Sexual labelling thus helps to maintain 'traditional' models of masculinity and femininity.

The material, social and symbolic relationships between gender and reproduction vary between social classes. Thus, for example, middle-class children are dependent upon their parents in a different way, and for a longer period, than working-class youth. Socially, middle-class young people expect to establish themselves in careers before reproducing families. Working- and middle-class youth also have different ways of defining desirable sexuality (Sarsby 1983). Here I shall concentrate upon working-class youth, since they suffered more severely from unemployment, and constituted the majority of my sample.

These three dimensions are in practice intertwined and mutually reinforcing. Moreover, they can also be contradictory. The social expectations of women as dependent 'home-makers' can be at variance with their position as an important or even dominant wage-earner in the family (especially with rising male unemployment). However, as Porter (1983) has indicated, the ideology of male 'breadwinner' and female 'home-maker' remains intact. Similarly, young women working in factories risk being labelled as 'vulgar', for this undermines symbolic codes of femininity whilst it reinforces those of masculinity (Pollert 1981). Thus in times of full employment these dimensions reinforce the position of young men, whilst creating tensions in women's position. The ways in which these dimensions operate during times of rising unemployment will be explored later in relation to my own empirical data.

Expectations and experiences of work

Most post-war studies of young people have emphasised the functional convergence between aspirations 'cooled out' or encouraged through the education system and experiences of employment. It is argued that the entry into employment is by no means a shock to working-class young people, because they have been schooled to accept their positions within a class society (Ashton and Field 1976, Willis 1977, Youthaid 1981). My research indicated that this traditional model may have changed. Many school-leavers in my sample rejected the work that they encountered on leaving school. This was not because they were inadequately prepared for working life, as recent government reports would suggest,[9] for all 153 school-leavers had had some work experience before leaving school; and, for a number, their first jobs were extensions of the part-time jobs performed whilst they were still at school. Rather, it was because many had had to accept jobs lower than their expectations due to a decline in the opportunities available in the local labour market.

On first leaving school, young people ranked local employment opportunities not just according to how much they paid, but according to the extent to which they fulfilled different gender-based identities. Hence, for boys, craft-work was the most popular aspiration (55 per cent) followed by outdoor labouring (29 per cent). These jobs conferred the most 'machismo'. Girls mostly preferred training in traditional feminine trades such as hairdressing and nursing (32 per cent), whilst 13 per cent preferred office work and others opted for retail work, these being the most 'feminine'. The least popular form of employment for both genders was factory work since it was heavily criticised by at least 80 per cent of the sample,[10] despite the fact that it was relatively highly paid and was indeed one of the main sources of juvenile employment. Thus, altogether one-third of the sample of 1979 school-leavers were downwardly mobile in relation to their original preferences. Adjustment to work had become a generational, rather than an individual, problem.

The aspirations of young people reflected traditional occupational roles and gender stereotypes. The fact that there were hardly any craft apprenticeships available did not prevent young males from wanting to become craftsmen; indeed the decline in oportunities seemed to reinforce aspirations offering a secure masculine status in circumstances where this was being eroded. Similarly, the absence of office work did not prevent young women from wanting to become secretaries. By the same token, the predominance of factory employment did not make it any more acceptable to school-leavers. This would suggest that aspirations were out of phase with labour market conditions. The 'reproduction' of such gender roles and expectations was inappropriate. One solution was to leave the local market altogether by joining the army, which around 10 per cent of the sample did, for it offered one of the only sources of secure employment.

Consequently, responses to unemployment should perhaps be

seen in the context of these reactions to employment. These
responses to unemployment were varied and depended upon the
domestic circumstances of the individual and the number of
friends or relatives who were simultaneously out of work.
However, at the ages of 16 and 17 many presented a proud and
defiant stance to the interviewer, claiming that they would not
stoop to doing some of the 'shit jobs' available anyway:

> There's Tesco's, the shirt factory and shit like that. Boring,
> repetitive jobs, sewing jeans and stacking shelves. I wouldn't do a
> lot of factory work unless I was really desperate because I would
> think it was a waste of my life. In a factory, doing the same thing all
> day. You need an awful lot of money to be able to stand that.
>
> (Unemployed girl aged 19)

> Well, I stayed six months but I was so pissed off with it I left. I'm just
> not cut out for factory work. It was terrible doing the same thing all
> day, and all those fiddling little bits you had to do [making fuses].
> You couldn't stop for breath and I started to get headaches. It was
> just so boring – and the noise and the dirt and that. It is like a rabbit
> hutch in there: no windows, and it's so hot. I never thought it would
> be so awful.
>
> (Unemployed girl aged 18)

> When I left school I wanted a decent factory job, working. Get some
> decent wages. I thought, you don't need qualifications to do that, to
> get on. I was quite content with a factory job till I left school and
> realised what a factory job was: how tedious and boring it was.
>
> (Unemployed by aged 18)

Although there was a negative reaction to many of the jobs
available and although aspirations were undoubtedly different to
actualities, this form of presentation may also have been a
defensive strategy, masking a more forlorn reality. Are such
attitudes examples of defence or defiance?

Expectations of domestic roles

As might be expected, boys and girls viewed future domestic roles
rather differently. At the point of leaving school in 1979, many
girls were indeed subscribers to the ideology of romantic love and
did see their lives as circumscribed by the inevitability of future
domestic status. However, they did not necessarily cherish
romantic illusions about the nature of this status. When I asked a

100

group of girls in a coffee bar what qualities they sought in a husband, they chorused in unison: 'No drinking. No gambling. No violence.' The unromantic realism of these attitudes has also been confirmed in other studies of girls at this age (Gaskell 1983). Indeed, even at 17 many girls still hoped to avoid or defer what they perceived as the unenviable fate of many of the women around them, as the girl quoted at the beginning of the chapter illustrates. These girls' expectations of domestic life could be characterised as one of critical ambiguity. Thus during my first round of fieldwork in 1979 I concluded that traditional domestic roles were being challenged by young women.

Domestic activity had a low status in the eyes of many girls, and they hoped instead to escape and do something more exciting, or to postpone it. Employment offered a way out because it provided money to do what they wanted; many hoped that it would also provide an alternative short-term career of sorts. There was thus some friction in the reproduction of domestic roles for girls, although symbolically many of the jobs they aspired to were 'feminine' ones.

However, this proved to be short-lived. A year after leaving school, one-fifth of the sample had already adopted domestic roles, having got married, started cohabiting or had children. For some, this was a carefully planned strategy, but most had just drifted, or claimed that this had happened 'by accident'.[11] Thus it appears that domestic roles tended to catch up with young women, despite some initial antipathy.

One reason for this was that, despite being critical of traditional employment and domestic roles when they first left school, young people nevertheless held very conservative views of their *long-term* careers. Men were supposed to become 'breadwinners' and women were supposed to become the wives and mothers to male breadwinners. This appeared to be as important for young men as for young women, for in answer to my question, 'What do you think you will be doing in five years' time?', I received answers such as, 'Oh, usual thing, council house, wife and kids. Having a rest, sort of thing. Nice steady job'; or, 'Married, I suppose, by then. In my own house. I wouldn't get married unless I could afford to own me own house anyway' – from men and women alike. By the time they were 21, young people tended to regard their lives in terms of progressional careers, moving from one domestic status to another, and from one house to another. This ideal assumed that at least one partner would be in full-time employment. The transition to

101

adulthood therefore required the assumption of new domestic roles, and this was equally important for male as for female youth.

Despite jibes about being 'trapped' or 'tied down' by women, a domestic status as head of the household was important for boys for them to assume their full status as adults in the community. Whilst for girls there was some tension between work roles and domestic roles, for young men the two were mutually reinforcing. Symbolic, material and social dimensions were aligned, assuming they could find a permanent job. Indeed, the evidence suggests that, if anything, a future domestic status was more important for young men.

Because this ideal assumed the presence of a male 'breadwinner', unemployment would have a potentially disruptive influence upon life-cycle transitions. Despite the high rates of unemployment locally, young men were unable to conceive of getting married and settling down without full-time employment. The anxiety that such a prospect provoked is illustrated in such comments as:

> I wouldn't get maried if I didn't have a job. I'd feel cheap living off me wife's work. I'd want to get a job behind me.
>
> (Unemployed man aged 18)

> I wouldn't get married on the dole. Where could you live? How would you get food in? You couldn't build nothing up on the dole. You'd be stuck with what you've got.
>
> (Unemployed man aged 18

Young women were equally confident that they would marry a partner with a full-time job, and this was more important than having a job themselves in the long term.

Differences between 16 and 21

Had I finished my research in 1980, when my respondents were 17, I might have concluded that new attitudes were being developed as a response to mass unemployment. Young people were critical of traditional domestic roles and traditional employment roles, even if they rather wistfully hoped to assume traditional roles in the long term. However, I would have been mistaken. Attitudes to employment, to unemployment and to domestic roles had changed by the time they were 21, and this appeared to be related at least partly to life-cycle transitions.

At the age of 21 respondents were beginning to assume adult domestic roles. Getting married involved considerable financial commitment from both partners, as well as extended family, so that young people were no longer able to resist employment: the search for work became less discriminating and more desperate. They were now willing to contemplate doing jobs that they would not have considered when they first left school. It was at this point that they became more 'instrumental' in their outlook, prizing financial rewards above most others. The adoption of domestic roles seemed to make many young people more likely to conform in other respects. Rather than be unemployed as one young unemployed father of a family expressed it:

> I'd do any job, anything. I've even been down the council to see if they want anyone to sweep the roads.

CW: 'Have your expectations gone down, then, do you think?'

> Yer, well, it's a real crusher, especially if you're two years out of work, like I was. In the end. You're hopeful at first. When I first got unemployed, I can remember, it was when Thatcher first got in and you could see the jobs disappearing then. Oh, it's a real killer being unemployed two years. See, it's not just me I get to think of now, it's them as well.

I asked another girl, who had left a series of factory jobs before having a baby, 'Have your ideas changed, do you think?' She replied: 'Yes, I would do machining work now, and I would stick at it.' Why? 'Because I've got somebody to look after now.'

It appeared from my respondents that unemployment was far more serious in its effects at 21 than at 16. One young father, looking back upon his experience of unemployment when he first left school and comparing this with his experiences at the age of 21, stated:

> Oh, I didn't mind then, it was just a laugh. All me mates were out of work, we used to have a good laugh. Although I did get bored, mind you. I wouldn't have minded more money, but then it was just a laugh. Now, though, I've got a kid and family to keep, and you think of all the things which they should be having. Nah, it's worse now, it definitely is.

Women, too, saw the man's job as important for family-building, as a man was likely to earn more and to determine the standard of living of the household as a whole:

103

CW: 'Do you think you would have got married if Steve (husband) had been on the dole?'
Well, no, I think it's silly. You start off on the wrong foot. You've got to have a good bank balance, I think, to get married, so you can get the things you want, get your house together. See, we had nice furniture when we moved in here. It was all new . . . We had a new kitchen and carpets and three-piece suite, and then we've just bought a new telly and video.

(Married women aged 21, two children)

Moreover, upon getting engaged or married, the dependence upon the extended family for donating items for the home meant that young people were forced to conform to their parents' expectations of good behaviour. This normally involved becoming a regularly employed 'respectable' worker, rather than, say, a punk or a skinhead.

The ideology of the home appeared to effect the behaviour of men and women as they grew up. The creation of a home ensured the reproduction of the work-force through *material* necessity; repaying a mortgage, renting a flat or taking on hire-purchase commitments required a regular income. *Socially*, the expectations of wider kin and community were more easily imposed at this stage, serving to reinforce internalised ideas of domesticity. Finally, *symbolically* the home represented security and adult status, which in turn had financial consequences for young people's behaviour. The ideology of the home required the acquisition of essential consumer items such as a three-piece suite, a television set, a bed. Together, these items symbolised the home and the status of the couple as a social unit. The acquisition of these items served to tie the youthful consumer into the capitalist economy more securely than work disciplines or training could ever do. In this way, the household as a consuming unit served to ensure the reproduction of the work-force.

The nature of this transition was class-specific. It took place at an earlier age for working-class youth than for middle-class, and earlier for girls than for boys. By the time they were 17, 5 per cent of boys in the sample were married or cohabiting and one had a child, whereas 20 per cent of girls were married or cohabiting and 10 per cent had children. At the age of 21, half the girls and one-third of the boys had either entered, or were moving towards, a new family unit.

The most striking pattern to be observed amongst this sample was the increasing divergence between those who had been regularly employed, and were therefore able to accumulate possessions and purchase a home, and those who were excluded from this process through unemployment. Elsewhere we have termed this process *social polarisation* (Pahl and Wallace 1985). This contributes to a trend described by Ineichen (1977, 1981), who argues that the nature of family formation and housing careers interact to determine the life chances of the family thereafter. Unemployment during this stage of family formation could therefore contribute towards a cumulative disadvantage later in life.

Ways of coping with the loss of status caused by unemployment

I have spent some time discussing the ways in which unemployment serves to undermine expectations of masculine and feminine roles in the long term. Unemployment also serves to undermine male and female status in other ways too. For example, Willis (1985), Walsgrove (1984), Jenkins (1983) and Seabrook (1982) have described the sense of loss, impotence and emptiness associated with the loss of the wage packet amongst male youth, and the exclusion from consumption that this brought. In the case of girls, Griffin (1985) has described the loss of status suffered as a result of unemployment and the movement back into the home that this involved.

Bearing these discussions in mind, I shall now turn to some of the compensatory status' constructed by the young when faced with these multiple losses. I shall be discussing only some of these 'solutions': those that seemed important because they shed light upon aspects of young people's behaviour discussed in other ways elsewhere, and that have been the concern of policy-makers. Once again, I shall concentrate upon the construction and reproduction of gender roles as an important explanatory variable.

Compensatory status adopted by unemployed male youth

To return to the three dimensions of social reproduction discussed previously: the material, the social and the symbolic. For male youth, the *material* and *social* bases of masculinity were undermined; they had no status as wage-earners and no money as consumers. Consequently, the *symbolic* expressions of masculinity were sometimes exaggerated. This was done in two main ways: through status-enhancing gestures or activities and through the retailing of such gestures and activities later as stories.

The stories through which masculine deeds were relayed and that helped to define masculine status seemed to undergo some dramatised embellishment amongst the young employed. This was partly a result of the need to create incidents in order to avoid 'doing nothing' (in the manner described by Corrigan 1979), and partly a consequence of the fact that story-telling was the one way of passing time. Stories about otherwise unremarkable incidents were therefore elaborated into ever more fantasised forms, and I heard many variations on these in the course of my interviewing. These stories, mostly recounting male adventures and designed to demonstrate masculine powers, fitted identifiable patterns; the form remained similar even if the characters changed.

These stories described such things as heroic (and otherwise irrational) acts of delinquency, great orgiastic binges of drinking or drug taking, and dramatic confrontations with the police, employers, the DHSS and others in authority. As well as recounting dramatic confrontations with others, such stories also tended to glorify accounts of *self*-destruction and to celebrate a form of self-immolating hedonism. The importance of such stories lay in their function as myths. They transformed potentially humiliating encounters with those in power into personal triumphs through their reconstruction as narratives. Thus, the narrator, who would normally be the victim in such encounters, was elevated into the status of hero, able to exact symbolic revenge even when the net result was further punishment for himself.

I shall give just one example of such mythical status creation: that of activity in the so-called informal economy. Consider, for example the following extract from a story collected whilst I was a participant observer:

> So I went down to sign on [to the DHSS], with me painting and artexing gear, didn't I? Parked the van outside. Covered in paint I was. Went in there, and I says to the geezer over the counter, I says, 'Hurray up, mate. I'm busy. Got things to do, money to spend. I can't afford to hang about here all day.' That makes 'em mad, see? I just like to see their faces.
>
> (Unemployed male aged 18

In practice, of course, few managed to elude the DHSS, and many resondents were not even getting the meagre benefits to which they were entitled. Apart from the financial benefits such activity might yield, what are the functions of such a story? Clearly, the belief that the authorities could be outwitted in some way helped to preserve some dignity for the young unemployed. Secondly, such stories demonstrated that the individual was not lazy, for young people feared the popular stereotype of the idle scrounger. Thirdly, the pursuit of these activities helped to demonstrate a masculine power to transform the world and exert power over the environment, the very capacity that being unemployed deprived them of. Fourthly, this enabled young men to pride themselves on their ability to live on their wits and to survive in a hostile world, where 'getting by' successfully involved being more cunning than the next person. Fifthly, participation in the 'informal economy' was often a means for learning and practising skills for which there were no opportunities in the labour market, particularly craft skills, which, as I have mentioned, were particularly prized at the very time when apprenticeship training was declining. Finally, of course, such stories had good entertainment value.

It can be seen that status-enhancing activities of the kind described above are difficult to distinguish from the *mythology* surrounding them, since it would appear that one of the reasons for undertaking such activity was in order to recount it as a story later. Hence, far from concealing their informal jobs and activities, young men often boasted of their abilities to manage. There were many stories of how they had managed to refurbish old cars and sell them for a vast profit, or performed clever and perhaps slightly shady deals. The rewards for these were more social than financial, for these individuals seemed no more affluent than the rest.

Participation in casual and informal activity of this kind was often an extension of the part-time jobs performed by school-leavers before they left school, since I have already mentioned that *all* school-leavers undertook some work of this kind. For young men, such jobs included working in scrap-yards, helping fishermen, attaching themselves to self-employed artisans as unpaid or casually paid assistants, self-employed work such as repairing cars and bicycles, and digging lug-worms to sell to fishermen. Amongst girls the most common forms of such work included undertaking factory outwork for friends and neighbours, informal nannying, cleaning and fruit-picking. I listed over sixty jobs of this kind amongst my respondents, and not all of these were illegal or necessarily directly remunerated. Altogether 5 per cent of the sample were working informally at the time that they were interviewed in 1984, all of them being young men (this was one in ten of the men in the sample). In 1980, on the other hand, nearly 16 per cent of the sample were doing jobs of this kind, and one-third of them were women.[12]

In practice many of these jobs were highly exploitative. Furthermore, only some young people had access to them, and the 'informal economy' tended to decline at the same time as the formal, meaning that such opportunities as did exist were drying up. It appeared that young people were consigned to the more marginal jobs, even within the informal sector.

Informal work of this kind was more available to young men than to young women, since it corresponded with traditional divisions in the labour market. There was a dual 'shadow' labour market too (Pahl 1984, Wallace and Pahl, 1985). Thus, whilst young men found higher-status and more lucrative jobs informally – such as fixing cars or doing painting and decorating – young women undertook the less well rewarded jobs, such as factory outwork.

For young men, then, participation in street-corner life was compulsory: they had nowhere else to go. Their 'solutions' were public ones, and whilst gathering in the amusement arcades and shopping precincts they passed their time recounting stories that helped to define their masculinity. Being excluded from access to more concrete forms of status, they created fantasised ones, often out of apparently self-destructive activities. (I am not claiming that it was only the unemployed who did this; they simply had more time to devote to these pursuits.) Whilst this 'solution' sufficed for a few years, in the long term, as we have seen, unemployment prevented the transition to full adult status of 'breadwiner'. Young men were condemned to a life of perpetual adolescence and street-corner bravado. Many of the stories circulating amongst them were the product of a need to bolster an increasingly fragile sense of masculinity.

Compensatory status adopted by unemployed female youth

The young woman's status within the natal home was more circumscribed than that of her brothers. In the case of employed girls, the acquisition of a regular wage transformed her status within the home; she could go out with her own money, decide upon her own patterns of consumption, and was excused a great deal of housework. Lack of a job, on the other hand, condemned her to the status of a junior within the home, and it was more likely that she would be given domestic chores to do as well. Whilst some girls might welcome this responsibility, this could also lead to a sense of claustrophobia as there were less opportunities for girls to escape on to the streets. Being more *financially* dependent upon parents than employed girls, unemployed girls were less able to assert their independence. Being also more *socially* controlled by parents, unemployed girls' lives were more limited than those of unemployed boys.

This could result in family tensions, which served to push the young girl out into a home of her own. It was no coincidence, perhaps, that girls who had been unemployed for longer than three months out of their five years after leaving school were twice as likely to have left home to live with a man, to have had children or got married than those who were regularly employed.[13]

Girls had less access to the public displays of bravado available to young men, and hence their 'solutions' in terms of compensatory status tended to be real rather than fantasised. These compensations were not consciously planned strategies: it was more a question of alternatives and possibilities that had appeared to be available when they were 16 becoming increasingly closed off. As I have indicated, enforced domesticity was not a universally welcomed prospect.

Employment was therefore important for young women in so far as it appeared to offer an escape from dependent domesticity. However, domesticity within the natal home was regarded as very different to domesticity in their own home. Unemployment in the natal home implied a form of extended adolescence, whilst domestic status in one's own home was an opportunity to attain a mature feminine status within the community. Thus there was more incentive to get married, cohabit or have children. In order to understand the pressure to pursue this option, we need to understand the difference between dependency in the natal home and that in the home of destination. In this way, the transition to new forms of domesticity was a short-cut to adulthood.

Conclusions

The research described here would support the conclusions of those who argue that there is an increasing *disjunction* between school and work in the context of rising unemployment. As jobs become more scarce, and some teachers use qualifications as the 'carrot' to encourage commitment to education, this may serve further to artificially raise expectations of regular employment. Educators should perhaps be aware that the journey into work is no longer a one-way ride and may take many detours. Increasing numbers of school-leavers are likely to spend their first year in the labour market doing odd jobs or drifting in and out of employment and government schemes – a prospect that the increasing emphasis on certification and submission to formal schooling is unlikely to equip them for. The introduction of the Youth Training Scheme has served further to fragment these early careers of beginning workers. On the other hand, anticipation of these kinds of initial career could make young people more sceptical of the value of formal education, and likewise tends to undermine traditional models of careers education based upon a 'traditional' model of full employment for everyone.

It would appear that the 'stick' that finally serves to beat young people into submission to the labour process is the long-term reproduction of the domestic life cycle. This is more important at 21 that at 16.

I have indicated that in times of full employment the material, social and symbolic dimensions of masculine roles in social reproduction were mutually reinforcing, whilst in feminine roles they were contradictory. In times of unemployment, masculine roles become contradictory too, and young men resort to exaggerating one dimension in the absence of others. For young women, their position between public and private spheres creates new cross-pressures. This persistence of traditional masculine and feminine expectations in conditions where they are unrealisable for many young people is reinforced by family and subculture. Gender expectations remain rigid and enduring despite the erosion of their economic basis. Indeed, if anything they become more entrenched.

The research has indicated the importance of the domestic and public sphere for both male and female school-leavers and has shown the essential interconnectedness of both. Although male youth tend to be described in terms of their relationship to the public sphere of street corner and work-place, the private sphere, too–in terms of their expectations of becoming 'breadwinners' – was of crucial importance in the transition from school to work. Female youth, on the other hand, have tended to be described in terms of their relationship to the private sphere of home and family, thus confusing the discussion of female unemployment. I have indicated that girls' experience of work and unemployment should be situated in the context of their position within the life cycle for greater empirical and analytical clarity. Male and female youth may stand in different relations to the private and public spheres, but both should be taken into account in the case of both genders.

In this context, the recommendations of the recent Social Security Review have important implications. It would appear that limiting young people's entitlement to supplementary benefits outside the natal home will serve to reinforce their dependence upon the family, and this is indeed the specific policy aim behind the legislation. This may in turn make the transition to a new home the only escape, and will certainly exacerbate tensions in families who traditionally regarded leaving school as the first step to independent adult status. Furthermore, it may reinforce many of the trends observed in the study by redefining the transition from adolescence to adulthood for working-class youth.

Social concern and social policy have tended to concentrate upon the initial entry of young people into work and the role that education and training play in this. My research would indicate that this is only one phase in a broader process of social reproduction. Viewed in this way gender identities and the role of the domestic sphere are an essential part of the process rather than something to be 'tacked on' when considering women. If education is to prepare young people for their broader roles as citizens in a changing society, it would seem that these wider issues need to be taken into account.

Notes

1 Reproduction is used in a number of confused and confusing senses (Edholm, Harris and Young, 1977). Here I am using it to mean the way in which one generation of children becomes the next generation of workers with values and attitudes appropriate to their position in the occupational hierarchy.
2 The original 153 young people were drawn from a cross-section of

students within a single division of a local comprehensive school. Not all of these were minimum-age school-leavers, although 109 of them did leave at 16. A cross-section were followed up in 1980 and 1984, although in this chapter I have concentrated upon the minimum-age school-leavers who were predominantly working-class.

3 These surveys were undertaken in an area that had already been extensively researched by a team at the University of Kent. This research was concerned with examining the relationship between work, the household and unemployment more generally. For the results of this research see Pahl (1984), Pahl and Wallace (1985), Wallace and Pahl (1985).

4 I recognise that 'full employment' is something of a misnomer, since there has been unemployment over the entire post-war period. However, it is a convenient term to describe the period before unemployment became widespread and endemic in Britain.

5 McRobbie (1978), McRobbie and Garber (1976) and Powell and Clarke (1975) have all criticised the literature on male youth sub cultures. They posed the question: were girls not present in youth subcultures or had they been ignored by researchers?

6 Many of the classic studies of unemployment have concentrated explicitly upon men (Hill *et al.* 1973, Marsden and Duff 1975). Jahoda (1982), for example, argues that unemployment is not so serious for women as they do have alternative domestic roles to turn to, but can the same be said about young unmarried women?

7 Some have assumed that the effects of unemployment upon young females would probably be the same as that upon young males (Stafford 1982, Bloxham 1983). Others have argued that they should be regarded differently (Markall 1980, Jahoda 1982, Walsgrove 1984, Griffin 1985).

8 Symbolic codes that define acceptable and unacceptable behaviour have been described by Bourdieu and Passeron (1977) and Martin (1983). In the case of girls, the distinction between 'slags' and 'drags' has been explored by Cowie and Lees (1981). My usage of this concept draws upon work by Wilson (1978).

9 The White Papers *A New Training Initiative* (1981), CMND 8455, and *Training for Jobs* (1984), Cmnd 9135, for example, emphasised the importance of training young people to prepare them for work, assuming that it was their ill-preparedness for work that prevented them from finding jobs. My own research indicates that this assumption is a complete fallacy.

10 These results refer to the 1979–80 sample.

11 These families happened 'by accident' because, despite extensive knowledge of contraception, many young people did not use effective methods of contraception, being morally circumscribed by codes of sexual conduct described elsewhere (Rubin 1976, Wilson 1978). Those girls who tended to be most disadvantaged in the labour market also

tended to be those most likely to fall pregnant 'by accident'. Those who had regular jobs and planned wedding ceremonies were also more likely to plan their families more single-mindedly. This association between irregular employment and drifting into pregnancy has been observed elsewhere (Jones *et al.* 1981, Jenkins 1983). However, the reasons for it are not clear.

12 Others who have documented the informal activity of young people have shown that this varies between geographical regions, and between social and ethnic groups (Roberts *et al.* 1981, 1982). Elsewhere, I have discussed the gender division in the informal sphere more fully (Wallace and Pahl 1985).

13 This association between unemployment and family formation could be an *indirect* rather than a direct association. It would therefore be rash to draw hasty conclusions about escalating teenage pregnancies on the basis of these data.

14 Some other researchers have observed this phenomenon too. Hence, Carter (1975) in his study of male youth in Sheffield has argued that although they may react against jobs in the steel industry initially on leaving school, family responsibility pushes them back towards these jobs. Moreover, Parker (1976) has charted this change in terms of delinquent careers.

References

Allat, P. and Yeandle, S. M. (1984) 'Family Structure and Youth Unemployment: Economic Recession and the Concept of Fairness'. Paper presented to the BSA Conference, University of Bradford.

Althusser, L. (1971). 'Ideology and Ideological State Apparatuses,' in *Lenin and Philosophy and other Essays*. London, New Left Books.

Anyon, J. (1983) 'Intersection of Gender and Class,: Accommodation and Resistance by Working-Class and Affluent Females to Contradictory Sex and Role Ideologies, In L. Barton and S. Walker (eds.), *Gender, Class and Education*. Lewes, Falmer Press.

Ashton, D. N. and Field, D. (1976) *Young Workers*. London, Hutchinson.

Bloxham, S. (1983) 'Social Behaviour and the Young Unemployed', in R. Fiddy, (ed.), *In Place of Work*. Lewes, Falmer Press.

Bourdieu, P. (1980) 'The Production of Beauty: Contribution to an Economy of Symbolic Good'. *Media, Culture and Society* 2: pp. 261–93.

Bourdieu, P. and Passeron, J. C. (1977) *Reproduction in Education, Society and Culture*. London and Beverley Hills, Sage.

Bowles, S. and Gintis, H. (1976) *Schooling in Capitalist America: Educational Reform and the Contradictions of Economic Life* London, Routledge & Kegan Paul.

Brake, M. (1980) *The Sociology of Youth Culture and Youth Sub-*

Cultures, London, Routledge & Kegan Paul.

Carter, M. P. (1966) *Into Work*. Harmondsworth, Penguin.

(1975) 'Teenage Workers: Second Chance at 18?', in P. Brann (ed.),

Clarke, J. and Jefferson, T. (1976) 'Working-Class and Youth Cultures', in Mungham and Pearson (1976).

Clarke, J., Hall, S., Jefferson, T. and Roberts, B. (1975) 'Subcultures, Cultures and Class: Theoretical Overview', in Hall and Jefferson (1975).

Cohen, P. (1972) *Subcultural Conflict and Working-Class Community*. Working Papers in Cultural Studies No. 2. Spring. University of Birmingham.

Connell, R. W. (1983) *Which Way is Up? Essays on Sex, Class and Culture*, London, Allen & Unwin.

Corrigan, P. (1979) *Schooling and the Smash Street Kids*. London, Macmillan.

Cowie, L. and Lees, S. (1981) 'Slags or Drags'. *Feminist Review* 9: pp. 17–31.

Davies, L. (1983) 'Gender, Resistance and Power', in L. Barton and S. Walker (eds.), *Gender, Class and Education*. Lewes, Falmer Press.

Deem, R. (ed.) (1980) *Schooling for Women's Work*, London, Routledge & Kegan Paul.

Delamont, S. (1980) *The Sociology of Women*. London, Allen & Unwin.

Donovan, A. and Oddy, M. (1982) 'Psychological Aspects of Unemployment: an Investigation into Emotional and Social Adjustment of School-Leavers'. *Journal of Adolescence* 5: pp. 15–30.

Edholm, F., Harris, O. and Young, K. (1977) 'Conceptualising Women' *Critique of Anthropology* 3 (9/10): pp. 101–29.

Finn, D. (1984) 'Leaving School and Growing up: Work Experience in the Juvenile Labour Market', in (I. Bates *et al.*, *Schooling for the Dole?*. London, Macmillan.

Gaskell, J. (1983) 'The Reproduction of Family Life: Perspectives of Male and Female Adolescents'. *British Journal of Sociology of Education* 4 (1): pp. 19–38.

Griffin, C. (1985) *Typical Girls?*. London, Routledge & Kegan Paul.

Hall, S. and Jefferson, T. (eds.) (1976) *Resistance through Rituals*. London, Hutchinson.

Hill, M. J., Harrison, R. M., Sargeant A. V., and Talbot V., (1973) *Men Out of Work*, Cambridge, Cambridge University Press.

Ineichen, B. (1977) 'Youthful Marriage: the Vortex of Disadvantage', in J. Peel and R. Chester (eds.), *Equalities and Inequalities in Family Life*. London, Academic Press.

(1981) 'The Housing Decisions of Young People'. *British Journal of Sociology* 32 (2): pp. 252–58.

Jahoda, M. (1982) *Employment and Unemployment: A Social Psychological Analysis*. Cambridge University Press.

Jenkins, R. (1983) *Lads, Citizens and Ordinary Kids: Working-Class*

Youth Life-Styles in Belfast. London, Routledge & Kegan Paul.

Jones, P., Williamson, H., Payne, J. and Smith, G., (1981) *Out of School: A Case Study of the Role of Government Schemes at a Time of Growing Unemployment:* Special Programmes Occasional Paper No. 4. Sheffield, MSC.

Leonard, D. (1980) *Sex and Generation: A Study of Courtship and Weddings*. London, Tavistock.

Macdonald, M. (1980) 'Socio-Cultural Reproduction and Women's Education', in Deem (1980).

McRobbie, A. (1978) 'Working-Class Girls and the Culture of Femininity', in Women's Studies Group Centre for Contemporary Cultural Studies (1978).

(1980) 'Settling Accounts with Subcultures'. *Screen Education* 34, 1980: pp. 37–50.

(1981) 'Just like a *Jackie* Story', in McRobbie and McCabe (1981).

McRobbie, A. and Garber, J. (1976) 'Girls and Subcultures: an Exploration', in Hall and Jefferson (1976).

McRobbie, A. and McCabe, T. (eds.) (1981) *Feminism for Girls: An Adventure Story*. London, Routledge & Kegan Paul.

Markall, G. (1980) *The Best Years of their Lives: Schooling, Work and Unemployment in Oldfield* Occasional Paper No. 3. William Temple Foundation.

Marsden, D. and Duff, E. (1975) *Workless: Some Unemployed Men and their Families* Harmondsworth, Penguin.

Marshall, G. (1984) 'On the Sociology of Women's Unemployment, its Neglect and Significance'. *Sociological Review* 32 (2): pp. 234–59.

Martin, B. (1983) *A Sociology of Contemporary Cultural Change*. Oxford, Blackwell.

Mungham, G. and Pearson, G. (eds.) (1976) *Working Class Youth Culture*. London, Routledge & Kegan Paul.

OECD (1977) *Entry of Young People into Working Life*. Paris, OECD.

Pahl, R. E. (1978) 'How School-Leavers See their Future'. *New Society* 46 (839), November: pp. 259–62.

(1984) *Divisions of Labour* Oxford, Blackwell.

Pahl, R. E. and Wallace, C. D. (1980) 7–19 and Unemployed on the Isle of Sheppey. Report to the Department of Employment, London.

(1984) 'Household Work Strategies in an Economic Recession', in N. Redcliff and E. Mingione, (eds.), *Beyond Employment: Household, Gender and Subsistence*. Oxford, Blackwell.

Parker, H. (1976) 'Boys Will Be Men: Brief Adolescence in a Downtown Neighbourhood', in Mungham and Pearson (1976).

Phillips, D. (1973) 'Young and Unemployed in a Northern City' in D. Weir (ed.), *Men and Work in Modern Britain*. London, Fontana.

Porter, M. (1983) *Home and Work*. London, Macmillan.

Powell, R. and Clarke, J. (1975) 'A Note on Marginality', in Hall and Jefferson (1975).

Pryce, K. (1979) *Endless Pressure*. Harmondsworth, Penguin.

Roberts, K., Noble, M. and Duggan, J. (1981) *Unregistered Youth Unemployment and Outreach Careers Work: Non-Registration.* Final Report Part 1. Research Paper No. 31. London, Department of Employment.

(1982a) 'Youth Unemployment: an Old Problem or a New Lifestyle?'. *Leisure Studies* 1 (2): pp. 71–182.

(1982b) 'Out-of-School Youth in High Unemployment Areas: an Empirical Investigation'. *British Journal of Guidance and Counselling* 10 (1): pp. 1–11.

(1982b) 'Out-of-School Youth in High Unemployment Areas: an Empirical Investigation'. *British Journal of Guidance and Counselling* 10 (1): pp. 1–11.

(1982c) *Unregistered Youth Unemployment and Outreach Careers Work*. Final Report Part 2. Research Paper No. 32. London, Department of Employment.

Rubin, L. B. (1976) *Worlds of Pain*. New York, Basic Books.

Sarsby, J. (1983) *Romantic Love and Society*. Harmondsworth, Penguin.

Seabrook, J. (1982) *Unemployment*. London, Quartet.

Shacklady Smith, L. (1978) *Sexist Assumptions and Female Delinquency*, in Smart and Smarst (1978).

Sharpe, S. (1976) *Just Like a Girl*. Harmondsworth, Penguin.

Sinfield, A. (1981) *What Unemployment Means*. Oxford, Martin Robertson.

Smart, C. and Smart, B. (eds.) (1978) *Women, Sexuality and Social Control*. London, Routledge & Kegan Paul.

Spender, D. and Sarah, E. (eds.) (1980) *Learning to Lose. Sexism and Education*. London, Women's Press.

Stafford, (1982).

Walker, S. and Barton, L. (1983) *Gender, Class and Education*. Lewes, Falmer Press

Wallace, C. (1980) 'Adapting to Unemployment'. *Youth in Society* 40: pp. 6–8.

Wallace, C. D. (1984) *School Work and Unemployment: Social and Cultural Reproduction on the Isle of Sheppey*. Ph. D. thesis. University of Kent.

(1985) *Growing Apart*. Report to the Joseph Rowntree Memorial Trust.

Wallace, C. D. and Pahl, R. E. (1985) 'Polarisation, Unemployment and All Forms of Work'. To be published in BSA Conference volume (forthcoming).

Walsgrove, D. (1984) 'Policing Yourself: Youth Unemployment, Individualism and the Amplification of Normality'. Paper presented to the BSA Conference, University of Bradford.

White Paper (1981) *A New Training Initiative* . London, HMSO.

(1984) *Training for Jobs*. London, HMSO.

Willis, P. (1977) *Learning to Labour: How Working-Class Kids Get*

Working-Class Jobs Aldershot, Saxon House.

(1984) 'Youth Unemployment 1. A New Social State'. *New Society*, 29 March: pp. 475–77; 'Youth Unemployment 2. Ways of Living'. *New Society*, 5 April: pp. 13–15.

Wilson, D. (1978) 'Sexual Codes and Conduct', in Smart and Smart (1978).

Women's Studies Group Centre for Contemporary Cultural Studies, University of Birmingham (1978) *Women Take Issue*, London, Hutchinson.

Youthaid (1981) *Study of the Transition from School to Working Life*, Vols. 1–3. London, Youthaid.

Acknowledgements

I am grateful for the support of the Joseph Rowntree Memorial Trust in funding this research.

CHAPTER SIX

The Social and Political Context of Black Youth
Unemployment: a Decade of Policy
Developments and the Limits of Reform

John Solomos

Introduction

In the mid-1980s, over fifteen years after the state had officially
recognised the 'special problems' faced by black school-leavers in
making the transition from school to work, the one certainty about
their current position in the labour market is that their
employment prospects are now much bleaker than they were back
in 1968.[1] During this period, and particularly since the mid-1970s,
many policy initiatives have been planned and undertaken as part
of the state's publicly announced objective of (a) ensuring equality
of opportunity for the 'second generation' of black Britons and (b)
providing 'special' help on those young blacks who were seen as
likely to drift away from the mainstream of society, particularly the
'educationally disadvantaged', homeless, marginalised or unemployed sections of this group (Solomos 1983a, Troyna and
Smith 1983). These measures have been pursued through a variety
of agencies, most notably the educational system, the Commission
for Racial Equality and its predecessors and more recently the
Manpower Services Commission.

There has been no shortage of expressions of concern about
disproportionately high levels of unemployment among black
youth, from within the highest echelons of government. This
became particularly clear during the violent confrontations
between the police and young blacks and whites on the streets of
Bristol, Liverpool, London, Birmingham and other urban areas

during 1980 to 1981. In this period 'black youth unemployment' became a source of anxiety to the state, to the extent that the Home Secretary made a forceful intervention calling for greater efforts to secure equality of opportunity in the labour market:

> It is a deplorable reflection on our society that in all too many instances young people from the ethnic minorities find it harder to get work than their white colleagues with the same background and experience. Employers must be ready to give young blacks a fair chance and to ensure that unreasonable barriers are not put in the way of capable applicants

(Whitelaw 1980:p. 3)

During the post-1979 period both the Thatcher administration and the Labour Party have in their own specific ways spoken out against the existence of 'unreasonable barriers' against young blacks (Solomos 1983b, Jenkins and Solomos, forthcoming). And this in the broad context of the pursuit by the Thatcher government of 'free market' policies in all areas of social and economic life over the same period.

Such expressions of concern can be read as a sign that the state is actually going to implement a fundamentally radical attack on all forms of racial discrimination and inequality in the labour market. But another reading of such policy initiatives has been articulated by sections of the black community, particularly the community groups involved in working with young blacks on an everyday level. Cecil Gutzmore, for example, in a sharp critique of policy developments in the aftermath of the 1980–81 'riots', has argued that such expressions of concern are larely tokenistic and ignore the deeply entrenched processes that marginalise young blacks socially and at the same time 'criminalise' them through the actions of the police and other government agencies (Gutzmore 1983). The *Caribbean Times*, which represents a radical voice within the Afro-Caribbean community, expressed a similar concern when it ran a series of reports during 1983 and 1984 about the bleak prospects for young unemployed blacks during the current recession.[2] According to this interpretation the impact of policy initiatives to help overcome unemployment among young blacks has been minimal, because (a) they have been symbolic rather than co-ordinated practical actions to overcome racial inequality in the labour market, (b) they ignore the wider structural roots of racism and concentrate on ameliorative help to individuals or groups, and (c) they ignore the actual demands of

119

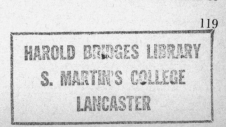

the numerous black community groups and define the 'problems' to be remedied from a purely administrative angle.

This chapter will attempt to analyse some of the underlying issues that lie behind the development of these viewpoints through an historical account of the various policy initiatives over the last decade. It will concentrate on the actual experience of measures that have been premised on either the reform of labour market inequalities or providing 'special help' to young blacks in the transition from school to work/employment. In addition, it will necessarily look at the ways in which young blacks are increasingly perceived as a 'problem' by the institutions of law and order, particularly the police. The order of presentation will be in three stages: first, a general overview of the relationship between the question of black youth unemployment and wider issues in employment and race relations policy; second, a critical analysis of the history of state intervention in relation to young blacks from the 1960s to the early 1980s; finally, the chapter will conclude by taking a look at the limits and possibilities for reforming or radically transforming the current position of young blacks in British society.

The Socio-political Context of Race Policies in Post-war Britain

Within the space of three decades 'race' has moved from the margins of dominant political discourse to the core, leading to what has been called the racialisation of political discourse (Miles and Phizacklea 1984). This politicisation has been accompanied by the arousal of fears about the impact of immigration on various facets of British society and the mobilisation of race as an important element in political debates. Within the broader context of the social and economic changes that took place during the 1960s and 1970s, the question of race and race-related 'problems' came to play an important role in fashioning policy responses in a number of areas, e.g. urban policy, welfare policy, employment policy, and law and order strategies. In quantitative terms, at least, race has thus become an integral element of the local and national political scheme.

A number of authors have, however, argued that there is a tendency to see these issues as in some way related to race, or at least as having a 'race dimension' in a negative sense (Hall *et al.* 1978,

Rex and Tomlinson 1979, Reeves 1983). Moreover, substantial evidence exists to suggest that this tendency to see 'race issues' as related to wider social problems had the consequence that ideologies blaming blacks (as individuals or as communities) as a cause of 'social problems' exerted an undue influence on the kind of policies emanating from both central and local government on 'race relations'. A good example of this blaming-the-victim approach to 'race' is the tendency to see urban problems in terms of the numbers of blacks in an area, either because of the demands they make on already scarce resources or because of their family patterns and communal life (Clarke *et al.* 1974). Another example, which is of some relevance to this chapter, is the tendency to interpret black children's under-achievement at school as related to differential patterns of child-rearing, language problems or differential cultural values attached to education (Carby 1982).

Perhaps the best way to appreciate the influence of a problem-orientated approach on official thinking about race is to look at the ways in which such issues as 'racial discrimination', 'racial disadvantage' and 'race prejudice' have been defined through the development of specific race policies since the mid-1960s. The racialisation of political and policy discourses that took place during the post-1962 period, with the passage of the various immigration and race relations Acts, involved the identification of 'special problems' faced by black minorities and remedial measures to help them either to 'adjust' or to achieve 'equality of opportunity' with the white majority. But it also led to the development of institutionally separate bodies to manage 'race relations' issues and to help the 'integration' of minorities in the wider society (Freeman 1979, Layton-Henry 1984). A large part of the effort of the 'race-relations industry' since the mid-1960s has been concerned with the communal weaknesses of minority communities, while the question of racism and its institutional manifestations has ben included as merely one issue among many.

The very notions of 'racial disadvantage' and 'special needs', which are the notions commonly used by government to define the position of black minorities, contain assumptions about these groups that have helped to reproduce a problem-oriented approach. A report by the Home Affairs Committee of the House of Commons on *Racial Disadvantage* contains the most articulate statement of this approach. The report argues that racial inequality is produced by the twin processes of *racial discrimination* and *racial disadvantage*. The first process was seen as not

121

necessarily the prime factor, because:

> Racial disadvantage is a particular case of relative disadvantage within society. With the exception of racial discrimination, the disadvantages suffered by Britain's ethnic minorities are shared in varying degrees by the rest of the community. Bad housing, unemployment, educational under-achievement, a deprived physi- call environment, social tensions – none of these are the exclusive preserve of ethnic minorities.
>
> (Home Affairs Committee 1981:para. 12)

The context of discrimination was seen as another 'handicap' from which blacks suffered, and one that could be dealt with by legal measures against discrimination. According to the committee the central problems of the 'complex of racial disadvantage' were (a) newness and problems of social and cultural adjustment, (b) the geographical location of minorities in inner city areas, (c) language and literacy problems and (d) educational disadvantage (ibid.: paras. 14–24).

The racialisation of policy initiatives over the last two decades has been based on various versions of this model of 'racial disadvantage plus discrimination', with the result that racism as an issue has been underplayed while assumptions about the weaknesses of minority cultures have played an imporant role in defining official responses to the 'race' question (CCCS Race and Politics Group 1982, Reeves 1983). In addition, however, it has also become clear that measures to combat racial discrimination have been ineffective in tackling the roots of the problem, and that the rhetoric of equal opportunity has not lived up to the reality. While numerous initiatives have been taken to deal with 'racial disadvantage', the legislation passed by successive governments seems to have done little to halt discrimination in relation to housing, employment, education or social welfare (Rhodes and Braham 1981, Brown 1984).

The paradox is that, although successive governments have promised equal opportunity for blacks, the measures they have taken have had more to do with overcoming the so-called handicaps faced by blacks because of cultural differences than with tackling racism. An example of this process at work is the recent debate about racism in the police force. While much effort has been placed on increasing contact between black communities and the police (by educating blacks about the police, and the police about blacks), little effort has been placed on tackling institutionalised racialism within the police.[3]

Similar problems arise when analysing state interventions in other areas, most notably in employment (Jenkins and Solomos, forthcoming). While there is by now a long history of government promises to overcome discrimination in the labour market, dating back to 1968, in practice such measures as have been taken have concentrated on remedial initiatives to meet 'special needs' (e.g. language needs, access to special training), which have been defined in terms of cultural or communal handicaps. Such explanations have been applied especially to young blacks, even though it is commonly recognised that unlike older black workers they do not suffer from problems of newness or language deficiencies. As the Home Affairs Committee report on *Racial Disadvantage* argued:

> These second and third generations are not themselves newcomers in any sense, but have inherited the disadvantages associated with migration to a complex society with its own settled economic and social patterns.
> (Home Affairs Committee 1981:para. 19)

Within the logic of this approach the rise of unemployment among young blacks, which has occurred steadily throughout the late the late 1970s and early 1980s, can be interpreted as a sign of this 'inheritance of disadvantages' rather than as a deficiency of opportunity brought about by racism. In this way the problem is located at the level of the ethnic minorities, and the 'settled social and economic patterns' are thus removed from debate. They are seen as the established structure to which minorities have to be helped to adjust, rather than as part of the problem.

In short, then, the increasing attention given by successive governments to the 'race question' cannot be seen as value-neutral. On the contrary,the experience of the last three decades has highlighted the ways in which the major concern of political institutions has been with managing the 'problems' seen as associated with blacks rather than tackling the socio-economic roots of racist practices in society. The established discourse of race relations policies that has been produced over these decades has increasingly been focussed on the concept of 'racial disadvantage', which is used as a policy tool to define the kinds of special help required by blacks in order to overcome 'their' handicaps. Within the terms of this established discourse the view never really comes across that racism is the central problem. Rather, the main emphasis is put on the handicaps of the black minorities, which are seen as only 'partly' produced by racism.

A measure of the effectiveness of this discourse is the way in which it is common in policy documents to talk of the barriers faced by blacks at work, in the neighbourhood or in schools as 'their' problems, or the use of metaphors equating being black in a white society to disability. The very language of what Edelman has called the 'helping professions' (Edelman 1977) has come to dominate common-sense views of race in contemporary Britain. No more so than in relation to young blacks, who have been stereotyped as a 'social problem' from the earliest stages of the development of the race-relations industry. It is to this specific group that an increasing amount of attention is devoted, both by bodies such as the Commission for Racial Equality and the Manpower Services Commission and by the mainstream government departments. It is to the story of how this categorisation of young blacks as a social problem has come about that we now turn.

Black youth, mass unemployment and the state: from assimilation to 'special needs'

As mentioned above, the basic objective of this chapter is to critically analyse the processes through which the question of young blacks (and specifically black youth unemployment) has been articulated in political discourse and in specific policy interventions. There is by now a consensus opinion that this is likely to remain one of the core elements of the domestic policy agenda for the next decade, and there are a number of studies on the history of the 'black youth question', on how racism affects the employment chances of young blacks, how they are differentially affected by unemployment and the impact of youth training schemes on the position of young blacks. While the specific problems facing young blacks in making the transition from school to work have been acknoweldged, this does not seem to have led to more critical studies of the processes that have resulted in the racialisation of debates about youth unemployment and the effectiveness of state interventions in this field.

This is not to say that the position of young or 'second-generation' blacks at school and in the transition from school to work have not been the subject of research,. Numerous studies have been made over the last fifteen years of 'education and race', and more recently some research has been carried out on post-school experiences and entry into the labour market. In addition some work on the complex links between the experience of schooling and the early experiences of the labour market and unemployment has produced some interesting results, particularly about differential patterns of job search, distribution of unemployment and participation in higher education and youth training schemes (Dex 1982, Troyna and Smith 1983).

It would be fair to say, however, that little critical research has been undertaken on how responses to the 'problems' faced by black youth have become increasingly politicised, i.e. subject to central and local government decision-making processes, and on the social construction of political discourses and debates about the 'crisis of black youth'. A recent Home Office report, which provides an overview of the issues covered by research on race since the 1960s, notes that the political dimension is the least developed (Mair and Stevens 1982). Apart from a number of recent studies that have looked specifically at the question of the police and black youth, the dominant concern of researchers has been with the subcultural, identity and family aspects of being young and black in contemporary Britain. The dominance of this approach can be traced back to the early stages of both academic and policy debates over the future of the 'second generation of immigrants' or 'black British'. As Fisher and Joshua argue:

> In order that black youth might be sociologically, that is 'scientifically', explained, first a recognisable social group had to be identified and isolated. This isolating/explanatory process, however, rather than an exercise in even conventional academic rationale and method, demonstrated from its very beginnings a greater empathy with the social formulations, concerns and designs of the body politic. In short, that body of sociological literature purporting to deal with black youth was not primarily informed by any overwhelming desire to document and order the myriad of situations and strategies applicable to the black second generation. Instead, by far the more discernible were the influences of successive crises posed by young blacks and the corresponding social and moral panic of the state; both instructed by the problem orientated sociology associated with the first generation colonial immigration.
> (1982;p. 131)

This tendency to look at the 'second generation' through a problem-oriented framework did not, of course, take shape in a vacuum, as has been shown above. The period since the mid-1960s has seen a number of fundamental changes in the organisation of race relations institutions in the role of central and local government departments and in the images that policy-makers have of the various social groupings composing the black communities in Britain. All of these fundamental changes have fed into debates about the 'second generation', not least because over this period this group has increasingly come to be seen as a test case of the success of 'good race-relations policies'. Moreover, as Fisher and Joshua correctly note, the various social and moral panics generated by young blacks over the last two decades have shaped and in turn been shaped by general policies on race, law and order and social welfare (1982;pp. 132–33).

In the same way that 'race' was invested with specific images implying both social conflict and cultural difference, the categories of 'second generation' or 'black youth' have been used as shorthand to signify a number of fixed social attributes that are then translated into immutable collective qualities: e.g. alienation, despair, criminality, school under-achievers, unemployable, muggers (John 1981:pp 155–56). In addition there has been a tendency to see such attributes, which have often been based more on guesswork than on research findings (Troyna and Smith 1983), as the basis for seeing the object of state policies as being one of rendering young blacks themselves subjectively different rather than transforming the conditions under which they live.

This perception of young blacks as a problem category, whether in terms of social policy or law and order, coexisted with a number of stereotypes of the supposed attitudes or values of the 'second generation', particularly young West Indians. Throughout the 1970s, for example, the commonest stereotypes of young West Indians were ones that perceived them as 'having a chip on their shoulder', as having no firm cultural roots, as having unrealistic job aspirations and as being alienated from the school system and academic values (Fisher and Joshua 1982, Field 1984). From such stereotypes there developed more general images of young West Indians as 'alienated' or 'at risk' of drifting into a tangle of pathology centred upon homelessness and a criminalised subculture. While some or all of these statements may be true of a small minority of young West Indians, the tendency through the 1960s and 1970s was to construct these mythological pictures as true for the 'typical' young black. In addition, while such stereotypes did not underlie policy in any precise way, they provided its background and selective problem framework.

These shorthand images of young blacks' 'deviant behaviour', and the popular media concern with subcultural grouping among young Afro-Caribbeans, have produced a number of studies of Rastafarianism and cultural politics (Hebdige 1976, Cashmore 1979), the involvement of specific groups of young blacks in sport (Cashmore 1982) and their involvement in subcultural forms of social expression and activity more generally (Brake 1980). Yet, despite the mounting evidence that the state's role in the development of specific ideologies about the 'crisis of black youth' has been crucial, this is perhaps the one area on which little research has been done. The preoccupation with ethnographic research on cultural and everday lifestyle patterns has tended to push research in the direction of looking at local communities and the position of youth within them, rather than analysing the political dimension or the role of the state in shaping the lives of young blacks. The one notable exception is the studies dealing with the mugging scare of the early 1970s, and more broadly with the emergence of confrontations between young blacks and the police as a general phenomenon in inner-city areas (Hall *et al.* 1978, Roberts 1982).

More recently Gilroy has attempted to develop this analysis in order to consider the more contemporary developments in police and popular ideologies about black youth and crime, and to insist on the political meaning of cultural forms such as Rastafarianism and black music (1982a, 1982b). Gilroy argues that in practice young blacks are categorised as a 'law and order' or a 'social' problem twice over: first through the institutionally racialist practices within schools and the labour market; second by the ways in which government agencies and the police define them as criminal, disruptive or violent. The development of policies towards young blacks, according to Gilroy, can be understood only if these twin processes of exclusion are analysed according to their concrete functioning over the last decades. In other words, it is important to link the current location of young blacks in the labour market to the complex economic, social and political processes that have served to categorise black youth as a specific problem for the state.

It is to these issues that the rest of this section is devoted. In particular attention will be focussed on (1) the historical background to the black youth question, (2) the categorisation of blacks as criminal and violent, (3) the categorisation of the 'special problems' of the young black unemployed and (4) the processing of

127

the black youth unemployment issue in the aftermath of the
1980–81 'riots'.

The 'second generation' and the future of race relations

The impulse for the first government initiatives towards the
'problems' faced by young blacks, can be seen as the outcome of a
number of pressures that grew apace during the 1960s and early
1970s. Apart from the politicisation of race at both local and
national levels, which has been briefly discussed above, these
factors were: (a) a fear that the 'second generation' would become
alienated from the dominant institutions and pose a political
threat; (b) a perception that relatively high levels of unemployment among young blacks were related to their differential
attitudes to the labour market and poor results in schools; (c) a view
of the 'second generation' as caught between two (sometimes)
conflicting realities, and in need of 'special' help in order to adjust
to the realities of their life in contemporary Britain.

The fear that the 'second generation' represented a kind of social
time-bomb that needed to be defused through positive action can
be located as a theme in government thinking from the 1960s
onwards, although it gained popular currency in the aftermath of
the mugging scare of the early 1970s. A combination of fears about
increasing youth violence in inner-city areas and the example of
race riots in United States cities during the mid-1960s provided the
impetus for both policy-makers and social scientists to single out
second-generation blacks as a potential destablising factor. In
addition the stereotype of the young black as enmeshed in a cycle of
poverty, cultural conflict and homelessness/unemployment was
beginning to take shape and exercise a certain influence on
political debate and the presentation of the 'second-generation'
issue in the mass media. As early as 1967 Roy Jenkins, then Home
Secretary, warned:

> The next generation . . . will expect full opportunities to deploy
> their skills. If we frustrate those expectations we shall not only be
> subjecting our own economy to the most grievous self-inflicted
> wound, but we shall irreparably damage the quality of life in our
> own society by creating an American-type situation in which an
> indigenous minority which is no longer an immigrant group feels
> itself discriminated against on the grounds of colour alone. One of
> the most striking lessons we can draw from experience in the United
> States is that once this has been allowed to happen even the most
> enlightened and determined government and voluntary action

cannot arrest outbreaks of racial violence . . . what we must ask ourselves, therefore, is whether the action we have so far taken is sufficient to avoid these possible dangers.

(Jenkins 1967:p. 216).

This was a theme also followed up in the influential report on *Colour and Citizenship* published by the Institute of Race Relations in 1969, and by the Select Committee on Race Relations and Immigration report on *The Problems of Coloured School Leavers* published in the same year. It was also a theme that recurred in political debate over this period and received some coverage in the media. The Select Committee report, apart from reaffirming the analysis offered by Jenkins, also warned that 'the second generation may be less patient in surmounting difficulties that confront them than their parents have been' (1969;p. 6). Given this climate of opinion it is not surprising that a prominent social scientist was moved to argue; 'The most obvious question to ask about the Black British is: will they revolt?' (Halsey 1970;p. 472).

The warning by the Select Committee that 'the second generation may be less patient' was related to another commonly held view that the aspirations of black school-leavers were too high, particularly in relation to jobs. An early study by Beetham (1967) argued that West Indian and Asian boys had rather higher aims and expectations than white school-leavers, and a limited number of specific jobs (e.g. engineering and work as an electrician) were mentioned by them as desired jobs. Beetham concluded that their aspirations were 'unrealistic'. This view of young blacks as suffering from 'unrealistic aspirations' exercised some influence on the views of policy-makers and in the practices of the agencies directly concerned with minority youth as a client group, e.g. the careers service, the youth service educationalists. Indirectly it also came to serve the function of providing a rationalisation as to why young blacks were more likely to be unemployed. The aforementioned Select Committee report accepted the implication of this argument about the 'second generation', by saying that 'so long as they are unwilling to consider other jobs, they are likely to miss opportunities of suitable employment and remain unemployed'.

The contradictions of this argument, and its possible dangers, were pointed out by a number of authors (Allen 1969, Nandy 1969). In particular, as Allen (1969) warned such a formulation could easily be transformed into a legitimation for ignoring the discrimination and racism that stopped young blacks from

129

entering the labour market on an equal basis. In addition there is little research-based evidence to suport the unrealistic aspirations model (Gaskell and Smith 1981, DES 1983). More importantly, as Nandy (1969) points out, any assessment of what constitutes 'unrealistic aspirations' cannot be seen as value-free or free of racist stereotypes about what is good for young blacks to aspire to. Despite these warnings, however, the 'unrealistic aspirations' argument remains part of the policy debate within the Manpower Services Commission, which has increasingly taken the leading role in managing the question of youth unemployment (MSC/CRE 1979).

The third influence on early responses to the black youth question was the view that the essence of the problem was a disjunction between minority cultures and British culture, which was seen as resulting in either the devaluation of the basis of minority cultures or their modification by Western influences. This in turn has led to the application of common-sense notions of 'culture conflict' and 'identity crisis' to describe the everyday experiences of being young and black in contemporary Britain. In part these views help explain why there has been an identifiable concern to remedy the 'identity problems' of specific groups of young blacks, e.g. Rastafarians, homeless youngsters and young Asian girls. Miles (1978), among others, has persuasively criticised the tenability of any notion of 'cultural conflict' that assumes minority cultures are somehow inferior to the majority culture. The ubiquitous usage of such notions in policy documents testifies to their broad influence, although there are indications that there is a growing awareness tht such ideas can in fact help undermine the self-concepts of minority youth rather than stregthen them. The CRE's document on *Youth in Multi-Racial Society*, for example, argued:

> It is sometimes easy for those in authority to regard young people as 'the problem'. To do so is to confuse cause and effect. The real 'problem' lies in the inadequacies of society and the inability to respond to the needs and challenges of new generations of young people – especially those with different ethnic backgrounds, colour and/or culture.
>
> (1980;p. 10)

Warnings such as this one apart, the influence exercised by notions of cultural conflict has remained strong. As will be argued later in this chapter, such notions remain influential partly because of their ambiguity and the use they make of common-sense images of young blacks as a 'problem' to be remedied by ameliorative and social control measures. But what is important to emphasise in this context is that from the very earliest stages of official concern about the 'second generation' the fear that this grouping represented a kind of social time-bomb exercised an important influence on the perceptions of policy-makers.

Street crime, urban violence and black political action
Whatever the contradictions apparent in the ideology of the second generation as a social problem, its component elements exercised a major influence on how the public and policy debates on the fate of young blacks were structured throughout the 1970s. Much as general policy initiatives on race were infused with some notion that either immigration or race relations were a special problem, the early concerns with the second generation were preoccupied by the need to define the problems with which they were associated. Mythological pictures were formed around these problem situations, which in turn informed policy indirectly and were then amplified further by the public debates following such initiatives. A good example of how this process worked was the focussing of public concern in the early 1970s around the supposed links between certain forms of street crime, particularly mugging, and sections of black youth in inner-city areas. Later on in the 1970s a similar development took place in relation to black youth unemployment, but it is to the mugging issue that we first turn.

As mentioned above, the history of the moral panic about black youth and mugging has been the focus of a number of important studies.[4] Hall *et al.* (1978), for example, have shown how the construction of black communities as problems was the ideological bedrock on which the black-youth urban-deprivation crime model of mugging was constructed during the 1970s. The image of the urban ghetto as the breeding ground for a culture of poverty, unemployment and crime came to dominate media coverage of race and youth. Mugging as a political phenomenon, according to Hall *et al.*, thus became associated with black youth, even when it took place in areas where they were a small minority of the total youth population:

> the three themes, subtly intertwined in the earlier treatment of 'mugging' were now fused into a single theme: crime, race and the ghetto. Accordingly, from this point onwards, the explanatory paradigms shift, bringing out more explicitly than before the social,

131

economic and structural preconditions of the black crime problem – and thus contributing the final link in the chain which fused
crime and racism with the crises.

(Hall *et al.* 1978:p. 329).

The institutional response from the police in areas like Notting
Hill, Brixton, Handsworth and Moss Side further accentuated the
stereotype that all black youth had a tendency to become street
criminals because they were part of a criminal subculture (Hebdige
1976). This in turn helped give further support to the notion that
that source of the problem lay in culture and attitude, with racism
and discrimination seen as playing only a subsidiary role (Clarke **et
al.** 1974).

This emphasis was partly the outcome of the earlier concern
with the second generation, but it was also linked with the
increasing confrontation between the police and groups of young
blacks in many urban areas. Gus John (1981) has demonstrated
how this process fitted in with successive stages of institutional
response to young blacks in British society, which have emobilised
images implying that they are both victims and a danger to social
order that should be contained and ghettoised:

> The state, the police, the media and race relations experts ascribe to
> young blacks certain collective qualities, e.g. alienated, vicious little
> criminals, muggers, disenchanted, unemployed, unmarried,
> mothers, truants, class-room wreckers, etc. The youth workers,
> community workers, counsellors and the rest start with these
> objective qualities as given, and intervene on the basis that through
> their operations they could render young blacks subjectively
> different, and make them people to whom those objective
> qualifications could no longer be applied. When this is done in
> collaboration with control agents themselves, as in police–com-
> munity liaison schemes, or instances in which professional blacks
> collaborate with schools in blaming black kids for their 'failure', it
> is interpreted as progress towards 'good community relations'.
>
> (P. 155)

Although it could be argued that other images of young blacks
have been used by various agencies, apart from those identified by
John, there are two important elements of his account that help
make sense of how the various responses to 'problems' faced by
young blacks have become part of the process of discrimination
against them, however well intentioned they may have been.

The first, and perhaps most important, element is the ascription
to young blacks of certain immutable collective qualities, which

are then transformed into taken-for-granted common-sense notions by policy-makers and officials working in control agencies. A good example of this type of ascription is represented by the way in which the 'second-generation' theme developed during the 1960s out of imprecise notions about 'disadvantage', 'social handicap' and the 'threat of violence'. Another is the response to 'black mugging' and unemployment through the adoption of police-crime-control and social-problem perspectives in relation to policy formation.

The second element, which in a sense grows out of the first, is the tendency on the part of government to intervene on the basis that through their operations they could render young blacks subjectively different. Because group deviance from the norm is defined as the problem, an inbuilt tendency exists for government agencies to seek causal explanations of the problems faced by young blacks through reference to cultural and group inadequacies that could be overcome by ameliorative actions. A pathology of the group and the individual predominates over a pathology of institutions, in the sense that the 'problems' that policies are supposed to remedy are personalised or attributed to 'cultural differences'.

The fusion of images of race, crime and the ghetto around personalised images of black deviance seemed to link the concerns of central government with the ideologies of the police at the local level, which increasingly come to see young blacks from a problem-oriented perspective. In the mid-1970s the Home Office, through its Research Unit, was expressing worries about the 'alienation' of young blacks from the 'values of majority society', and plans were put into operation for research to show the extent of such disaffection and to propose possible remedies aimed at avoiding future social disorder.[5] Similar fears were expressed through the 1970s, and were given some support from the emergence of evidence that young blacks in localities such as Brixton, Handsworth and Toxteth were between twice and four times as likely to be unemployed as young whites from a similar background (Brooks 1983). Within this broader context rising unemployment came to symbolise more specific fears about the future of young blacks in British society.

Racial disadvantage, mass unemployment and 'special needs'
The emergence of black youth unemployment on to the political agenda during the late 1970s was particularly traumatic because it

133

coincided with (a) the broader crisis of the post-war full employment consensus and (b) the collapse of the youth labour market. It is against this background that public and policy debates focussed on the issue of rising unemployment among young blacks as a possible cause of future urban unrest and opposition to the forces of law and order. In addition, however, the rise of unemployment among young blacks became an issue that attracted much attention from within the black communities, leading to pressures on the government to take some initiative to remedy the situation.

According to Moon (1983) youth unemployment became a major issue precisely because it emerged as a political problem during the mid-1970s. Certainly during the period after 1975 the issue of the young unemployed came to occupy a disproportionate amount of public attention, both in Parliament and in the media. This was not simply because young people were disproportionately affected by the rise in unemployment. It was largely because of the political and social attributes that were attached to the young unemployed, and the over-arching fear that the growing numbers of unemployed and 'never employed' youngsters in inner-city areas could become a source of political instability. Media coverage of youth unemployment during this period, for example, emphasised linkages between the young unemployed and violence, crime and political extremism of both the left and right (Mungham 1982, Loney 1983, Pearson 1983).

To these fears about the young unemployed generally were added the fears about specific sections of youth becoming increasingly alienated from the dominant values of society. Given the history of official reactions to young blacks from the late 1960s onwards it is not surprising that by the late 1970s they were increasingly seen as a very problematic category. Reports dating from the mid-1970s onwards about young blacks were increasingly dominated by the question of unemployment.[6] Black youth thus became a cause of concern for both the 'race relations industry' (Fisher and Joshua 1982) and the 'unemployment industry' (Moon and Richardson 1984). For example, during 1978–9 both the Commission for Racial Equality and the Manpower Services Commission began to show interest in the question of the 'special needs' of the 'ethnic-minority young', leading to a joint report produced by a working group briefed to look into the question of how the unemployment services could best respond to the needs of minorities in relation to youth training (MSC/CRE 1979). This report, along with others produced during this period, carried the warning that there was a danger of young blacks becoming a group apart from society, and in addition becoming increasingly politicised. The fear was, as one report from this period expressed it, that such a development would 'pose the sort of problem for our society for which we have no solutions other than firm control' (quoted in John 1981;p. 152).

It was during this period that a number of common-sense assumptions were articulated about the inadequacies of young blacks, which needed to be remedied by the state. The common thread that runs throughout these assumptions is the notion that young blacks were a 'special group' that has 'special problems'. One element of these problems is racial discrimination, or according to official language 'racial disadvantage'. But in the context of the overall 'complex of racial disadvantage' discrimi-nationn was defined as only one factor among many, including lack of skills, educational disadvantage, language problems and newness, residence in inner-city areas. It is on these broader categories of 'needs' and 'problems' that attention was focussed during the late 1970s, since the question of discrimination was seen as something to be dealt with by anti-discrimination legislation.

The articulation of the ideology of the 'special needs' of the young black unemployed thus involved an attempt to locate two levels of 'disadvantage': first, that type of 'unequal access' resulting from discrimination or the location of blacks in inner-city deprived areas; second, that type of 'special problem' resulting from the cultural background or personal characteristics of young blacks. During the late 1960s and early 1970s this dual framework resulted in numerous attempts to define the 'special needs' of young blacks and to develop remedial measures to cater for these needs. It also resulted in a sometimes uneasy balance between a 'race-blind' and a 'colour-conscious' approach to the question, which to some extent continues until today. A good example of this tension is the following argument from an MSC document reviewing its services:

> The needs of the ethnic minority unemployed are related partly to their having a relatively greater share of certain characteristics than the general population (e.g. more young people, unskilled) and partly to problems specific to the ethnic minorities (language skills, educational disadvantage, racial discrimination). The first type of disadvantage can be alleviated by services available to the unemployed generally . . . The second type of disadvantage requires

measures specifically geared to the needs and problems of this group.

MSC 1981: parag. 3.24).

Around the same time as this report the special needs ideology was also being applied to the disabled, educationally disadvantaged, young people with a criminal record and other 'handicapped' youngsters. The argument was that such groups required remedial attention in order to allow them to benefit equally from existing services.

In this way the emergence of black youth unemployment as a policy issue was linked by notions of 'disadvantage' and 'handicap' to the cruder idea that it was not so much the system that was the problem – since young blacks themselves had failed and required remedial action to help them catch up. Just as in educational ideologies the notion of 'compensatory education' relied on the notion that those who failed educationally needed remedial help, so the special needs ideology saw minority groups as having 'failed' because of personal or cultural inadequacies.

The 1980–81 riots, Scarman and youth unemployment

The events in Bristol, Brixton and Toxteth (among other inner-city areas) during 1980 and 1981 added a further spur to the politicisation of black youth unemployment. Even though there was much dispute about whether the 'riots' could be linked to high levels of unemployment, there seems no doubt that they had an important influence on how young blacks were perceived by the state and by the agencies of the unemployment industry. This influence was partly direct, as in the case of the immediate reponses to the riots, which linked the riots to social deprivation and high levels of unemployment (Benyon 1984:pp. 163ff). But this politicisation was also achieved indirectly through the increasing concern of the Manpower Services Commission and other components of the unemployment industry with the question of so-called 'ethnic-minority youth'.

During the height of the riots in Brixton, Mrs Thatcher defended her government against charges that the riots were linked to increased poverty and unemployment brought about by her policies by arguing that 'nothing that has happened in unemployment would justify those riots'; she justified this by reference to the role of agitators and subversive elements in places such as Brixton and Toxteth ((*Financial Times* 1981). Similar denials by Mrs Thatcher were issued during the events of July 1981, which spread over the major urban conurbations in England (see, for example, Hansard, 7 July 1981; cols. 260–62). In addition, even in the aftermath of the Scarman Report, which linked the Brixton events to a wider structure of racial disadvantage, there was a notable reluctance to link the riots to unemployment as such. This was due, no doubt, to the Thatcher administration's fears that wide public concern with unemployment could damage support for its policies on inflation and economic rationalisation.

Such denials notwithstanding, the role of the young unemployed in the riots did become a major issue in media debates about the events, and even within the limits of his brief Lord Scarman felt moved to comment about the 'wider social context' in which the events in Brixton had to be located (see Benyon 1984). Moreover, it is interesting to note that the degree of public attention given to the youth unemployment issue increased drastically in the aftermath of 1981 (Solomos 1985). This trend was even clearer in relation to the young black unemployed, who were singled out as the leading edge behind the riots in Bristol, Brixton, Toxteth, Birmingham and other centres (MSC 1982:para. 5.20).

Perhaps one way of encapsulating the change is to be found in the marked increase in the public and media debate about unemployment among young blacks. While the theme of youth unemployment had been a constant reference point in debates about the social context of unemployment, it was only in the aftermath of the riots that widespread media attention was given to the 'double disadvantage' suffered by young blacks.

More important, perhaps, are the changes in policy emphasis and orientation that took place in the aftermath of 1981. Such changes were clearest in relation to the policy issues, but important shifts also took place within those agencies charged with helping the unemployed or with 'helping' to better integrate blacks within British society. In relation to the Manpower Services Commission, the main government agency charged with managing the unemployment issue, the riots pushed it to adopt (a) a higher profile on the 'special needs' of the black unemployed and (b) a commitment to equal opportunity as part of its objectives (MSC Special Programmes Division 1982, MSC Youth Training Board 1983). Since 1981 also, the Commission for Racial Equality has placed much more importance on the question of youth, and has intervened a number of times in debates about youth unemployment to ensure that adequate provisions were made for the black unemployed. It is difficult to imagine that either the MSC or the

137

CRE would have adopted such a high profile had it not been for the disturbances during 1980 and 1981.

Equally, however, it is important not to equate changes at the formal level with real change in the material conditions that confront young blacks in the labour market. The MSC has stated, for example, that it will continue to make its services available to all, 'regardless of sex or ethnic origin', but that it sees the need for the Youth Training Scheme to play a role in 'ensuring that an ethnic minority school-leaver's first taste of the world of work is in every way possible as satisfactory as that of other school-leavers' and in 'ameliorating the disadvantages' that young unemployed blacks face (MSC Youth Training Board 1983, 1984). Moreover the Commission's annual reports of 1981-2 and 1982-3, which reflect the direct impact of the events of 1980-81, include important references to the 'particular labour market needs' of ethnic minorities and fretting calls for more attention to be paid to those needs (MSC 1982, 1983). At the same time, the MSC has forcefully rejected attempts to move in the direction of positive action to overcome the effects of past discrimination, or attempts to make receipt of MSC grants conditional upon the implementation of an equal opportunity policy. It also has maintained a clear connection between the new equal opportunity stance and the established view of black deficiency as an important explanation of high levels of black unemployment.

The clearest example of this continuity is the manner in which equal opportunity is defined as 'meeting the needs of young people from the ethnic minorities' (MSC Youth Training Board 1983). Given this perspective the 'problems' that have to be overcome are located at the level of the black unemployed, since it is they who have to be helped to compete equally with their white counterparts. This has the effect of removing from serious consideration the issue of racism, and also creates the impression that any inequality in the labour market or in training schemes between black and white is the result of the attributes of those who lose out; it is after all they who have to be helped to adjust.

To summarise: the policy impact of the 1980-81 riots has been more at the level of rhetoric than reality on at least two counts: (1) the promise of measures to bring about equality of opportunity has not been matched by action; (2) the shift towards the ideology of special needs has not been accompanied by a break from the deficiency explanations of black youth unemployment. What of the future? It is to this issue that we now turn.

138

Schooling, black youth unemployment and the recession

The substance of the argument developed so far in this chapter can be summarised as saying (a) that a central theme of state interventions to 'help' the young black unemployed has been to conceptualise their higher levels of unemployment in terms of notions that amount to 'blaming the victim', and (b) that state interventions have done little to put into practice the promise of 'equality of opportunity' underlying their public policy agenda.

In some respects these arguments can be extended to cover state interventions towards the young unemployed as a whole. Indeed, this is the point made forcefully by Loney in a recent paper arguing that there is an inherent tendency for supply side interventions in the labour market to 'blame the victim' for being unemployed:

> Governments who are reluctant to change the way in which the economy is run, and who lack policies for economic growth, naturally welcome the idea that what is at fault is not the socio-economic system but the individuals who are its victims. If we can tackle youth unemployment by retraining youth, and giving them work experience, then why tamper with the existing mechanisms for distributing wealth and opportunities?
>
> (Loney 1983:p. 30).

While there is a danger of over-generalising this point, to the extent of seeing all types of state intervention as manipulative attempts to 'blame the victim', there does seem to be an inbuilt tendency within current thinking to conceptualise 'training' as a kind of solution to unemployment. This in turn supports the mythology that there are in fact jobs waiting for those who are suitably trained or willing to take them.[7]

Because they are already categorised as a 'problem group', as a result of being black and 'culturally different', young blacks are doubly affected by these ideologies that blame unemployment on the social and skill characteristics of those who are unemployed. The context of recessionary policies and economic restructuring puts extra pressure on those groups that suffer most from unemployment, especially when associated with the neo-conservative policies of the Thatcher administration since 1979. Just as the current administration blames unemployment on those who are unemployed or on the workings of the international economic system, so it sees unemployment among the young or among minorities as rooted in their conditions and specific characteristics.

Given the background of the last decade, what are the prospects for the young black unemployed in the current situation? More specifically, is it possible to foresee any radical change for the better or will the pursuit of current initiatives lead to the reproduction of the inequalities in employment chances that characterise the present? In broad outline, there seems to be three main reasons why change is likely to be limited short of radical changes in political priorities: (1) the symbolic and tokenistic nature of the intiatives undertaken in relation to the problems that young blacks face; (2) the limitations of equal opportunity polices that result from the recession and the collapse of the labour market; (3) the failure to link changes in training policy to the overall reorganisation of the education system and the youth labour market. Although it is not possible to discuss all these issues in detail, some comments are necessary about each of them.

Symbolic regulation and the structures of racism

The major limit on the effectiveness of measures to deal with black youth unemployment is the failure to combine measures for 'equal opportunity' in training with a concerted effort to challenge the operation of racial discriminiation at all levels of the labour market. As argued above, this is partly because there has been a tendency to see policies for equal opportunity as separate from the overall struggle against racism. But it is also, and perhaps more importantly, the outcome of a failure to distinguish questions about racism from common-sense ideologies about the personal and cultural handicaps of young blacks.

As a result of this confusion the objective of providing 'training' for young blacks has been detached from the question of having to deal with actual high youth unemployment levels among blacks and other disadvantaged groups. This separation was reflected most clearly in the efforts by the Conservative government during the riots of 1980–81 to help young blacks overcome 'unreasonable barriers', while insisting that the policy of producing a 'strong economy' (which in turn resulted in higher levels of unemployment) would 'benefit the ethnic minorities' (see Whitelaw 1980, Benyon 19884). Such a distinction served to explain black unemployment as resulting partly from 'unreasonable barriers' (which could be controlled by government) but largely from the absence of a 'strong economy' (which was beyond the boundaries of political control).

This detachment of 'special training measures' to help young blacks from a policy on jobs has resulted in largely symbolic measures that tackle black youth unemployment in tokenistic terms. Because it is the lack of a 'strong economy' that produces too few jobs then the most that can be done for the young unemployed is to train them to compete more effectively for existing jobs. Thus the whole question of why there are too few jobs or too few opportunities for particular groups has been politicised in a specific way. It has been transformed into a question of the inadequacies of the unemployed or the 'unreasonable barriers' that hinder the free functioning of the market economy, and the focus has been placed on 'training' rather than economic expansion or job creation.

Equality of opportunity and the context of the recession

The vast difference between the discriminatory processes facing young blacks and the largely symbolic measures taken to 'help' them has produced a contradictory situation. On the one hand the role of agencies such as the Manpower Services Commission in 'helping' young blacks meet their 'special needs' has achieved a higher profile over the last five years. On the other hand the deepening of the recession has further undermined the effectiveness of equal opportunity measures, and widened the divide between the rhetoric and reality of government interventions to achieve greater equality of access to jobs for young blacks.

The massive task facing any radical strategy against racial inequality in the youth labor market has been further accentuated by the stark decline of employment opportunitites for young blacks in inner-city areas (Richardson 1983), and by the reproduction of discriminatory recruitment practices (Lee and Wrench 1983). According to Rhodes and Braham (1981), during a period of recession and overall decline in employment opportunities black workers are likely to be disadvantaged because: (a) they occupy jobs in industries that are most likely to be affected by closures and restructuring; (b) discriminatory practices are likely to increase in a period of recession; (c) the 'colour-blind' consequences of a changing economic climate and of government economic policy will outweigh the 'colour-conscious' effects of equal opportunity policies. In these circumstances the basic issue is not the so-called 'special needs' of young blacks or ameliorative training to increase their 'employability'. On the contrary, the question of how to overcome structural and conscious forms of racial discrimination in relation to employment is the key issue. This is also precisely the question that policies over the last decade, or more, have not addressed.

141

Because these issues have been inadequately addressed it is difficult not to see that while promising 'equality of access' the majority of schemes offering training do not lead to any jobs. This is true for white youth, but doubly so for young blacks in declining and de-industrialised inner-city areas. It is not surprising that a reasoned study of the period after the 1980–81 riots concluded that 'from the streets of Brixton and Toxteth, the new intiatives look like old wine in new bottles' (Roberts 1984:p.182).

Against this background, the changing pattern of industrial restructuring and unemployment during the past decade represents a fundamental barrier to equal opportunity, because no effort has been made to make sure that young blacks gain access to jobs rather than to training that leads nowhere. According to an important study emanating from research funded by the MSC there is at least a strong likelihood that this will not change as a result of the Youth Training Scheme (Fenton *et al.* 1984). As one critical study concluded: YTS thus seems unlikely to advance the position of . . . ethnic minority youth in the labour market (Fairley 1983–4:p. 49). We may be witnessing during the current recession the emergence of a strategy similar to the one pursued in the United States for the last three decades, whereby the state has made sure that resources are provided to keep young blacks off the streets and 'in contact', while doing little to solve the real problems they face in relation to employment, the police and other 'street-level bureaucrats'. Such a development may seem to create the image that change is actually taking place while masking the degree of continuity (and even deterioration) in the socio-economic standing of first- and second-generation blacks.

The educational system and the reproduction of racial inequality

The main thrust of the above account has emphasised the limits of policies that promise equal opportunity for young blacks while doing little to address the deep-seated inequalities reproducing racism in the labour market. Given this line of argument, what possible role can there be for anti-racist initiatives within the educational system? The relationship between school and work in the current recessionary context is a complex one, and one which has been the subject of a major debate (Solomos 1985). It would clearly be impossible to address all the complex dimensions of this issue in this chapter. But what I want to do here is reflect upon the question of how the educational system can help in transforming entrenched patterns of racism and discrimination.

A vast amount of research on the racialisation of educational policy has demonstrated that policies aimed at producing a more multicultural, 'multiracial' educational system cannot in themselves compensate for the racism of society as a whole (Troyna 1984, Williams 1984). In addition, it is also questionable whether equal opportunities policies within schools can help young blacks achieve more equal access within the youth labour market particularly since those young blacks who achieve some form of certification at school still suffer from discrimination in the transition from school to work (Jenkins and Troyna 1983).

Given the limits of 'multiculturalism' any co-ordinated strategy to tackle high levels of unemployment among the second- and third-generation blacks involves not only questions about training but, crucially, about the role of schooling in relation to the labour market. More specifically, there is a need to see measures to overcome racial inequality in the labour market as one dimension of a broader strategy to challenge racist practices as they affect the life chances of young blacks in British society. Ambiguous charter phrases such as 'multicultural education', 'equal opportunities' and 'anti-racist education' provide only a partial glimpse of the multiplicity of barriers faced by young blacks at all levels of the educational and employment processes. They do not capture the depth of the marginalisation they encounter at all levels of British society, and function more at the level of symbolic politics than concrete political change.

A more radical strategy for tackling the crisis facing young blacks in the labour market needs to situate the educational system as a core area for change but place it in the context of a broader anti-racist strategy. The danger, however, is that the obsessive concern with 'multicultural' or 'anti-racist' education in schools and 'training' in the post-school period may obfuscate the fundamental barrier confronting young blacks in both areas: namely, racism. Ths is not to deny the value of even limited initiatives to change attitudes to 'race' or to question common-sense stereotypes. But such initiatives cannot themselves transform the material and ideological relations that produce racism, least of all if they ignore the connections betwen the barriers that marginalise young blacks into a second-class position in the labour market and the processes that label them as 'criminal' or as 'culturally deficient'.

The question that must be addressed within the educational system is not principally 'How can education be made more multicultural?' but, 'What role can education play in challenging

143

the racist barriers inside and outside the school?' Within the current recession it would be naive to imagine that merely by improving the performance of black pupils in schools one also enhances their life chances. Rather, it becomes increasingly important to develop a more rounded view of the role of education in a broader alliance of struggles against racism. Such a shift of direction would in turn question the platitudes and mis-conceptions on which existing educational policies are based, and bring to the fore questions about racial inequality and how it is reproduced routinely in all the main institutions of British society.

Conclusion

The legacy of the past fifteen years of state intervention to 'help' young blacks improve their position in employment has served to remind us once again of the difficulty of effectively tackling racism and other forms of oppression without challenging the structural basis for their production and reproduction. The general argument of this chapter is that the changes brought about by policy intiatives have been both superficial and symbolic. It is clear, for example, that in a number of crucial policy areas in the broad field of 'race' (education, transition from shcool to work/unemployment, law and order) there has been a noticeable shift in the ideology and symbolic language used to legitimise state interventions: from a desire to achieve assimilation through a 'race-blind' approach to the stated objective of achieving integration through the ideology of 'special needs'. Yet it is also clear that in all these areas there is a mismatch between stated objectives and actual outcomes, with the prospects for black youngsters becoming even more bleak as a result of the recession (Rhodes and Braham 1981, Jenkins and Solomos, forthcoming).

The picture that this chapter has painted emphasises the limits of what has been achieved by policy initiatives over the last decade. Yet it would be too deterministic to argue that nothing can be achieved within the current socio-economic system to enhance the life chances of young blacks. Limited reforms can be achieved, and to some extent the impact of the 1980–81 riots would lend support to the argument that direct and unconventional forms of protest can achieve some kind of political pay-off. It must be recognised that policy initiatives to deal with social problems are not neutral bureaucratic programmes, but comprise an elaborate dialectical structure, reflecting the tensions, ideologies and ambivalence that flow from social inequality and conflicting interests. There is thus some possibility for pressures resulting from the actions of disadvantaged groups to produce changes in policy orientation (Dearlove and Saunders 1984, Offe 1984). But, as numerous studies have shown, 'in a capitalist society egalitarian goals are formal and rhetorical, while an inegalitarian social structure shapes implementing decisions'.[8]

Any successful strategy for overcoming racism and discrimination as it effects young blacks in the labour market must take as its starting point the following two points. First, the role of the state and political institutions in relation to the 'race question' over the last three decades cannot be understood as that of a neutral arbiter between contending interests. The political system is no more separate from the racist structures of British society than it is from the structures of social inequality. Second, the relative powerlessness of blacks as a political force must be overcome if there is to be a concerted campaign against racial inequality. The idea that blacks can be 'helped' from the top is both paternalistic and unrealistic in the context of an unequal distribution of power and socioeconomic resources.

The current recessionary situation requires drastic measures to prevent racial inequality from becoming more entrenched and divisive. The experience of the last decade provides massive evidence against any naive optimism, but the political and ideological struggle against racism remains a vital task for those interested in progressive social change in contemporary Britain. As this chapter has argued, however, such change will not be achieved through platitudes about equal opportunities and compensatory training, but by effective measures to tackle racism and unemployment as they affect young blacks and other sections of the black communities. The experience of the last decade indicates that such a radical shift in policy orientation is not going to come about without more effective political action to challenge racism at all levels of British society.

Notes

1 The first major investigation into the prospects of young blacks in the labour market was conducted by the Select Committee on Race Relations and Immigration during 1968–9. It has been a regular theme in debates about race relations in the last fifteen years, a trend analysed in some detail in Fisher and Joshua 1982, Solomos 1983a.

145

2 Examples of the coverage given to this issue in *Caribbean Times* (and other black weeklies such as *West Indian World* and *The Voice*) are numerous, and the coverage has steadily increased over the last two years.

3 This is an issue discussed in some detail in Gilroy 1982a, Gilroy and Sim 1985.

4 For an overview of this issue see (Gilroy 1982b, Roberts 1982, Gutzmore 1983.

5 In November 1977 the Research Unit proposed to the Home Office's Advisory Committee a study of the attitude of the ethnic minority young. The study was thought to be necessary because this group was seen as drifting away from the mainstream institutions of government, particularly in a context of rising unemployment and urban poverty. This proposal was made in the context of a climate of opinion that perceived the increasing numbers of unemployed young blacks as a possible danger to law and order.

6 To some extent this may be said to reflect the broader preoccupation with youth unemployment among the population as a whole. But there were also specific factors in relation to the 'race' question in mid-1970s Britain that influenced this situation. See Small 1983, Solomos 1983a.

7 Such ideologies have been a recurrent theme in discussions of unemployment in a number of countries. See Edelman 1977, Richardson and Henning 1984.

8 Edelman 1980; similar arguments about the specific case of youth unemployment have been made by Loney 1983.

References

Allen, S. (1969) 'School-Leavers: Problems of Method and Explanation' *Race Today*, October: pp. 235–7.

Bates, I. *et al.* (1984) *Schooling for the Dole? The New Vocationalism*, London, Macmillan.

Beetham, D. (1967) *Immigrant School Leavers and the Youth Unemployment Services in Birmingham*. London, Institute of Race Relations.

Benyon, J. (ed.) (1984) *Scarman and After*. Oxford, Pergamon.

Brake, M. (1980) *The Sociology of Youth Culture and Youth Subcultures*. London, Routledge & Kegan Paul.

Brooks, D. (1983) 'Young Blacks and Asians in the Labour Market', in Troyna and Smith (1983).

Brown, C. (1984) *Black and White Britain: The Third PSI Survey*. London, Heinemann.

Carby, H. (1982) 'Schooling in Babylon', in CCCS Race and Politics Group (1982).

Cashmore, E. (1979) *Rastaman*. London, Allen & Unwin.

  (1982) *Black Sportsmen*. London, Routledge & Kegan Paul.

CCCS Race and Politics Group (1982) *The Empire Strikes Back: Race and Racism in 70s Britain*. London, Hutchinson.
CEDEFOP (1982) 'Young Migrants: the "Less Equal" '. *Vocational Training* 10: pp. 18–49.
Clarke, J. *et al.* (1974) 'The Selection of Evidence and the Avoidance of Racialism: a critique of the Parliamentary Select Committee on Race Relations and Immigration'. *New Community* 3 (3): pp. 172–92.
Commission for Racial Equality (1980) *Youth in Multi-Racial Society*. London, CRE.
  (1983a) *Equal Opportunity, Positive Action and Young People*. London, CRE.
  (1983b) *Equal Opportunity and the Youth Training Scheme*. London, CRE.
Community Relations Commission (1974) *Unemployment and Homelessness*. London, CRC.
Cross, M. *et al.* (1983) *Ethnic Minorities: their Experience on YOP*. Sheffield, Manpower Services Commission.
Dearlove, J. and Saunders, P. (1984) *Introduction to British Politics*. Oxford, Polity Press.
Department of Education and Science (1983) *Young People in the Eighties*. London, HMSO.
Dex, S (1982) *Black and White School-Leavers: The First Five Years of Work*. Research Paper No. 33. London, Department of Employment.
Edelman, M. (1977) *Political Language: Words that Succeed and Policies that Fail*. New York, Academic Press.
  (1980) 'Systematic Confusions and the Evaluation of Implementing Decisions'. Unpublished paper.
Fairley, J. (1983–4) 'The YTS and Democracy'. *Youth and Policy* 2 (3): pp. 47–56.
Fenton, S. *et al.* (1984) *Ethnic Minorities and the Youth Training Scheme*. Research and Development Paper No. 20. Sheffield, Manpower Services Commission.
Fiddy, R. (ed.) (1983) *In Place of Work: Policy and Provision for the Young Unemployed*. Lewes, Falmer Press.
Field, S. (1984) *The Attitudes of Ethnic Minorities*. Home Office Research Study No. 8. London, HMSO.
Financial Times (1981) 'Thatcher Rejects Wider Terms for Riot Inquiry'. 15 April.
Fisher, G. and Joshua, H. (1982) 'Black Youth and Social Policy', in E. Cashmore and B. Troyna (eds.), *Black Youth in Crisis*. London, Allen & Unwin.
Freeman, G. P. (1979) *Immigrant Labor and Racial Conflict in Industrial Societies*. Princeton University Press.
Gaskell, G. and Smith, P. (1981) *Race and 'Alienated Youth': A Conceptual and Empirical Enquiry*. London School of Economics, Department of Social Psychology.

Gilroy, P. (1982a) 'Steppin' Out of Babylon – Race, Class and Autonomy', in CCCS Race and Politics Group (1982).

(1982b) 'The Myth of Black Criminality', in *Socialist Register 1982*. London, Merlin Press.

Gilroy, P. and Sim, J. (1985) 'Law, Order and the State of the Left'. *Capital and Class* 25: pp. 15–55.

Gleeson, D. (ed.) (1983) *Youth Training and the Search for Work*. London, Routledge & Kegan Paul.

Gutzmore, C. (1983) 'Capital, Black Youth and Crime'. *Race and Class* 25 (2): pp. 13–30.

Hall, S. *et al.* (1978) *Policing the Crisis: Mugging, the State and Law and Order*. London, Macmillan.

Halsey, A. H. (1979) 'Race Relations: the Lines to Think On'. *New Society*, 19 March: pp. 472–4.

Hebdige, D. (1976) 'Reggae, Rastas and Rudies: Style and the Subversion of Form', in S. Hall and T. Jefferson (eds.), *Resistance through Rituals*. London, Hutchinson.

Home Affairs Committee, Subcommittee on Race Relations and Immigration (1981) *Racial Disadvantage*. London, HMSO.

Jenkins, R. (1967) 'Address by the Home Secretary to the Institute'. *Race* 7 (3): pp. 215–21.

Jenkins, R. and Solomos, J. (eds.) (forthcoming) *Equal Opportunity and the Limits of the Law: Racism, Regulation and Employment*. Cambridge University Press.

Jenkins, R. and Troyna, B. (1983) 'Educational Myths and Labour Market Realities', in Troyna and Smith (1983).

John, G. (1981) *In the Service of Black Youth*. Leicester, National Associations of Youth Clubs.

Layton-Henry, Z. (1984) *The Politics of Race in Britain*. London, Allen & Unwin.

Lee, G. and Wrench, J. (1983) *Skill Seekers – Black Youth, Apprenticeships and Disadvantage. Leicester, National Youth Bureau*.

Loney, M. (1983) 'The Youth Opportunities Programme: Requiem and Rebirth', in Fiddy (1983).

Mair, G. and Stevens, P. (1982) *Abstracts of Race Relations Research*. Research and Planning Unit Paper No. 7. London, Home Office.

Manpower Services Commission (1981) *Review of Services for the Unemployed*. Sheffield, MSC.

(1982) *Annual Report 1981–2*. Sheffield, MSC.

(1983) *Annual Report 1982–3*. Sheffield, MSC.

(1984) *Corporate Plan 1984–8*. Sheffield, MSC.

Manpower Services Commission, Special Programmes Division (1982) *Special Client Groups*. Unpublished memo.

Manpower Services Commission, Training Services Division (1982) *TSD's Provision and Services for Ethnic Minorities: An Issues Paper*. Unpublished paper.

Manpower Services Commission, Youth Training Board (1983) *Equal Opportunities for Ethnic Minorities*. Unpublished paper.
(1984) *Equal Opportunities in the Youth Training Scheme*, Unpublished paper.

Manpower Services Commission and Commission for Racial Equality (1979) *Ethnic Minorities and the Special Programmes for the Unemployed*. London, MSC.

Miles, R. (1978) *Between Two Cultures? The Case of Rastafarianism*. Working Papers on Ethnic Relations No. 10. Birmingham, ESRC Research Unit on Ethnic Relations.

Miles, R. and Phizacklea, A. (1983) *White Man's Country: Racism in British Politics*. London, Pluto.

Moon, J. (1983) 'Policy Change in Direct Government Responses to UK Unemployment'. *Journal of Public Policy* 3 (3): pp. 301-30.

Moon, J. and Richardson, J. J. (1984) 'The Unemployment Industry'. *Policy and Politics* 12 (4): pp. 391-411.

Mungham, G. (1982) 'Workless Youth as a Moral Panic', in T. Rees and P. Atkinson (eds.), *Youth Unemployment and State Intervention*. London, Routledge & Kegan Paul.

Nandy, D. (1969) 'Unrealistic Aspirations'. *Race Today*, May: pp. 9-11.

Offe, C. (1984) *Contradictions of the Welfare State*. London, Hutchinson.

Pearson, G. (1983) *Hooligan: A History of Respectable Fears*. London, Macmillan.

Reeves, F. (1983) *British Racial Discourse*. Cambridge, Cambridge University Press.

Rex, J. and Tomlinson, S. (1979) *Colonial Immigrants in a British City*. London, Routledge & Kegan Paul.

Rhodes, E. and Braham, P. (1981) 'Black Workers in Britain: from Full Employment to Recession', in P. Braham *et al.* (eds.), *Discrimination and Disadvantage in Employment*. London, Harper & Row.

Richardson, J. and Henning, R. (1983) *Unemployment: Policy Responses of Western Democracies*. London, Sage.

Richardson, R. (1983) *Unemployment and the Inner City: A Study of School-Leavers in London*. London, Department of Environment.

Roberts, B. (1982) 'The Debate on "Sus" ', in E. Cashmore and B. Troyna (eds.), *Black Youth in Crisis*. London, Allen & Unwin.

Roberts, K. (1984) 'Youth Unemployment and Urban Unrest', in Benyon (1984).

Rose, E. J. B. *et al.* (1969) *Colour and Citizenship*. London, Oxford University Press.

Select Committee on Race Relations and Immigration (1969) *Problems of Coloured School-Leavers*. London, HMSO.

Small, S. (1983) 'Black Youth in England: Ethnic Identity in a White Society'. *Policy Studies* 4 (1): pp. 35-49.

Solomos, J. (1983a) *The Politics of Black Youth Unemployment*. Working Papers on Ethnic Relations No. 20. Birmingham, ESRC

Research Unit on Ethnic Relations.

(1983b) 'Black Youth Unemployment and Equal Opportunities Policies', in Troyna and Smith (1983).

(1985) 'Youth Training, Unemployment and State Policies'. *Sociological Review* 33 (2): pp. 343–353.

Troyna, B. (1984) 'Multicultural Education: Emancipation or Containment?' in L. Barton and S. Walker (eds.), *Social Crisis and Educational Research*. Beckenham, Croom Helm.

Troyna, B. and Smith, D. (eds.), (1983) *Racism, School and the Labour Market*. Leicester, National Youth Bureau.

Whitelaw, W. (1980) Speech to Birmingham Community Relations Council. 11 July. Birmingham.

Williams, J. (1984) *From Institutional Racism to Anti-Racism: The Relationships between Theories, Policies and Practices*. Unpublished MSc. thesis. Birmingham, University of Aston.

CHAPTER SEVEN

The Classification and Control of Vocational Training for Young People

Paul Atkinson, Hilary Dickinson and Michael Erben

Introduction

The following chapter will outline and discuss some possible analytic perspectives for the understanding of a number of contemporary vocational training programmes. Such programmes have emerged in response to youth unemployment and to a concern with the real or supposed inadequacies of traditional secondary-school curricula and traditional vocational training. (For recent collections containing descriptions of such developments see, *inter alia*, Eggleston 1982, Rees and Atkinson 1982, Gleeson 1983, Watson 1983.) In doing so we shall draw on recent work in the area of structuralist sociology and cultural reproduction. This perspective enables us to identify certain anomalous and contradictory features in vocational training programmes.

The rationale for such a task is twofold. On the one hand, there is need for analysis that provides sociological frameworks for a comparative understanding of these developments, and draws out their *formal* similarities and differences. On the other hand, the empirical focus of the chapter allows us to explore the possibilities of such formal models.

Classification and framing

We wish to invoke some of the insight to be gained from Basil

Bernstein's work on the classification and framing of educational knowledge (Bernstein 1971); the relevance for this approach to vocational curricula has been suggested elsewhere (Dickinson and Erben 1982). Here one is concerned not primarily with the content of educational experience but with its formal organisation. Bernstein's work is rooted firmly in a Durkheimian anthropology and a structuralist theory of knowledge (cf. Atkinson 1981, 1985, Manning 1982). Such a perspective is concerned with cultural domains of meaning, with the relationship between domains and the overlap – or absence of overlap – between them. Curriculum is portrayed as a formal arrangement whereby elements are separated out of the field of experience and combined in temporal, spatial and organisational arrangements within the socialising institution.

When classification is strong, then knowledge domains (e.g. school 'subjects') are tightly bounded by symbolic membranes, their contents clearly kept separate from one another, and there will be an emphasis on the 'purity' of such categories. There will likewise be clear demarcation between what is to be counted as 'proper' educational knowledge and the impure, 'profane' world of mundane experience. But when classification is weak, boundaries will be absent or highly permeable; subjects and disciplines will be intermingled and there will be much weaker membranes between the 'educational' and the 'extramural'. By the same token, when framing is strong, the selection, pacing and organisation of educational knowledge will be tightly bounded. That is, the agenda for pedagogic encounters will be tightly controlled. (The locus of control may vary from a central Ministry to the individual teacher. It may also be inscribed in the technology of teaching materials, apparatus and the like; this aspect will be developed later.) Where framing is weak, such matters will be more flexible and open to negotiation between teachers and taught.

Bernstein's conceptual framework is open to criticism on several counts. The main ideas are extremely abstract, general and diffuse. They are open to a wide range of interpretations, and empirical exemplification is not easy to establish. For the purposes of our argument here, however, we intend to gloss over these difficulties, and will take Bernstein's notions as heuristic sensitising devices rather than as definitive concepts. We shall argue that the value of Bernstein's approach lies in the analysis of change in the classification and framing of educational knowledge and in accounting for differences, tensions and contradictions both between and *within* curricula.

In Bernstein's original treatment of these themes – and in subsequent commentary – there is some ambiguity as to whether the theory is intended to capture features of everyday practice, or ideology, or both. Classification and framing potentially refer to 'theories' about knowledge and pedagogy, embodied in official syllabuses, public examinations, teacher-training programmes and so on. Equally they may refer to observed characteristics of curriculum and pedagogy in practice – at school or classroom level. In this chapter we shall draw on evidence relating to both levels of analysis, including official reports and recommendations, and the investigation of particular programmes in action. The applicability of Bernstein's analysis to both theory and practice is a virtue of his approach. No prior assumption should be made that the two are congruent. Indeed, it is a particular merit of the approach that it sensitises to the possibility of ambiguity and competing message systems within and between the two.

We take as the focus of our analysis the major curricular and institutional changes that have been taking place in recent years in order to confront the problem of youth unemployment, and the deficiencies (real or supposed) in traditional school curricula and methods of vocational training. We refer particularly to the New Training Initiative launched via three documents of this name in 1981 (a government White Paper and two publications from the Manpower Services Commission: Department of Employment 1981, Manpower Services Commission 1981a, 1981b) and in particular the proposal to introduce the Youth Training Scheme in 1983. Many of the methods of training – for example, training workshops – and curriculum innovations had precursors in the Youth Opportunities scheme (which YTS replaces) and in local initiatives; for example, training workshops or college-based vocational preparation schemes. There are also some striking similarities, as well as some interesting differences, in the major reforms being initiated in France arising from a government report of 1981 on the integration of young people into society and working life: the Schwartz Report (Schwartz 1981).

In order to explore possible tensions and contradictions we intend to focus in particular on situations where classification and frame vary independently; for example, strong classification and weak framing. Bernstein discusses this issue, but somewhat tentatively, and the main body of his work is concerned with overall variations between codes – classification and framing

153

changing together. The four possible associations are: strong classification and strong framing (+C+F), strong classification and weak framing (+C-F), weak classification and weak framing (-C-F) and weak classification and strong framing (-C+F). While it would be to pursue a chimera to expect to trace perfect correspondence between C and F in any particular curriculum, none the less striking contrasts between C and F suggest the presence of contradictory or ambiguous message systems, as would striking contrasts between boundary-maintaining systems in different elements of a curriculum or course of training. This is because the underlying cultural message systems of collection and integrated code are very different and imply a very different kind of engagement on the part of the learner. Under the diffusely bounded and negotiated integrated code the learner has, and must have, considerable autonomy. It may well be that the autonomy is enforced rather than chosen, the outcome of an individualised and interpersonal socialisation pattern, but the result is that the learner must take responsibility for his/her own learning is imposed on the learner, with or without his/her co-operation.

We make the observation that curricula clearly exhibiting weakened boundary maintenance fall into two categories. There are those where both aspects of boundary maintenance are weakened (-C-F) and where the control of the learner over what is to be learned is present. Dissertations and projects at under-graduate and graduate level are in this category (Walford 1981). For younger age groups such curricula are hard to point to with certainty. Possibly the curriculum at Summerhill (at least in the years before formal examinations) is rare in being clearly open. What characterises these curricula is that they exhibit weak boundaries for both C and F, and that they are curricula that maintain their recipients on the route to academic success. The second category of curricula exhibiting weakened boundaries – and it is these on which we focus here – are for people on the margins of the educational field, the failures and potential failures. A further characteristic of such curricula is that, though accompanied by a rhetoric leading one to expect -C and -F, their realisation indicates that the framing is not weak from the learner's point of view. There is tight control over selection and pacing of material by the teachers.

In his 1977 paper Bernstein extends the discussion of knowledge codes, previously confined to schooling, into the sphere of production. He notes that the code of production is typically that of very strong external control over the worker (++C++F) and also notes the contradiction that educational provision for those destined for the lowest, and most closely controlled, levels in the work-force has shown a tendency to weakening of C and F. However, with the introduction since the late 1970s of the curricula that we discuss here (YOP, YTS, community- and college-based training workshops and vocational preparation courses) this weakening of boundaries has been apparent in vocationally oriented training programmes. Traditional vocational training courses have been emphatically +C+F. City and Guilds craft courses exemplify strong boundary maintenance. Curricula for the newer TEC and BEC courses (now amalgamated as B/TEC) showed a clear intention to modify boundary maintenance at least at the level of content (C), although this intention has not always been realised in practice.

The context of curriculum innovation for vocational education - a comparison with France

The context and wider intentions of curriculum innovation for the vocational training of young people have a bearing on the curriculum as implemented. We wish here to look at the wider aims of curricula reform and the structures proposed to realise them in France as well as the UK. A systematic comparison is not intended; rather, the French proposals are used to highlight absences in the British context.

Government intentions in this field in both countries since 1981, and before, show considerable similarity both in perceived problems and needs and in the solutions proposed. But there are also important differences. The principal sources of information for the UK that we draw on are the three New Training Initiative (NTI) documents already referred to. Our particular focus is the Youth Training Scheme, which is only one part of the NTI. The other two concern the reform of apprenticeship and adult training and retraining. In addition to the NTI documents the Further Education Unit (FEU) publications give more detailed guidance on how the aims of YTS may be implemented. The most important source of information in France is the Schwartz Report (Schwartz 1981). In these documents both governments initiated proposals for major changes in the vocational training of young people at about the same time, and in response to similar perceived problems: unemployment, particularly youth unemployment; problems of technological change and the difficulty of relating vocational training to such change; and the deficiencies in the education that young people had received to date.

There are important similarities in many of the curricular changes proposed. The most important of these similarities are that:

(1) planned work experience should form part of all vocational training, and that this planned work experience should be more systematically related to off-the-job training than has been the case;

(2) both work experience and off-the-job training should be more flexible and continually related to the needs of individual learners – the principle of *negotiation*;

(3) work experience should introduce the learner to the whole context of the work-place, rather than be related to a single skill;

(4) assessment and certification should be more flexible and more closely related to the needs of individual learners and to the tasks they are actually performing than has been the case with traditional modes of industrial training.

These are moves that would have the effect of blurring boundaries – between work experience and off-the-job training, between different kinds of skills and between the actual skills a learner may have to acquire and formal qualifications.

There are at least two important differences between the French and the British proposals. These relate first to the emphasis in each country given to the general education and social welfare needs of young people on the one hand and to industrial requirements on the other hand; and secondly to the kind of qualification to be conferred.

The differences between the respective emphases (in the documents referred to) on the general educational and social welfare of young people is considerable. As we stated earlier, YTS is only one part of the New Training Initiative, the others being the reform of apprenticeship and adult training and retraining. The needs of young people are clearly embedded in a context primarily to do with training in relation to industrial and technological requirements, and the problem of unemployment. As Blackstone and Lodge (1982) comment, it is youth unemployment and not egalitarian reform that has kept provision for 16–18-year-olds on the agenda in the UK since the Conservatives took office in 1979. The Schwartz Report on the other hand is concerned with much wider objectives than youth unemployment and skills training, as it considers the whole context of young people's lives and is concerned with the amelioration of social and educational inequalities generally: 'Our proposals do not therefore relate solely to the fight against unemployment, but form part of the wider objective of the economic and social reintegration of young people' (Schwartz 1981: p. 11). In keeping with this intention, while there is a large section concerning the structure, content and assessment of vocational training, there are also important sections on leisure opportunities, health, housing and the general welfare of young people. The Schwartz Report is only one of a series of educational reports commissioned by the French government (Legrand Report 1982, on schools for 11–16-year-olds; Prost Report 1983, on *Lycées* for 16–18-year-olds) concerned with measures to reduce the divisiveness and elitism of the French educational system and to improve the quality of education. The improvement in quality refers as much to social justice and broad educational aims as to the promotion of industrial efficiency.

The Schwartz Report cannot be compared directly with the NTI proposals. It is a report to the government, not, like NTI, a statement of government intentions. The proposals of the Schwartz Report have been accepted in principle, and some measures have been taken to implement them, but not on the scale of the YTS scheme in the UK. However, the scope of the French proposals highlights some of the contradictions and anomalies of the YTS initiative, and its precursors. We discuss these contradictions in the final section of this chapter in relation to vocational curricula. The issue we wish to point to here is that the proposals of the Schwartz Report provide a framework that *might* allow the principles of negotiation, blurring of boundaries and individual needs to be realised effectively. The UK initiatives, with their focus on industrial and technological need, yet with curriculum guidelines pointing to some degree of openness, imply some inherent contradictions in the various curriculum aims.

We turn now to a consideration of proposals for reform in qualifications in France and the UK. The intention in France is to use the existing qualifications, but to reform them in content and style of assessment, and also to increase those with some formal qualification at 18-plus from the present 60 per cent to 80 per cent by 1993. At present concern for reform is focussed on the lowest levels of vocational qualifications. The principal qualifications in this category are the Certificat d'Aptitude Professionnelle (CAP) (a three-year course, if taken in full-time education) and the Brevet d'Etudes Professionelles (BEP) (a two-year course, if taken full time). These can be taken in full-time education (from as early as age 14 and 16 respectively), as part of an apprenticeship or by evening class and/or private study. The CAP and BEP cover a wide range of occupations: office work, catering, engineering, craft skills and many more. A consideration that probably influenced the decision to use existing qualifications is the fact that in France an employer has to pay a national minimum wage to a qualified worker.

In Britain YTS has its own certificate. This is a record of the trainee's activities and achievements while on the scheme, in the form of a profile. The record may include a trainee's success in existing formal qualifications, such as City and Guilds certificate. But the YTS certificate itself is not a nationally recognised and standardised qualification. This will almost certainly have implications for the relative value of different YTS certificates, which is likely to be compounded by important differences between two modes of delivery of the scheme, Mode A or Mode B. In a Mode A scheme the employer is managing agent and is responsible for the whole programme of work experience and off-the-job training. In a Mode B scheme the Manpower Services Commission is the managing agent and subcontracts the programme to (for example) a college or training workshop. There is a tendency for Mode A schemes to follow traditional vocational training models: regular on-the-job experience plus day release at a local college, often enrolled on a traditional course such as a City and Guilds certificate, and with the possibility of the YTS year being treated as the first year of a traditional apprenticeship. Mode B schemes are often more innovatory, and make explicit provision for negotiation, for counselling and guidance and for time specifically devoted to interpersonal skills such as 'personal effectiveness'. Unpublished research by Clive Seale at Garnett College indicates that this is happening; also that in many Mode A schemes the relationship between on- and off-the-job training remains much as it was before YTS, the intended closer liaison not having been achieved. Differences between types of scheme in Britain relate to more general principles of differentiation in further education.

Types of further education curricula

Denis Gleeson (1983), writing specifically about further education, draws attention to stratification between courses and the relationship between tightly classified schemes on the one hand, and weakly classified schemes on the other, with the different strata:

- 'Tertiary modern'. The 'new' FE; incorporating the unqualified, unemployed and unemployable. Curricular emphasis is on 'generic skills' via remedial vocational education, 'voc prep', work experience and 'social and life skills'.
- 'Craft'. Mainly day release craft tradition (male dominated); but now incorporating female craft skills: hairdressing, beauty therapy, catering, nursing and so forth. Curricular emphasis is on training for home and non-work.
- 'Academic–technical'. Full- and part-time academic/technical tradition incorporating the concept of 'educated' skilled labour. Here the curricular emphasis is on 'education' via English, maths and science. Students include those following GCE, social work, technician, management, secretarial and other courses that assume 'academic competence'.

Looking at YTS, it appears that there is a tendency for the Mode A schemes to approximate to the 'craft' model, and for Mode B schemes to the 'tertiary modern'. It is on the tensions and contradictions within this 'tertiary modern' level that we focus, exemplified by YTS and its precursors, in particular training workshops in South Wales.

The weakening of classification exhibits variable and anomalous features. The first is that, while classification is weakened, framing is relatively strong. The second is that not all aspects of the training programme show equal weakening of boundary, in that the closer the curriculum experience is to production processes (work experience, training workshops) the more both C and F remain strong. The third is that the weakening of C occurs most markedly in those sections of the curriculum that are innovator (not forming part of a traditional craft course), that can generally be grouped as 'social and life skills', 'personal effectiveness' and 'communication' (whatever the title given by a particular course), and are related to notions of personal development rather than technical expertise or technical theory. This last category is largely absent from such programmes. This personal development aspect

159

of such courses exhibits a particular kind of weakening of boundary in that, as 'academic' subject matter may be curtailed, ever more domains of everyday life are treated as relevant to training.

We find in such contexts, therefore, that in principle any and every aspect of everyday life, and of the student's biography, can be incorporated and transformed into educational contents. Such contents are then the focus of increasingly strongly framed surveillance and evaluation. The latter is often inscribed in the technology of pupil 'profiles' 'cf. Stronach 1984). (This is not to imply that education or traning becomes identical with everyday experience. The former is always a 'version' or 'reproduction' of it, subject to its own transformation rules. This point will be touched on again later.) The weakening of boundary in this instance is in part realised by the highly variable locales of training and education (in the 'community', on employers' premises, in outdoor pursuits or leisure centres and so on, as well as within the institutional confines of college and classroom). The rhetoric used to describe such initiatives sometimes carries connotations of such boundary weakening and interpenetration: 'infusion', 'transition', 'link' and the like.

In the rhetoric of both French and British schemes, therefore, we find changing emphases upon the bounding of educational experience, in C and F. There are, too, differences in C and F that reflect the stratification of courses and students. The weakening of classification in such contexts is not necessarily accompanied by a weakening of frame, however. Indeed, schemes for the less able may display a somewhat paradoxical mixture, of –C and +F. This is illustrated in the case study of industrial training to which we now turn.

The classification and framing of industrial training

By way of illustration of some features of 'training' in practice, we turn to a discussion of industrial training for 'slow' learners. These have been documented in some detail elsewhere (e.g. Atkinson, Rees and Shone 1981, 1983), and the detailed ethnography is not reproduced here. These units illustrate in practice the format characteristics we have already explored at a more general level. The working of just one unit is drawn on here to illustrate the co-presence of weakened classification and strong frame.

The relatively weak classification of contents in the industrial training was reflected in the diverse topics that were introduced by the staff as the basis for 'discussion' with the students. These were *not* part of any specifically timetabled components, but were introduced 'spontaneously'; they arose out of specific incidents on the shop floor. In our own reports (e.g. Shone and Atkinson 1982) we have referred to these features in terms of 'social and life skills', 'training for adult life' and 'training for work life'. But these are terms for our own analytic convenience, and do not correspond to any member-identified curricular boundaries.

A brief exemplification of the range of topics introduced will perhaps suffice here: motivation, attention span, confidence, smoking, interpersonal relations, appearance and self-penetration, capitalism, democracy, advertising, literature, classical music, mortgages, taxation. In these contexts in our unit, the framing of even these domains was remarkably strong; coverage was accomplished primarily through staff-initiated lectures, homilies and harangues.

These lectures arose out of the contingencies of everyday work in the unit, and they were intimately related to staff commentary and criticism directed against student conduct and demeanour. This latter point emphasises the extent to which the students were subject to scrutiny and diffuse evaluation by staff. Evaluation was for the most part directed towards the recognition and production of 'good workers'. This included aspects of cognitive and motor skills, attention, attitude and motivation, self-presentation, deference, punctuality, common sense and aspirations. The workshop thus became a sort of panopticon wherein each and every aspect of the student's moral being was open to inspection and commentary.

The framing of knowledge and experience was linked intimately to the framing of production. It was part of the philosophy of the unit that it should include a substantial proportion of 'real' work on contract from local firms, rather than simulation. It was believed by the manager that this guaranteed 'meaningful', 'worthwhile' and 'purposeful' activity. It was explicitly contrasted with what he saw as the 'meaningless exercise' of the academic curriculum, in which his students had demonstrably failed (and which had failed them).

The contract work introduced constraints within which the staff and students worked. The level of tolerance of staff in training students can be severely curtailed by the risk of ruining customers' raw materials and failing to meet the order. Likewise, the contract

161

work meant that staff were careful to match production tasks to students' perceived capacities.

Students were assigned to those tasks where they were felt least likely to cause damage, especially in the case of the least able. This meant that certain students could be assigned to the same job and the same item of equipment for long periods of time; retraining on other tasks – especially more demanding ones – was uneconomical in terms of staff time, materials and lost production.

In undertaking contract work the unit had to meet certain obligations. The staff had to ensure that the standards of production were adequate for their customers' needs, and that schedules were kept to. It thus imposed on them something of a strait-jacket, in accordance with the somewhat limited capacities of the students themselves.

Equivalent constraints were set by the machinery installed in the unit. There was, of course, an intimate relationship between the content of the contract work and the plant available. Together, they defined many of the students' activities as the repetitive performance of productive tasks such as simple drilling or stamping operations. While it would be a distortion to suggest that the unit was identical to a small factory, shop-floor production methods and schedules furnished parameters that 'framed' the training.

Discussion

In the 'new' FE programmes that we have been considering here, we note the following features:

(1) Variation between courses in respect of strength of boundary (tending to be strong in Mode A courses, weak in Mode B).
(2) Variation within courses between elements showing marked boundary-maintaining features and those showing weakened boundaries; those elements showing weakening boundaries are those that focus on the student as an individual rather than as a person learning a skill.
(3) The weakening of boundary applies largely to the content (C), while the framing (F) remains strong.

This last aspect is particularly worthy of note.

We argue that the combinations of classification and framing of

+C+F, +C-F and -C-F are logically consistent variations in tightness of control over the content of a curriculum and its pedagogy. Traditionally, and typically, curricula have been controlled from above; what is to be learned and how it is to be learned have been closely prescribed (+C+F). If the learner is to be offered some autonomy it is relatively easy to allow some choice over selection, organisation and pacing of a still prescribed content (+C-F). If the learner is to acquire more autonomy the content may also be negotiable (-C-F). But we argue there are inherent contradictions in the -C+F combination. The basis of any curriculum is its content (C). Where social relationships are hierarchical and interpositional, or where – and this is typically the case where the curriculum is closely allied to production – the student is learning a process that will be applied in prescribed ways in a prescribed context, this content will be prescribed in detail and be subject to tight boundary maintenance (+C). Where social relationships are interpositional curriculum content will become open to negotiation (-C). But if the boundaries are weakened (-C) while control over the learner remains strong (+F), the content is given meaning neither by external control, and by the fact that acquisition of content provides access to occupations or to further training, nor by the learner's progressive understanding (-C). The learner cannot apply the rule for +C: learn what you are told and you will become a qualified hairdresser/dentist/fitter. But neither can the learner apply the rule for -C: see what other people have done, see how you can utilise and develop what has been done before you; because the learner is constantly controlled, following closely prescribed activities.

A further effect of a -C+F curriculum is that it appears to impose a greater inequality between teacher and learner than a +C+F curriculum, where the teacher shares, albeit to a lesser extent, the external constraints. The spontaneity of some of the curricula observed – where curricula were adapted to immediate needs – is largely teacher-generated. Moreover, the increasing strength of frame, coupled with weak classification, means that ever-widening aspects of student life and identity may be brought within the bounds of scrutiny. Hence the possibility is created for ever stronger forms of social control and the 'pedagogic colonisation of everyday life'. Affective aspects of education may thus be redefined as instrumental; the hidden curriculum of student behaviour and demeanour is rendered central to the manifest curriculum. This is an integral feature of the broader process of 'technicisation' manifest in recent educational innovations.

The strength of the framing for the learner is largely an unintended consequence of the curricula we have discussed. Many teachers wish to pay more than lip-service to principles of negotiation and learner autonomy. The difficulties these teachers face are many. Lack of resources to offer real choices and the lack of self-motivation of many of the learners (understandable in that they often perceive that the courses they are on are unlikely to lead into employment) are important ones. We pointed earlier to what may be a significant difference between YTS and the reforms in France initiated by the Schwartz Report: that the latter intends to reform the existing and nationally recognised diplomas. This approach increases the possibilities of offering more autonomy for learners, and more opportunity for the validation of informally acquired skills linked to publicly recognised, and so more desirable, objectives.

We noted earlier that many of the 'high status' YTS schemes incorporate existing and largely traditional qualifications into their programmes in addition to the YTS certificate. The very openness of the curriculum guidelines for YTS seem, paradoxically, to work against the intended move towards flexibility and negotiation, by imposing so little control that managing agents can and do fall back upon existing patterns of training. This is in some contrast to the Business Education Council (now B/TEC) where assessment procedures, for example by enjoining cross-modular assignments and so ensuring some integration, have some inbuilt pressures towards weakening of classification and frame. Even so there are variations in the extent to which colleges have responded to the intentions of the curriculum (Barnes and Barnes 1984).

Any programme of vocational education is working in a context where the tradition is of strong classification and frame, and, further, in a situation where the context of production itself exerts strong pressures to a collection code. The Durkheimian origins of Bernstein's ideas are of importance here. The collection code is held to correspond to the Durkheimian notion of mechanical solidarity, resting on structurally equivalent sections. The integrated code corresponds to the individualistic division of labour characteristic of organic solidarity. An important part of Bernstein's analysis is his treatment of the process of social change that regulates and is regulated by transformations in the structuring process. He suggests that contemporary schooling shows a shift from mechanical to organic solidarity, from collection to integration, and that the moral order of the school is transformed from the externally imposed order of interpositional control to the individualised negotiation of interpersonal control. We argue that the openness, flexibility and negotiation of YTS stand in contradiction to the context of production where the externally imposed order of interpositional control remains dominant. When the experience or simulation of 'work' based on strong classification and frame is introduced into educational contexts, then ambiguous or contradictory message systems may be created in the structuration of curriculum and pedagogy.

References

Atkinson, P. (1981) 'Bernstein's Structuralism'. *Educational Analysis* 3 (1): pp. 85–95.

(1985) *Language, Structure and Reproduction: An Introduction to the Sociology of Basil Bernstein*. London, Methuen.

Atkinson, P., Rees, T. and Shone, D. (1981) 'Labouring to Learn? Industrial Training for Slow Learners', in L. Barton and S. Tomlinson (eds.), *Special Education: Policy, Practice and Social Issues*. London, Harper & Row.

(1983) 'Industrial Training for the Disadvantaged', in D. Gleeson (ed.) *Youth Training and the Search for Work*. London, Routledge & Kegan Paul.

Atkinson, P., Rees, T., Shone, D. and Williamson, H. (1982) 'Social and Life Skills: the Latest Case of Compensatory Education', in Rees and Atkinson (1982).

Barnes, D. and Barnes, D. (1984) *Versions of English*. London, Heinemann.

Bernstein, B. (1971) 'The Classification and Framing of Educational Knowledge', in M. F. D. Young (ed.) *Knowledge and Control: New Directions for the Sociology of Education*. London, Collier-Macmillan.

(1977) 'Aspects of the Relations between Education and Production', in B. Bernstein (ed.) *Class, Codes and Control, Vol. 3* (2nd edn). London, Routledge & Kegan Paul.

Blackstone, T. and Lodge, P. (1982) *Educational Policy and Educational Inequality*. Oxford, Martin Robertson.

Department of Employment (1981) *A New Training Initiative: A Programme for Action*. London, HMSO.

Dickinson, H. and Erben, M. (1982) 'Technical Culture and Technical Education in France: a Consideration of the Work of Claude Grignon and its Relevance to British Further Education Curricula'. *British*

Journal of Sociology of Education 3 (2): pp. 145–59.

(1983) 'The Technicisation of Morality and Culture: a Consideration of the Work of Claude Grignon and its Relevance to Further Education in Britain', in D. Gleeson (ed.), *Youth Training and the Search for Work*. London, Routledge & Kegan Paul.

Eggleston, J. (ed.) (1982) *Work Experience in Secondary Schools*. London, Routledge & Kegan Paul.

Further Education Unit (1983) *Supporting YTS: Guidance for Colleges and Others Involved in the Youth Training Scheme*. London, Further Education Unit.

Gleeson, D. (1983) 'Further Education, Tripartism and the Labour Market', in D. Gleeson (ed.), *Youth Training and the Search for Work*. London, Routledge & Kegan Paul.

Legrand, L. (1982) *Pour un College Democratique: Rapport au Ministre de l'Education Nationale*. Paris, La Documentation Francaise.

Manning, P. (1982) 'Structuralism and the Sociology of Knowledge'. *Knowledge–Creation, Diffusion, Utilization* 4 (1): pp. 51–72.

Manpower Services Commission (1977) *Young People and Work: Report on the Feasibility of a New Programme of Opportunities for Young People* (Holland Report). London, MSC.

(1981a) *A New Training Initiative: A Consultative Document*. London, MSC.

(1981b) *A New Training Initiative: An Agenda for Action*. London, MSC.

(1982) *Youth Task Group Report*. London, MSC.

Prost, A. (1983) *Les Lycees et leurs Etudes au Seuil du XXI$_e$ Siecle*. Paris, Centre National de Documentation Pedagogique.

Rees, T. and Atkinson, P. (eds.) (1982) *Youth Unemployment and State Intervention*. London, Routledge & Kegan Paul.

Schwartz, B. (1981) *The Integration of Young People in Society and Working Life*. Trans. R. Sayer. Berlin, CEDEFOP (European Centre for the Development of Vocational Education); published originally in French: Paris, La Documentation Francaise.

Seale, C. (1984) 'FEU and MSC: Two Curricular Philosophies and their Implications for the Youth Training Scheme'. *The Vocational Aspect of Education* 36 (93): pp. 3–10.

Shone, D. and Atkinson, P. (1982) *Everyday Life in Two Industrial Training Units for Mentally Retarded Young People in Mid-Glamorgan*. Cologne, IFAPLAN.

Stronach, I. (1984) 'Work Experience: the Sacred Anvil', in C. Varlaam (ed.) *Rethinking Transition*. Lewes, Falmer Press.

Walford, G. (1981) 'Classification and Framing in Postgraduate Education'. *Studies in Higher Education* 6 (2): pp. 147–58.

Watson, K. (ed.) (1983) *Youth, Education and Employment*. Beckenham, Croom Helm.

CHAPTER EIGHT

Leaving School: Structures and Agencies in New Zealand

Roy Nash

New Zealand in many ways serves as an ideal social laboratory. Its systems are small and generally uncomplicated; and although there is not an abundance of research data, information can readily be obtained, if necessary through the provision of the recent Official Information Act. The secondary-school system is now struggling to cope with the twin effects of falling rolls and comparatively high levels of youth unemployment. This chapter presents a compressed analysis of the processes by which pupils leaving New Zealand secondary schools each year find (or fail to find) a place in further education or the permanent work-force. The discussion will be structured theoretically by a framework of concepts taken from several discrete areas of academic knowledge: (1) family reproduction strategies, (2) credentiallism, (3) labour segmentation, (4) cultural production and (5) rational choice or game theory. It is possible to do no more than sketch the outline of a brief introduction to the central ideas. This inevitably means a certain over-simplification, but each element of the argument advanced here has been developed by extensive research, and the literatures– excepting perhaps rational choice theory –are widely known in the contemporary sociology of education. What has not been done, so far as I am aware, is to work these elements into a coherent account of particular aspects of the schooling process. It is hardly possible to do that and do much more than state the nature and relevance of the concepts involved.

(1) Bourdieu's (1978) emphasis on strategies of family reproduc-

tion and the continuing importance of educational systems as a resource for such strategies marks an important shift in our understanding the mechanisms of the schooling process and its driving force. All available New Zealand research shows the expected relationship between social class (or socio-economic status) and level of educational attainment. Moreover, historical research demonstrates this to have been established from the earliest days. McKenzie (1980), for example, shows a markedly greater examination success rate for middle-class pupils by 1880. At present it is likely that about two-thirds of all middle-class children reach university. Social mobility is always difficult to measure, and the New Zealand research is limited in scope and in size. A recent study by Davis (1979) shows, in broad outline, that 31 per cent of sons were in occupations of the same status as their fathers and 35 per cent had moved down. This indicates a level of social mobility similar to that in Australia and the USA. But these figures are accounted for in great degree by movement between the large lower-middle and upper-working-class groups. Outside this band it is a different picture; for example, 78 per cent of higher professional workers' sons remained middle-class and only 7 per cent were demoted to semi-skilled or unskilled manual work. Similarly, 60 per cent of semi-skilled manual workers' sons remained working-class, and fewer than 4 per cent were promoted to the higher professional class. This is a pattern of social reproduction, not social mobility. There can be little doubt, and census data confirm the point, that educational qualifications are becoming increasingly necessary both for entry to employment and for promotion within it. The best explanation of all this is captured by Bourdieu's concept of family reproduction strategies. Generally, parents try to 'do the best for the kids', and these endeavours can be interpreted as evidence for strategies of family reproduction. Families may be understood to possess financial, social and intellectual resources that in certain social conditions are interchangeable, convertible, one to another. The transmission of these resources or capitals from one generation to its successors ensures class and status reproduction of family units and, therefore, of the social structure of the class system itself.

(2) Since the rise of the reformed public school and formal credentialling a century ago the educational system has become increasingly important and is now essential to the reproduction strategies of large sections of the population. The basic concept of credential inflation (Dore 1976) is all too easy to grasp in the

context of the New Zealand experience. In 1963 the proportion of school-leavers gaining University Entrance, the senior school award, was 16 per cent; twenty years later the proportion is 32 per cent and can increase no further without major changes to the regulations. From the standpoint of employers UE now signifies not the upper sixth of all school-leavers but close to the upper third. From the standpoint of the UE-credentialled school-leaver a level of attainment that once virtually assured a higher education place or white-collar occupation cannot now guarantee entry to any occupation. It is necessary to exaplain how securely the examination straight-jacket constrains school awards in New Zealand.

The two most important examinations are School Certificate (SC) and University Entrance (UE). School Certificate is sat by almost all students who complete Form 5, and University Entrance is attempted by almost all students who complete Form 6. Both SC and UE examinations are scaled to ensure that pass rates are linked to the total number of candidates taking the examinations in any one year and are thus norm-referenced tests with a pre-determined distribution and an arbitrary pass mark. In 1982 SC pass rates varied from 87.2 per cent (Latin) to 37.2 per cent (Clothing and Textiles). This typical pattern of variation is caused by scaling procedures that tie performance in all subjects, including practical-craft subjects and Maori language (but this has led to protest and is to be discontinued), to performance in English. These fixed ratios and scaling procedures determine, as they are apparently intended to do, that the overall number of candidates gaining SC in three subjects (the recognised useful standard) is about half of all school students (in 1982 the figure was 54.3 per cent). Students are permitted to proceed to Form 6 study without SC English, but this is unusual and most schools require students without this qualification to repeat Form 5. The proportion of students able to enter Form 6 cannot, therefore, rise much above 50 per cent of the year cohort. At UE the pass target is maintained by regulation at a little less than 60 per cent, which ensures that only that proportion of school candidates can obtain the full award. In 1982, 31.6 per cent of all school-leavers gained UE, and it will be realised that the system is working to capacity; it is simply not possible to go beyond this point within the existing regulatory structures. These scaling procedures arithmetically determine the proportion of pupils who can succeed at these levels of attainment in the New Zealand school examination system. Not much more

169

than half can obtain a useful SC result and in practice only this group can be accepted as UE candidates. Of these only 60 per cent can obtain UE, and so the maximum proportion of the total school population able to gain this credential is 30 per cent. Thus, when the system is working to capacity, as it now is, the ratios are: a little less than half of all pupils leave with less than three passes at SC, one-sixth leave Form 6 with SC but without UE (most with Sixth Form Certificate introduced specifically as a qualification for that group), and close to one-third leave with UE.

(3) The concept of labour segmentation offers an analysis of some power. In Edwards's (1979) analysis the labour market is understood to be divided between the primary and the secondary sectors. Within the primary sector two levels are distinguished, independent and dependent. Independent workers are engaged in professional, technical and managerial occupations characterised by a high level of initiative and a recognisable set of internalised 'professional' attitudes. Such positions command respect, authority and high social status. Dependent workers, in contrast, have a lower level of intiative, are closely supervised and are responsive to externally set goals. These occupations typically offer fewer personal satisfactions to the worker and convey a lower status. Employment within the primary sector is structured by the bureaucratic authority of government or large-scale commercial enterprise, and provides for workers the possibility of a career of upward mobility within the institution or profession. In the secondary sector jobs are characteristically unskilled, temporary, physically demanding or dangerous, and often provide little personal satisfaction. Edwards's analysis is not concerned with other labour market segmentions. There is, in principle, no limit to the possible non-labour process divisions that may arise within a labour market or employment structure. In New Zealand the labour market has, in fact, become noticeably divided and fractioned, with young people, women and Polynesians concentrated in the secondary sector. The implicatons of this are obvious. Most unemployment is concentrated in the secondary sector; moreover, the entirely justified demands of the trade unions for the retraining of those workers in the primary sector whose skills are made redundant by technology cannot ease unemployment in the secondary sector. Labour segmentation theory helps to explain, by focussing on structures and the resources necessary to progress within them, why unemployment is highest among the least powerful – that is, least resourced – sectors of the community:

young people, women and ethnic minorities.

(4) Cultural studies have acquired a particular meaning after the sustained investigations of the Birmingham Centre for Contemporary Cultural Studies and those influenced by the work produced there. The concern is with the lived culture of the working class (and ethnic groups) and with reading the expressions of those groups as a system of produced signs. Among others Hall and Jefferson (1976) have shown how groups with readily and self-consciously identifiable stylistic markers – many youth groups (teddy boys, mods, bikers), for example – can be analysed with considerable insight. The concept of symbolic resistance encapsulates the realisation that these are systems of subcultural meaning, which must be read as symbols of antagonism and resistance to aspects of the dominant culture that are experienced as oppressive. This method reads culture as a system of culturally produced signs and as such responds to emergent subcultures. What groups emerge and how they will be marked cannot be predicted. Once their existence is noted it can be read and in some cases shown to be related to objective social conditions including the structures of the labour market and the divisions of class, age, sex and race.

(5) Rational choice theory has been persuasively advocated by Boudon's (1982) models, which assume that individuals act rationally in pursuit of those ends they perceive to be within their grasp. It is thought, not least by these writers themselves, that the explanatory theories of Boudon and Bourdieu are incompatible. It is important, since the argument advanced here draws on both sets of work, that this be established as a misunderstanding. Bourdieu's theory is understood to state that the possession of cultural capital is given recognition by the school and credentialled as an 'objective' valuation providing access to professional occupations. Boudon's statistical theory is understood to state that individuals act rationally in their best interests as they perceive them within their decision field and so create statistical structures of class mobility that, in fact, seem quite close to random allocation. Yet both theories are based on the same broad notion of game theory, or rational choice theory, at least in its general principle that people try to do the best with the resources they possess (and acquire more) and employ them rationally in decision fields bounded by culturally available information. It is particularly noteworthy that, despite polemical sniping between them, Boudon and Bourdieu both cite the same reference group theory as the

171

psychological field within which people act to create the structures that sociology identifies as the enabling and constraining structures of social life and that it also constitutes as causal factors in models of the interaction between social structures. If university entrance seems a possible ambition to a middle-class student and entirely unconsidered by a working-class student, that may be due to the existence of these classes as cultural groups in which collective ideas about what is possible for 'people like us' can emerge. Boudon insists that these can be regarded in theory (if not in psychological reality) as rational choice fields. If the possibility of attaining a certain goal – for example, university entrance – is statistically high in return for a known and affordable stake and its opportunity costs then the 'bet' is rational. The force of Bourdieu's elaboration of cultural/individual structuring by *habitus* is to take the study of culture beyond reference group theory and transcend the conventional analysis at that level. Where conventional theory concentrates on the choice field Bourdieu emphasises the cultural structuring of the decision field and the causes of that structuring itself. Interpretation of the statistical results of these struggles to make the best of life is a complex question. But that the allocation of credentials and jobs may seem to be not far from that expected by chance, on certain models, does not in the least reduce the necessity to work at the business of getting them. In reality people are not awarded educational certificates and occupations at random. If social reproduction is far from assured that only makes the struggle to achieve it more intense and anxiety ridden. If cultural capital cannot always be exchanged in the market, is devalued, if it can be acquired by non-elite individuals, none of this invalidates the concept or the processes involved in social, family, reproduction.

The theoretical divisions within sociology are essentially about how to construct a theoretical language able to give structure and agency the same importance and emphasis. In this chapter structures are regarded as having a real existence that confronts people whose actions in their individual interest (remembering that individual interests may often be subsumed by individuals to group interests; in the argument of this chapter employers are assumed to act in the interests of their firms, parents in the interest of their families and job-seekers in their own interests) cannot but bring about the continued existence of those structures. Labour market structures, for example, confront school-leavers all too obviously, and nothing in the power of those young people can alter their oppressive facticity. But not for one moment does that

Leaving School: Structures and Agencies in New Zealand

imply that labour market structures are not the result of the actions of others–largely, in fact, of individual employers acting in the interest of their firms. Moreover, that structure is one that school-leavers must *act* within, to accept or resist in their several collective ways. Only these structures that make their actions intelligible.

Modelling the flow from school to work

The models presented below assume that young people leave shool with one of three levels of attainment: (1) University Entrance and above (UE), (2) School Certificate (including Sixth Form Certificate) at three passes or more (SC) and (3) lesser credentials or none (LC); and that they move from school to, (a) further education (FE), (b) the technical and clerical category (TECH), (c) the production category (LAB) and, (d) to unknown positions or unemployment (UN). Department of Education statistics from which these categories are derived are no longer published in this form, and the most useful cross-tabulations can only be estimated. Table 8.1 is derived from data published by the Department of Education in 1964. Table 8.2 provides the most recent equivalent. It will be noted that the analysis of anticipated destination is here by level of schooling rather than by highest credential attained.

Table 8.1 Destinations and qualifications, non-Maoris* Maoris, 1963

		FE	TECH	LAB	Total
UE plus	NM	4,134	1,594	510	6,238
	M	46	14	5	65
SC of Form 6	NM	1,310	4,299	2,264	7,873
	M	43	80	56	169
No SC	NM	522	9,817	15,155	25,454
	M	13	537	2,853	3,403
Total	NM	5,966	15,710	17,889	39,565
	M	102	631	2,904	3,637

173

Table 8.2 Classification and probable destination of school-leavers, 1979

	FE	TECH	LAB	UN		
Form 6/7	11,137	11,197	3,382	5,040	NM	28,845
					M	1,911
Form 5	793	3,715	2,383	2,870	NM	8,464
					M	1,297
Other	371	5,349	6,689	8,860	NM	15,486
					M	5,783
Totals						
NM	11,605	18,456	10,055	12.679		52,795
N	696	1,805	2,399	4,091		8,991

No single agency collects information in this form, so assembling the necessary data is not entirely straightforward and involves making certain plausible deductions. It is necessary to know the number of 15–19-year olds, (a) in educational institutions, (b) on training programmes, (c) in regular employment, (d) on special work programmes, (e) registered as unemployed and (f) non-registered but unemployed. The 15–19 age cohort is estimated as 316,255. Of these there are 44.6 per cent in full-time education, 41.3 per cent in permanent employment, 8.3 per cent registered unemployed, less than 1 per cent non-registered unemployed, 3.8 per cent on special work projects and less than 1 per cent on young people's training programmes. (The numbers held in other institutions, especially prison, are comparatively high, but not significant in these percentages.) These statistics are static in the sense that they describe reality at one point in time. There is a considerable degree of mobility from training courses to work to unemployment and back. About one-third of the 15–19 group not in higher education are at risk to this kind of 'career'.

There is a similar difficulty, but of greater dimensions, in obtaining useful data on labour segmentation. The most complete information is available only from the census and is not routinely published. It will be assumed that the TECH category adopted here reflects, if only in a distorted image, the subordinate division of the primary sector (the independent division is now recruited almost entirely from college and university graduates), and that the LAB category reflects the secondary sector. Given these assumptions Table 2 shows that the TECH category employs 28 per cent of school-leavers, the great majority of whom are credentialled; and the production sector employs 22 per cent of school-leavers, somewhat more than half of whom are credentialled. The destination of 29 per cent of school-leavers is unknown. About half of these will, in all probability, be unemployed for a period after leaving school, and a further substantial proportion will find special work or gain acceptance to a training programme. Well over a third of those without a known destination on leaving school had reached in Form 6/7. UE is gained by approximately 60 per cent of those completing Form 6, and surveys confirm that many of these leavers hold that qualification.

The following explanatory models use approximately proportionate data in recognition of the difficulties of obtaining accurate information and in order also to allow ready comprehension of the procedures. They are based on 33 per cent UE and higher, 25 per cent three passes SC or SFC and 42 per cent lesser qualifications. Reference can also be made to Table 8.2 as the nearest equivalent having regard to the comments made above. The models are based on the familiar image of a bus queue.

The biased conductor

Imagine three (long) queues. The buses are destined for FE, TECH and LAB. The FE bus loads first, weighting UE applicants 2.75 more than chance. (By chance there will be (10,000 × 20,000) ÷ 60,000 = 3,333 in this cell; 3,333 × 2.75 = 9,166.) TECH loads second, with UE applicants weighted 2.0 above chance – adjusting the marginal frequencies in recognition that 9,166 have been taken out. Then FE takes SC applicants, weighted 2.0. TECH then takes SC applicants, also weighted 2.0. The LAB bus now begins to load with 1.5 weight (only 50 per cent above chance) to UE and SC in that order. The expected frequencies are continually adjusted to account for the different order of loading, and the six marginal totals are completed last. A third of the queue is left standing on the pavement. These weightings are those necessary to meet the conductor's preference above the level of chance.

175

Table 8.3 A biased distribution

	FE	TECH	LAB	UN	Total
UE	9,166	6,400	2,610	1,824	20,000
SC	564	5,660	4,581	4,195	15,000
LC	270	2,940	7,809	13,981	25,000
Total	10,000	15,000	15,000	20,000	60,000

The model draws attention to the possibility that much of the distribution of school-leavers to occupations, particularly in the LAB category, could easily result from chance; which is to say that employers could largely be indifferent to school credentials at this level. This seems the only reasonable interpretation of Table 2, which indicates that 12,454 jobs in the LAB category were open to 8,422 Form 6/7 leavers, 5,253 Form 5 with SC leavers and 5,549 lesser credentialled leavers, assuming that other sector positions have been filled. These jobs were distributed almost randomly between those with these levels of educational attainment. In fact, those with UE get proportionately less than their fair share. It is possible, of course, that many with high attainments do not compete in this sector, but the figures are illuminating nevertheless. The preferences on which Table 3 is based have been worked out backwards from what is likely to be proportionately approximate, to the actual situation. It is necessary to remember that in reality the 'buses' load simultaneously (in some ways a better image might be that of a huge taxi fleet) and that, most importantly, some seats may be reserved. This last consideration leads to the second model.

Reserved places

Imagine the buses arriving at the queue with strictly reserved seats. The FE bus has reserved 90 per cent of its seats for UE holders and 70 per cent of its remaining places for SC holders. The TECH bus reserves 40 per cent of its places for UE holders and 60 per cent of the remaining places for SC holders. The LAB bus reserves 15 per cent of its places for those with SC. The result is shown in Table 8.4.

Table 8.4   A reserved distribution

	FE	TECH	LAB	UN	Total
UE	9,000	6,000	2,250	2,750	20,000
SC	700	5,400	6,375	2,525	15,000
LC	300	3,600	6,375	14,325	25,000
Total	10,000	15,000	15,000	20,000	60,000

Again this is probably not far from the true proportionate distribution. The basis of this calculation is quite different from the first. What matters here are not the preference weightings theoretically necessary to prevent a random distribution but the power of gatekeepers to impose a series of quotas. The model reflects the real practices of admissions bodies, professional associations and employers to reserve places. Such reservations are made in relation to the expected numbers of appropriately credentialled applicants, which itself is a function of the relative attractiveness of the occupation determined in turn by the alternatives available and the level of salary and other incentives offered.

The model also accommodates the preferences of employers who do not reserve places but differentially weight educational and other unspecified qualifications. As labour turnover proceeds (as job holders move), those with educational credentials initially excluded gain further opportunities and may be expected to improve their position. The actions of those who weight educational credentials or reserve places for those with educational credentials serve the same ends, and both practices are based on a knowledge of the relative attractiveness of their positions and the importance of credentials to their placement procedures. Thus it is not possible for LAB employers as a whole to reserve 80 per cent of places for UE holders because they have gone elsewhere. This gives an indication of why it occasionally happens that some less attractive occupations 'overbidding' for highly credentialled

177

labour can have difficulty in obtaining sufficient applicants to meet their self-imposed level of restriction. Some employers may have a high ideal preference for educational credentials, but the smaller the proportion of such labour competing for positions in that sector the less likely is the possibility of their ideal preference being realised. Of the two models this is probably the most useful since it refers to the relative power of different credentials in different sectors of the labour market. It matters little to this theory whether the quotas are actual and result from formal bureaucratic procedures or whether they are a product of the informal collective preferences of employers.

Discussion

The fact that employers generally prefer educated labour to the extent that they do, and demonstrate that preference by weighting and reservation practices, cannot show how necessary a given level of education is to the actual performance of an occupation. It does seem plausible to assume that employers' willingness to meet the cost of educated labour is directly related to the contribution that labour makes to productivity. However, all efforts to demonstrate an empirical relationship, especially at this level, have been markedly unsuccessful. There are probably three other and sufficient reasons for the general preference for educated (or schooled) labour: credentials (1) demonstrate a capacity for instruction and training, (2) indicate possession of the appropriate habits of order and discipline required by this labour sector and (3) provide an objective means of career grading. The rhetoric of employers in the secondary sector is not, in fact, difficult to decode and it reduces to a demand for an attitude of co-operative common sense combined with acceptance of any cultural norms of presentation associated with the occupation. These desirable qualities are only contingently related to academic ability, although schools put much effort into tying them together. (There is a difference and a tension between education and schooling and this is where it becomes apparent.) In the FE and TECH sectors UE is worth more than SC, and SC is worth more than LC. The position is unclear in the LAB sector. Some employers probably do prefer high levels of educational attainment but they may be equally matched by those with a negative preference. (In Britain it has become commonplace for well educated job-seekers forced to apply for routine manual work to conceal their credentials, which they have learned to be in no sense 'qualifications'.) Clearly, a substantial number of those with UE and SC will be unemployed or without permanent work in the first year after leaving school. This will necessarily mean that about half of those without work will have good levels of educational attainment. There is nothing much they can do about getting work, except keep applying for jobs in the hope of maximising their chances of success.

These models can be adjusted for any parameters. Table 8.5 shows a 'reserved places' model prepared in the light of recent projections on population and school enrolments. It is assumed that the retention rate to Form 6 completion will rise from 55 to 73 per cent and that the historic formula for determining UE numbers will be maintained. (The Labour government elected in 1984 has, in fact, announced plans to abolish UE, but the analysis presented here is worth following through.) It is assumed further that the actual numbers entering FE will fall slightly but rise proportionately. There are no current plans to expand entry to higher education, and this seems a realistic assumption. Estimating future levels of unemployment is more difficult. The temptation is always to err on the side of caution since to project high levels of unemployment is to invite charges of alarmism. A nonprofessional economist can only note that there is no convincing evidence to suggest that the number of jobs will significantly increase in New Zealand in the medium term, or that a greater proportion will be obtained by school-leavers; and more than a little evidence suggests that both the number of jobs and the proportion available to school-leavers will decline. The figures for 1979 have thus been reduced by 10 per cent.

This is a cautious, even timid, estimate and projects a situation considerably more favourable than that currently existing in Britain. Those of a more apocalytic frame of mind may recalculate the figures to their own level of pessimism. The labour division preferences follow the discussion above. For example, FE institutions have a 90 per cent preference for UE over all other credentials (or qualifications) and a 70 per cent preference for SC over LC. The preferences of the TECH and LAB categories are given in the table. It is unlikely that the 'preference' (the distribution could be random) of employers in the LAB category for UE will be much greater than 20 per cent over other qualifications even given the anticipated further devaluation of this credential.

Roy Nash

It can confidently be predicted that such unemployment so distributed will generate intense pressure on government and on schools to find ways of setting the system to rights. Table 8.1 shows that in 1963 17 per cent of school-leavers with SC entered further education, 54 per cent entered technical and clerical occupations, and virtually all found work of some sort. In 1979, as far as can be ascertained, only 9 per cent of those with SC (Form 5) gained further education places, 32 per cent entered technical and clerical work, and 32 per cent were without known work. If the model shown by Table 8.5 for a decade hence is worth anything, this last figure is unlikely to rise.

Table 8.5 A possible future distribution

	FE	TECH	LAB	UN	Total
UE	(.9) 10,350	(.45) 6,750	(.2) 2,200	2,700	22,000
SC	(-7) 805	(.35) 2,887	(.4) 3,520	5,788	13,000
LC	345	5,363	5,280	4,012	15,000
Total	11,500	15,000	11,000	12.500	50,000

Boudon's arguments from game theory suggest that before long substantial numbers of pupils will disqualify themselves from this game. With the odds of obtaining work at little better than 50:50 even with School Certificate, there are many young people to whom the effort of attaining it will not seem worthwhile. Unemployed young people will make their own way of life, their own lived culture, one that will become for many working-class (and Maori) youths of both sexes a real alternative to be weighed against a heavy investment in School Certificate with a not much more than even chance of being any better off in the end.

Unemployment as it is experienced by most young people in contemporary New Zealand is not so much unemployment as marginal involvement in the secondary sector of the labour market. Typically, young workers in this sector now move in and out of the labour force perhaps several times in the course of a year.

180

Moreover, unless the economy goes disastrously wrong, they will not be 'unemployed' even in this sense for more that five to ten years. These young people are really being put into a holding pattern and so long as they can keep circling around and retain their work habits intact (which Labour Department schemes are intended to ensure) most will end up with more permanent jobs before the end of the decade. This is not intended to sound complacent; large-scale youth unemployment is entirely unnecessary, but what one would like to happen and what an objective appraisal of social and economic forces suggests will happen are two different things.

These pressures make rational 'bets' that much more crucial. The structures mean that some school-leavers with good educational qualifications will fail to find appropriate employment, or even any employment. As far as the middle class are concerned, young people – their young people – who work hard to attain UE are not supposed to be unemployed. If they are, and if their children start to choose and create a resistant subculture of the urban unemployed and marginally employed (and why would they create a conformist subculture in celebration of a social order that dashed their hopes and offered nothing better than this aimless marking time?), the political pressure to take greater control of the system will be hard for democratic politicians to ignore.

But what could politicians do? Before they can do anything they need to learn what is going on. At the moment most senior state education officials, most secondary-school principals and perhaps most teachers have a shrewd idea. Yet it is hardly possible for them to theorise adequately the central issues within a liberal discourse of equality of educational opportunity that regards the school as a potent mechanism for generating social equality through social mobility. Boudon and Bourdieu have each demonstrated after their individual fashions the error of this view. Officially, education administrators maintain the struggle against reproduction theory (ironically in view of their implicit structural functionalism), but they accept it tacitly. Until it becomes politically acceptable to discuss publicly what the social reproductive effects of schools really are, their room for manoeuvre is likely to remain restricted. It is thus all the more necessary for those of us in a position to speak to begin to shift this aspect of the public discourse on schooling. It is for such reasons of discourse that 'band-aid' schemes for youth training will not be advocated in this paper.

181

There are persuasive arguments to support removing the 16–18 year group from the labour market (but not from contact with production) by providing places in schools and colleges and with independent (perhaps ethnically based) educational foundations. This could become possible only through the introduction of a living allowance provided for all young people whether in formal institutions or not. Such an allowance could replace current unemployment benefits and student bursaries. There would be some additional cost if the level were set realistically but this could be set against reduced expenditure on social control measures as some of the stress generated by unemployment was relieved.

At the same time the inevitability of permitting market forces to concentrate unemployment on this age group should be resisted. There is a widening discrepancy between the amount of human labour power required to produce culturally necessary goods and the number of people forced by the capital accumulation crisis to seek waged employment in order to purchase them. (Marx was right about this.) It is hard to imagine a worse or more cruel way of managing the unemployment so created than to let market forces dump it on those who have the least responsibility for creating it and the least capacity to cope with it as individuals. Professional as well as popular progressive educational forces need to be rid of the idea that these are matters outside their legitimate area of concern. As a society we can leave the allocation of work to those who benefit from an uncontrolled labour market (and they are not many) or we can insist on non-market intervention policies. A socially rational approach to the reduced need for labour can open many possibilities. But nothing is possible unless this nettle is grasped.

There is not much that can be done about credentiallism. If the present level of inflation is considered a problem, that could be minimised by several strategies. An additional level of qualification could be introduced to reserve or weight FE and TECH places, or the growing percentage of pupils with UE and SC could be reduced by decreasing the efficiency of teachers (through worsening staffing ratios and so on) or by raising the level of difficulty of the examination (for which there are historical precedents). Neither of these approaches, to say the least, are at all desirable. As monetary inflation cannot be reduced without economic restrictions that bring about their own unwelcome consequences, so it is with credential inflation. It is precisely because no further inflationary movement is possible that the senior school examination system is to be overhauled. Collins (1979) advocates entirely removing the examination function from schools, but that would, other things being equal, lead to employing bodies setting up their own examination system. The best that can reasonably be hoped for in New Zealand is the development of a broader-based curriculum that integrates, rather than divorces, theory and practice and a suitable competency-based examination system recognising that pupils will leave school at different points (although the school-leaving age should certainly be raised to 16) in the foreseeable future. Such reforms could be successful only if linked to a coherent policy to relieve youth unemployment. In other words it calls for intelligent political policies.

It is at the cultural level that most schools will face their greatest problem. Their task is unenviable. On the one hand they have to hold open to pupils the possibility of attaining credentials that will be true qualifications and so motivate as many as possible, and on the other they have to close off and contain those who make what must be recognised as a theoretically rational cultural choice to passively reject or actively resist the processes of schooling. Schools might find that it wold make more sense to point out that there are so many school-leavers and so many fewer, jobs that these qualifications seem to count for so much and not much more when applying for jobs of this or that sort, and so on. Pupils already know this in a taken-for-granted sense as it affects their lives but once pupils are formally aware of the structures of opportunities that exist they can be encouraged to discuss the nature and cost benefits of the cultural choices open. Good teachers do this already, but a great deal remains to be done. One fights against despair at the utter lack of comprehension shown by school counsellors on this issue. There still seem to be some who think that with 45,000 school-leavers chasing perhaps 35,000 jobs the 10,000 at the back of the queue need to comb their hair. The greater the proportion of young people who decide that their objective chances of success are too slim to make the game worth playing, the greater are the chances of those who remain in competition. Such is the perversity of ideology, however, that this in no way prevents many of those whose own youngsters so benefit from condemning the kids who opt out, or in perceiving that choice to be not the result of objective structures but their cause. (The existence of such subcultures is a threat to family reproduction and is feared on that account, but so long as one's own children are unaffected this self-disqualification of competition is an advantage.) These are complex matters but they are not incomprehensible and there is no real excuse for the confusion that bedevils this discussion.

This chapter has been implicitly structured within the traditional problematic of social class. Women (or girls in this context) are slightly worse off than boys in almost all respects. Maori young people are a great more worse off; even now more than half have no permanent occupation. The data are given in the tables and stand without further comment. In future years the proportion of Maori pupils in school will rise and, other things being equal, a greater number will obtain School Certificate and University Entrance. Whether it will do them much good in the labour market is another matter. If the number of further education positions or real jobs is less than the number of credentialled school-leavers – and the situation is already close to that – then other qualifications become increasingly relevant and apparent. If all have equal credentials then credentials count for nothing.

In any case the lower the level of educational credential held and the less preferred the division of labour the more important factors other than education credentials have always been. There is no reliable information on the customary methods of labour recruitment for school-leavers in the secondary sector. It is known that a quarter of all New Zealand employed men have the same occupations as their fathers, which may have less to do with social and psychological modelling than with the power of some fathers to 'speak for' their lads at the appropriate time. Many customary recruitment practices based on such inalienable qualifications must objectively disadvantage Maori pupils. For example, firms that privilege their workers' children for vacancies thereby privilege more non-Maori (since they are the greater proportion employed) than Maori workers. Thus, even leaving aside the degree of outright racial discrimination that undoubtedly exists, Maori will be disadvantaged. An analysis of census data from the 1981 10 per cent sample shows that Maori youths aged 15–19 with SC or UE are now as likely as their non-Maori counterparts to obtain an appropriate level of employment. But those Maoris without school credentials were much less likely to find employment than non-Maori in a similar position. It may nevertheless be the case that in the sector of the labour market open to most Maori school-leavers School Certificate is of only marginal value.

The model of schooling advanced in this chapter supposes that class-located families concerned to 'do the best' for their offspring are engaged in practices of family reproduction (thus ensuring, at the cultural level, social class reproduction); that the real (non-inflationary) distribution of educational credentials, which give access to the segmented labour market, is strictly controlled; and that the processes by which pupils are rationally both allocated and self-allocated to what can seem almost predestined statistical fates are processes of structured cultural production. Agency must not be confused with the political possibility of structural transformation. Of course, labour market structures can be changed to make space for all school-leavers, but not without almost totalitarian government intervention. And parents, teachers and school-leavers must act within the structures that exist – and to that extent help perpetuate them. The whole purpose of this analysis is not to deny agency, or to limit agency in the face of structure, but to make possible the identification of enabling and constraining structures shaping the processes examined. If we are concerned with the structural element of higher education places, then their number is fixed by government in response to sectoral pressures, specifically the professional classes and the professions. As for the collapse of the youth labour market, the reasons for that are extremely complex but essentially reduce to the fact that the overall demand for labour has fallen, which again must be explained by a combination of factors; and that since school-leavers have fewer resources than other labour market contenders they are unable to make a successful bid for employment. No one suggests that the collapse of the youth labour market is not caused by human agency, but how to correct it is far from being a simple matter. Effective interventions could be made only by government. Certainly, elected goverments will respond to popular pressure, but, while that is being built up, teachers, parents and pupils must act within the structures that exist, and that, as I have pointed out, must help maintain them. (One element that is comparatively easy to transform by non-government, popular, agency is the sex differentiation within these structures; it leaves everything else untouched and simply redistributes the sex of those who hold positions within them. I am not opposed to this but I shall make the point.)

The schooling processes analysed in this chapter are ever active and are simply intensified by the recent collapse of the youth labour market. The problems of politics and pedagogy must be discussed elsewhere, In conclusion it will be noted only that it seems necessary to give up completely the idea that educational systems can be effective agencies of social mobility for an entire class and hence so foster, in that way, a society in which the resources of intelligence, capital and political control are more equally distributed. What schools can do, at least, is confront the pressures that structure the lives led within them, in the belief that however little may be within the power of teachers and pupils even that depends on a correct analysis.

References

Boudon, R. (1982) *The Unintended Consequences of Social Action.* London, Macmillan.

Bourdieu, P. and Boltanski, L. (1978) 'Changes in Social Structure and Changes in the Demand for Education', in S. Giner and M. Archer (eds.), *Contemporary Europe.* London, Routledge & Kegan Paul.

Collins, R. (1979) *The Credential Society.* London, Academic Press.

Davis, P. (1979) 'Social Mobility in New Zealand: Preliminary Results from a National Survey'. *Australia and New Zealand Journal of Sociology* 15 (3): pp. 50–56.

Dore, R. (1976) *The Diploma Disease.* London, Allen & Unwin.

Edwards, R. C. (1979) *Contested Terrain.* London, Heinemann.

Hall, S. and Jefferson, T. (eds.) (1976) *Resistance through Rituals.* London, Heinemann.

McKenzie, D. (1980) 'Scholars and Mobility: an Account of the Operation of the Scholarship Scheme in Otago, 1878–1889'. Paper presented to the tenth annual ANZHES Conference. Newcastle, Australia.

CHAPTER NINE

Work, Education and Democratisation

Knud Jensen

Introduction

Politics is the distribution of benefits and burdens; politicians will not distribute these benefits and burdens in the same manner. The research project that I discuss in this chapter has been used and is still used by the political left wing in Denmark; but it is also used by some of the new liberals who, at the local level, work towards the decentralisation of political power.

The particular research material I intend to discuss here concentrates upon only part of a larger project. The broad research problem that occupies me is a curiosity about the kind of understandings workers build up during work. Analysts from a wide range of disciplines – philosophy, psychology, pedagogics, sociology, politics and economics – seem to have been able to acknowledge that *people's basic experiences arise or are learned in relation to work*. So what is it that one actually learns? What sort of understanding is it that these analysts have of work and learning, and what kind of knowledge and understanding do workers achieve during their work-related experiences. In this chapter I will introduce and discuss a single facet of my research, namely the relationship btween vocational education (or, as I prefer, 'work education') and democratisation. This research strand centred on an experiment in autonomy and democratisation in the classroom, jointly mounted by a group of researchers and teachers. The analysis of this experiment derives its point of origin, its direction and its critical strength from a dialectic–materialistic background; and as it progresses I will touch upon certain problematic aspects of Marxist analysis, especially where I am in disagreement with some of the economistic or structuralistic versions of this approach.

Working conditions: schooling and research in Denmark

Before I begin the description of the research work, it is necessary to provide a brief sketch of the context in which the experiment was conducted. The legislation determining the system of schooling in Denmark and the status of researchers within the system have certain unique properties that bear directly upon the research itself.

The Folkeskole

Primary and lower secondary schooling in Denmark is provided in the Folkeskole. The objectives and organisation of the Folkeskole are both strictly defined by the Danish School Act of August 1976. The juridical side of activities in the Folkeskole, then, is determined by statute, and this includes a formal statement of the general objectives of the Folkeskole, incorporating the following three interesting elements:

- to contribute to the all-round development of the pupil;
- to create possibilities of experience and self-expression that allow pupils to develop their ability for making independent assessments, evaluations and opinions; and,
- to prepare pupils for participation in the processes of a democratic society.

According to these objectives, the education provided by the school and its entire daily life must, therefore, be founded on intellectual liberty and democracy – as the following Ministry of Education statement shows:

> The aim of the Folkeskole is, in co-operation with parents, to give pupils a possibility of acquiring knowledge, skills, working methods and ways of expressing themselves which will contribute to the all-round development of the individual pupil.
> In all of its work, the Folkeskole must try to create possibilities of experience and self-expression which allow pupils to increase their

desire to learn, expand their imagination, and develop their ability for making independent assessments, evaluations and opinions.

The Folkeskole shall prepare pupils for taking an active interest in their environment and for participation in decision-making in a democratic society, and for sharing responsibility for the solution of common problems. Thus, teaching and the entire daily life in school must be based on intellectual liberty and democracy.

(Danish Ministry of Education 1976)

It can, perhaps, be difficult to comprehend that an ideological state apparatus can explicitly impose such objectives. But it is of great significance for the possibilities for change in the ideological state apparatus itself and, moreover, it is a result of political and ideological struggle in Denmark. (A central point in this context is that the law directs that the teacher co-operate with the pupils in the choice of curriculum content and structure, of pedagogic style and of how learning is organised:

The more detailed planing and organisation of educational activities, including the decision on teaching forms, methods and material, shall as far as possible take place in co-operation between the teachers and the pupils.

(Danish School Act 1976:clause 16.4)

Today, an average course of schooling will start at 6 years of age in a nursery-school class, followed by nine years of obligatory education that, more often than not, take place in the Folkeskole. The average number of pupils in a class is around twenty. The Ministry of Education provides guidelines to local authorities on what subjects are to be taught in school and how they might be taught. The allocation of lessons suggested in these guidelines (Table 9.1) shows two interesting features. For every year group of form there is one weekly lesson, designated 'the class's lesson'; and in the eighth to the tenth forms there are three weekly lessons in contemporary studies. Further to this there are some obligatory subjects that must be dealt with; for example, traffic safety, sexual instruction, foreign religions and philosophies.

A myth

A living legend concerning the Danish Folkeskole has it that changes in legislation arise as a result of changes that have taken place in the school's everday life. This is a myth, but it has a progressive signficance, the reason being that it gives relatively easy access for experimentation, though not with widespread financial support. This access to variations and experiment is, in

Table 9.1 Lesson allocation in the Folkeskole

Compulsory topics: traffic safety, sexual instruction, Norwegian and Swedish, other religions and philosophies of life, educational and vocational guidance, health and information on the most prevalent stimulants and intoxicants.

Subject	1	2	3	4	5	6	7	8	9	10
Danish	9	8	7	6	6	6	6	6	6	6
Free class discussion	1	1	1	1	1	1	1	1	1	1
Arithmetic/maths	4	4	4	4	4	4	4	4	4	
Phys. ed. and sport	1	2	2	2	2	2	2	2	2	3
Christian studies	1	1	1	2	1	2		1	1	
Creative art	1	2	2	2	1					
Music	1	2	2	2	1					
History History Contem					2	2				
Geography Geography porary			3	3	3	2	2	3	3	3
Biology Biology studies					2	2				
Needlework				2	2					
Woodwork				2	2					
Home economics					2	3				
English					3	3	3	3	3	3
Physics/chemistry								2	2	2
Non-compulsory subjects in all							3[3]	8	8	14
Total number of weekly lessons	18	20	22	24	26	28	30	30	30	30
Minimum number of lessons according to the Act	15	15	18	20	23	24	24	24	24	24
Maximum number of lessons according to the Act	20	20	23	25	29	30	30	30	30	

fact, used to a considerable degree, even though these do not necessarily lead to particularly progressive changes in the long run.

Researchers
Most research people in the higher institutes of educaton are public servants, and most often they define their own research within their fields of employment; ostensibly this should provide possibilities for more controversial research. Some of them are appointed on a group contract basis, but in principle they all have the same conditions. There is a tendency, however, to carry out more and more contract research for both the public institutions (governmental, county and municipal) and private concerns. This is made possible by the greater number of qualified young people who have a higher education but are without permanent employment. For the research project described here, my own situation was that I abandoned my university work and was instead employed as principal of the Folkeskole in a Copenhagen suburb where the experiment was developed.

Shaping and reshaping the research problem

As a starting point for the research, I selected the following title for the project in an attempt to articulate a concise version of the research problem: 'A descriptive analysis of the relationship between participation in a work process and the education gained as a consequence'. I chose to illuminate the problem through the use of different analytical strategies; namely, consideration of pedagogic–philosophical debate, of Danish school history, of the political economy of education and, of course, of the experiment itself. A crucial concern in the early stages of the research was an exploration of variations in how the relationship between work and education has been conceptualised.

The pedagogic-philosophical perspective
In the formation of pedagogic theory, a great deal of the discussion from the turn of the century and some decades afterwards was taken up by the work concept and its educational value. A systematic representation will point at three dispositions towards the 'work school'. In autocratic Europe, mercantilism as an economic principle gave rise to a rapid development of individual countries'

191

own production systems, for which there was a shortage of the necessary and qualified labour force with sufficient knowledge and skill. Workhouses, where the necessary training could take place, are known from several places in Europe, and these were continued in the industrial schools in the eighteenth century. The central issue in this connection was the emphasis on trade skills, and these schools were based solely on the desire to educate for work.

The second disposition crops up in connection with the violent structural changes related to nineteenth-century industrialisation. New traits were necessary for the labour force, and the greatly increased work distribution made trade education inadequate. By considering the provision of trade skills as a didactic task, however, not only was education *for* work extended but also the possiblity was created for an education *through* work, and thus, at the same time, for an understanding of work's character-forming significance.

In the third approach, the work concept has been set into a community–theoretical model. Trade skills came to be seen as a part of humanistic education. The two elements that radically separate this approach from the former are the thesis concerning the class character of child-rearing and the thesis with regard to the necessity of combining school education with productive work, thus making technological training a part of all-round education.

I found that Spencer, Kerschensteiner, Dewey and Krupskaja were fruitful exponents for this part of the study. Starting from different viewpoints concerning the existing and the future society, they reached different conclusions with regard to the educational value of work. They represent a collection of varying but important points of view on work, helping us recognise that the concept of work varies, for example:

- in relation to education and training;
- in relation to the social structure;
- in relation to class and stratum;
- in relation to work distribution and power; and
- in relation to interest, need and motivation.

Some features of Danish school history

In the Danish debate surrounding children's work and education in the 1920s and 1930s there is a pronounced interest on the political and on the pedagogic level. The key concept was self-activity. Self-activity involves two elements; the first is that one is active, and the second is that one decides for oneself what one is

192

active with. Supporters of pedagogic 'work' in school, and thus of the pupil's self-activity, worked for a ban on child labour. Those who thought that the children came to no harm by doing a bit of paid labour for strangers were very doubtful about just how self-active, and thus self-determinative, children could be allowed to become in an educational context. The same discussion was continued into the 1960s, but the connection between the practical subjects (arts and crafts) and the commercially oriented subjects (vocational training/career education) in the Folkeskole's senior classes took on a different slant. The debate went so far that one discussed whether woodwork, metalwork and the like should provide a particular occupational competence in relation to the training of apprentices.

However, it is the combination of work and self-activity that is interesting, which I have shown has received legal status in the School Act 1976.

The political economy of education

Political economy and the renaissance it received within the educational sector in the 1960s and 1970s showed particular interest in the connection between developments in the methods of production and developments in the educational system. The interest in the function of education, and especially qualification theories, is fruitful because it attempts to capture the relationship between the changes in the structure of the labour market and that qualification structure with which the educational system equips the future labour force.

Today, I regard much of the analysis as having a restricting effect on our understanding of school processes. The restrictions to which these analyses gave rise were most often that they did not respect their own premises, such as the theory concerning relatively autonomous state apparatus; or, theories that reduced their points of origin from illumination of the connection between several factors to the dominance by some factors of other factors. A type of limitation is involved that often arises when the angles of approach to an analysis are too technical or narrow.

Reshaping of the problem

At the beginning of my research I held the view that, on the basis of the three areas mentioned above, I would be able to carry out an analysis of how significant the changes in courses of study and in educational practice were that moved in the direction of greater self-activity and greater occupational orientation. Reflection on the lesson of the three debates – philosophic, historical and political – forced me to consider whether my working title adequately encapsulated my problem and, since it did not do this, to reformulate it. The orignal problem formulation was: 'A descriptive analysis of the relationship between participation in a work process and the education gained as a consequence'. The changed problem formulation became: 'A description and an analysis of the work process as a learning process, with regard to the participants' relations to their own and to others' conceptions, actions and benefits'.

My original formulation of the problem had contained a reduction of the problem's complexity and of the elements of the working process. I could hardly have found this reduction if I had used only *one* of the three angles of approach, and my investigation would have been related only to the reduced problem. I will illustrate this shortly.

The experiment: the school at Magelhøj

The scene

The place is a municipal borough with approximately 10,000 inhabitants, thirty kilometres from the centre of Copenhagen. During the course of the last twenty years the borough has changed from being a small village community to a fully developed suburb, politically dominated by the conservatives and the liberals. Some quite serious problems with the young opened up the possibilities for establishing a work school. The setting-up of an experimental school as part of the normal school created many kinds of conflict. But the extension of activities was agreed upon, despite the fact that this gave rise to increaed public expenditure; it was election year.

There was talk in the community of extensive criminality and the start of deviant behaviour by smaller groups of school pupils. Where the school was concerned, the problems were reflected in absenteeism and thus in intensified scholastic and social difficulties. The problems made themselves felt most seriously at the senior class levels. The problems resulted in a discussion between school staff and politicians about the lack of youth activities and of the possible prevention of corresponding problems with the pupils of the future.

The disinclination to go to school, a distaste for the school and problems of behaviour manifest themselves more and more frequently among children in the sixth, seventh and eighth classes. Behind the suggestion concerning the establishment of a work school lay my already-mentioned considerations and the assumption that it is also possible to teach academic subjects as an integrated part of practical work. The town council decided to establish a work school at an abandoned farm in the borough for a trial period of three years. The experiment was to take into account the already 'school-tired' pupils from the eighth and ninth classes, and the 'potentially school-tired' at the sixth and seventh levels.

It was agreed that an experimental school should be established in which pupils in the sixth and seventh forms would follow programmes that mixed their regular curriculum with project weeks built up around practical work – and practical work aimed at democratising their involvement in the work process and at preparing them for participation in work outside the school. The school at Magelhoj was born.

The curriculum

The curriculum at Magelhoj was built up around horticultural production, building crafts, mechanical production, administration and housekeeping. The Folkeskole's main subjects, Danish and arithmetic, were integrated in this teaching in the form of work programmes, work descriptions, surveys, etc. All work and education contained planning, presentation and evaluation of the work. At the start of their stay at the school a working programme was drawn up for the individual pupils. Great emphasis was placed on the fact that at the end of their stay there should be no vocational obstacles standing in the way of the pupils' return to their home classes. The project weeks for the young pupils were also built up around a limited subject, and also involved planning, production and evaluation.

The school at Magelhoj has now been in existence for seven years; it is still the subject of political and pedagogic discussion in the local area. However, since my employment at the Royal Danish School of Educational Studies some four years ago, I have not had any direct association with it. I have chosen to include this description because I regard it as important that my data and the conditions for its collection be open to question.

Knud Jensen

The experiment itself

When learning is organised as a work process it will, in its simplest form, involve three phases:

- the first in which the impression of the work is formed;
- the second in which the work is carried out; and,
- the third in which the efforts are evaluated in relation to the applicability of the product.

Two theses formed the basis of organising education in work processes. The first was that learning is made easier when the form in which it takes place can be directly understood; the second was that experience gained from solving practical problems could perhaps the transferred to other situations and thus be of general significance for the pupils. These assumptions are not new, but are based precisely on the work-school experiences developed in the 1920s and 1930s. This, incidentally, is also in agreement with Marx's ontological work concept. In *Capital*, Marx notes:

> In the first instance the work is a process in which both the person and nature participate–a process in which the person on his own initiative puts into effect, regulates and controls his metabolism with nature. As a force of nature he sets himself up as a counterpart to the material of nature itself: he sets the powers of nature with which he is equipped, namely arms, legs, head and hands, in movement in order to appropriate the nature products in a form which is adjusted to his own needs. At the same time, through this movement, he influences and changes the nature outside himself, and he changes his own nature.
>
> (Marx 1976:p. 302)

There is such an enormous amount of school work that does not have the character of real work (at least not in the Danish schools); and this is due, among other things, to the fact that the relatively autonomous agents of the ideological state apparatus (the teachers) have not discovered this problem, or that they act in accordance with a restricted conception of work. Consideration of Engels's conception of work will, I think, illuminate this. He comments that 'Labour which creates use-values and is *qualitatively* determined is called "work" as opposed to labour; labour which creates value and is only measured *quantitatively* is called "labour" as opposed to "work" '(Marx 1976: ch. 1, part 3, footnote by Engels).

School labour with the alien quantitative requirement creates a capacity for work. But our aim was the development of the versatile, democratic and socially aware person. This is why progressive teachers must use their relative autonomy to recreate qualitatively determined work in school for the pupils and to minimise quantitative school labour.

In the early phase of our research I described the didactic consequences of this understanding of work as follows:

> If we hold to the basic assumption that the pupils can learn to use experiences within new areas, then it is a new condition that the conception with regard to new work is common to both teachers and pupils; not in the sense that we know an equal amount, but in the sense that the pupil has an understanding of and accepts that a concept can be realised. If this condition is not fulfilled, then the rest of the process will only partly take on the character of work, at least not of conscious work.
>
> (Jensen 1978).

In this connection it was interesting to note the pupils' experience of work in relation to our conception of the work process. From observation, I was able to describe the teachers' deliberations in a series of logical steps, and I realised that the pupils' influence would not make itself felt until the work tasks had been given an order of priority. Thus:

(1) The teachers agree upon the next step.
(2) Some of the teachers draw up a rough plan.
    (a) Which remedies are the pupils going to use in order to acquire knowledge?
    (b) What are the instructions going to be for the groups that are to carry out the plan?
    (c) How much time will it be acceptable to use for the pupils' preparations?
    (This is where the pupils' influence starts.)
    (d) How is the planning group going to inform the others of the basis of decisions?
    (e) How is the final decision going to be made.
    (f) What further planning is needed regarding materials, tools, the sequence of work and timetable?
(3) Production of working plan for the subject.

At this point there was no doubt about the legitimacy of this form of teaching process, neither amongst the teachers nor among those in charge. Likewise, there was no doubt among the pupils: they did *not* consider the procedure as being legitimate. (In this

197

context I choose to use the word 'legitimate' as almost synonymous with 'reasonable' and 'justified', as in everyday language). Even though they could not formulate the viewpoint in verbal criticism, it was expressed clearly and distinctly in their behaviour. Their attitude towards a lot of work was that they did not take it seriously. Later, somewhat vaguely, I wrote about these cirumstances as follows: 'Despite the difficulties in putting our theoretical starting point into practice, it happens more and more frequently that the practical work forms the *starting point* for the school's remaining activities.' I could just as well have written: 'In fact, things are not going too well.' It was the first time that I had had personal doubts concerning the teachers' and the management's legitimate rights to interpret the *conception* phase *for* the pupils. My assumption had to be altered and be based on the actual situation.

Data collected at Magelhøj

Before describing the changes in my assumptions with regard to the relationship between work and learning, I should give an account of the data we collected concurrently during the experiment. The most important data types were as follows:

- *The pupils' work-sheets.* The pupils filled these out every day with the title of the work task, the number of working hours and possible remarks.
- *Work schedules.* For the concrete tasks.
- *Observation notes.* From work situations and meetings.
- *Reports of pupils' conversations.*
- *The pupils' reports concerning pupil meetings.* The pupils' conditions.
- *The teachers' reports concerning teacher meetings.* Instruction, pupils, learning problems.
- *The management's reports concerning management meetings.* Instruction to pupils, teaching problems and problems in relation to the commune.
- *Teachers', pupils' and own reports of joint meetings.* Participants were pupils, teachers and management; all problems could be raised.
- *Decision and negotiation records of all political plans.* The parent–teacher committee, teachers' council, school and leisure-time committee, financial committee, town council.

Decisions in the work process

I realised that the difficulty lay in getting the pupils to see *through* the whole process and in getting the teacher group to work *with* the whole process, even though the pupils lacked a number of prerequisities for being able to see through the work process and thus also to take joint responsibility for implementation.

I committed the considerations to paper in the following way:

> In the simplest form, the work process can be described in progressive steps. A decision (1) is taken to convert something (2) to something else (3). What is involved is a conscious conception during which one prepares oneself for the consquences of that action which one will undertake, and where the possibilities of control lie in the finished product.
>
> In our society the process is far more complicated because it is socially organised and financially dependent and conditoned. A further simplified presentation of the process can throw some light on some fundamental difficulties.

In diagrammatic form, these 'difficulties' can be grasped as in Table 9.2.

It was here that I discovered the problem between the conception's sequences. I had come to write teacher conception as if it were a joint conception. When the aim is for the work process not to be restricted to acting as a consequence of the conception of others, then it is necessary for both *conceptions* and *evaluations* of the result to be included in the process analysis, and this holds true not only for the individual's work, but also for the work of larger and smaller groups and not least for participants with varying power.

The work process as a didactic model

Although at this time we had worked on the categorisation of assertions and behaviour, we could make neither head nor tail of our observations. This was naturally the case because our methods were incomplete and founded on theoretically incorrect premisses.

Each of the three phases in the work process can be looked upon as being a part-work-process. We called the elements in the part-work-processes sequences. On the theoretical level, each of the three phases can be considered as an independent work process, the approach shown in Table 9.2.

My new didactic model came to look like Table 9.3.

(This model is built up on the classical model of work. One has a conception of something, one acts to achieve this something and one gets a result of one's actions. One is placed in another situation.)

Table 9.2

Conception	Action	Result
1 Whose conception?	2 Who is to act?	2 To whom does it belong?
2 Which conditions?	1 On which conditions?	1 Which advantage?
3 Whose decision?	3 Which consequences?	2 How necessary for whom?
3 Which intention?	3 For whose benefit?	

Table 9.3 Didactic model of the work process

	Phase 1 Conception/ decision	Phase 2 Action with regard to change	Phase 3 The product and its utility
Sequence I: Idea/consideration/ examination	Idea: whose conception or idea concerning change is it?	Conditions: obtaining the necessary materials and means	Product: how did it proceed? Can it be used?
Sequence II: Change/possibility	Argumentation: what and why does on want to change?	Action: which actions are going to take place and when?	Effect: did it change anything compared to the former situation?
Sequence III: Decision/evaluation/ control	Decision: who is going to effect the change and how?	Control: who accomplishes and controls the relation between aims and action?	New conception/idea: how necessary was it? Which possibilities does the new situation involve?

◀━━ The process of democratisation ━▶

Let me explain the model. When education is organised as a work process, in its simplest form, it will give rise to attention to three phases:

- The first phase is that in which the conception of the work is formed; i.e. one conceives a situation converted to another situation with new possibilities.
- The second phase is that in which the work is carried out; one changes the situation or the conditions.
- The third phase is the new situation; the changed conditions and the possibilities that lie therein.

More often than not, the three phases cannot be so sharply separated, and consequently it happens that work must be given up provisionally in order to revise the conceptions. Nevertheless, the phases are a help when education has to be organised, and when the contents of education have to be determined. If we consider the conception phase as an example, then the conditions for its progress and the result will depend partly on the external conditions, partly on the participants' world of experience and not least on the attitude taken by the participants towards these two aspects. What perspective and what possibilities does the participant see in the situation?

The conception phase

The first sequence is the concept. One gets an idea concerning the making of a change. One is prepared to act. The second sequence involves the considerations covering what is to be done, and how the pattern of action may/can be. What is involved here is an examination, an argumentation and bringing one's experiences into readiness. One acquires knowledge. We could talk about intellectual action. The third sequence involves making a decision concerning the course of action and the initiation of its implementation (or its rejection), on the basis of the two previous sequences.

I then re-analysed my data in accordance with the participants' attitude and power. Consequently, my interest changed from classification and numeration to *recording how the participants failed to exercise influence on the work process*. My strategic interest became concentrated on getting participants to take a steadily increasing part of the control over the whole chain of events.

I carried out the re-analysis by removing 'noise' from my data;

that is, I included only observations and behaviour that had a bearing on the matter, and this gave an interesting picture of both the work processes and educational situations. In Tables 9.4, 9.5 and 9.6 I try to illustrate the power of the model for an analysis of work experience in educational settings. The tables allow for a graphic representation of shifts in the degree of influence by participants in different phases, and in different sequences of different phases, of the three action levels of the work process. The examples of work process are of three specific projects that formed part of the experiment. The projects are:

(1) The manufacture of a product for the first time; in this case, the production of tables and benches for the school.
(2) The mass production of the same product; in this case, production for use and for exchange.
(3) Some new production suggested by a participant; in this case, a pupil's suggestion to set up a chicken farm.

The examples are not empirical in the sense that they show only figurative and selective representations of what took place. They are actual, however, in the sense that they describe the power-levels in different phases and sequences of the work, when irrelevant elements have been removed. To put it another way, they are objective but laundered.

In reality, what I had done was to make the didactic model three-dimensional. I could see that unless *all* participants took part in the *whole* of the process, then the education was unsatisfactory and my research meaningless, because the transfer from work and education that one could expect in a given case must immediately appear to be in the criteria for *decision*, in the abilities to *act* and in the criteria for *evaluation*. My research design changed character. *What use was there in trying to answer the question: What has the pupil gained out of participation in the concrete work process, when the work process in the mind of the pupil lacked parts of the process and was thus different to what I had thought?* In this situation it was immaterial how much data I put together, because it did not throw any light on the problem I wanted to examine.

It is thus primarily in the conception phase that the two sides of self-activity–action and joint consultation–must be coupled together. If the work has a quality that can be used for other than social control, then the coupling of work and democratisation is inevitable in the school; unless, that is, as a teacher one actually wants to exercise one's social control by concealing parts of the

203

Table 9.4 Didactic model of the work process for the first-time production of tables and benches for the school's outside rooms

	Phase 1 Conception* decision	Phase 2 Action with regard to change	Phase 3 The product and its utility
Sequence I: Idea/consideration/ examination	Idea: oooo xxx	Conditions: xxxx xxxx sss	Product: xxxx xxxx ssss
Sequence II: Change/ possibility	Argumentation: oooo oooo xxxx xx s	Action: xxxx xxxx ssss ssss ssss	Effect: oooo oooo xxxx sss
Sequence III: Decision/ evaluation/ control	Decision: oooo xxxx ss	Control: xxxx xxxx ssss	New conception/idea: oooo oooo xxxx xxxx ss

◄──The process of democratization──►

Key: o = leadership; x = teachers; s = students.

Explanation: The different amounts of hatching symbolise the extent of the registered interest of each of the three power layers (their purpose), the amount of resources used by the class, e.g. time, knowledge, finances, and their registered activity in order to reach to the next sequence in the work process. The re-analysis has sought to determine the participation by all three layers in all phases and all sequences in the work process.

Table 9.5 Didactic model of the work process for the mass production of the same product, partly for other schools and partly for sale

	Phase 1 Conception decision	Phase 2 Action with regard to change	Phase 3 The product and its utility
Sequence I: Idea/consideration/ examination	Idea: oooo xxx s	Conditions: xxxx xxxx ssss	Product: xxxx ssss
Sequence II: Change/ possibility	Argumentation oooo oooo xxxx ssss	Action: xxxx ssss ssss ssss	Effect: xxxx xxxx ssss ssss
Sequence II: Decision/ evaluation/ control	Decision: xxxx xxxx ssss	Control: xxxx xxxx ssss ssss	New conception/idea: xxxx xxxx ssss

←The process of democratisation→

Key: o = leadership; x = teachers; s = students.

Table 9.6 Didactic model of the work process for new production on pupil initiative: setting up a chicken farm

	Phase 1 Conception/ decision	Phase 2 Action with regard to change	Phase 3 The product and its utility
Sequence I: Idea/consideration/ examination	Idea: ssss x	Conditions: ssss ssss ssss xxxx	Product: ssss ssss xx
Sequence II: Change/ possibility	Argumen- tation: ssss ssss xxxx	Action: ssss ssss ssss	Effect: ssss ssss xxxx
Sequence III: Decision/ evaluation/ control	Decision: ssss xx	Control: ssss ssss xxxx	New conception/ idea: ssss ssss xxxx

◄—— The process of democratisation ——►

Key: o = leadership; x = teachers; s = students.

work process and thus obstruct insight. It is also here that the liberating strategic element is revealed: to get the teachers to democratise *their* work process. One of the ways in which this can be brought about is by the teachers using the model as a tool for anlaysis, not only of manual work but also of normal teaching. The move from the didactic determination of work to a determination of education is, on the theoretical level, relatively simple; on the practical level the world is always more complicated.

However, before returning to the assertion that the didactic model also includes power levels, I will exemplify briefly the point that teachers, either consciously or unconsciously, often create work and learning processes without the conception possibility for the pupils, and without the pupils' control of the utility of their own work. At Magelhoj we were able to ascertain that the teachers' execution of education in connection with the development of proficiencies in, for example, Danish, mathematics and foreign languages formed the following pattern (Table 9.7), or what I call the outer frame; the inner frame is the pupils' pattern.

It often proved to be the case that the action by the pupils was that they were told what they had to make and where, why and how they should make it. The control thus rested solely with the teachers. These teachers were open to democratisation. A simultaneous representative investigation into the teachers' starting point for education provided the following picture: 69 per cent of teachers in the Danish Folkeskole always or often use as a starting point for their teaching subjects that are formulated in ready-made educational materials. This does not necessarily say anything about education and democratisation; but it indicates that very many of the teachers have left the whole of their conception phase to the best publishers they happen to know.

Teachers are the potential for change

To begin with, it is on the teacher level that it will be possible to make changes, the reason being that teachers, at least in Demark, are relatively autonomous agents. The most noteworthy aspect of the teachers' position is that *there are no work orders attached to their work situation: they work within a framework that can and must be interpreted.*

Instead of summarising or concluding, I prefer to stipulate those

Table 9.7 Frames of control

	Phase 1 Conception/ decision	Phase 2 Action with regard to change	Phase 3 The product and its utility
Sequence I: Idea/consideration/ examination	Idea: whose conception or idea concerning change is it?	Conditions: obtaining the necessary materials and means	Product: how did it proceed? Can it be used?
Sequence II: Change/possibility	Argumentation: what and why does on want to change?	Action: which actions are going to take place and when?	Effect: did it change anything compared to the former situation?
Sequence III: Decision/evaluation/ control	Decision: who is going to effect the change and how?	Control: who accomplishes and controls the relation between aims and action?	New conception/idea: how necessary was it? Which possibilities does the new situation involve?

◀── The process of democratisation ──▶

Table 9.8 The basis for teaching in Denmark (2,693 teachers)

The basis comprises	Always + often	Some times	Seldom + never	Total
	%	%	%	%
Subjects formulated in ready-made teaching media	69	16	16	101
Subjects formulated by the teacher	37	47	16	100
Subjects formulated by teacher and pupils	14	39	58	111
Subjects formulated by the teacher and colleagues	10	24	65	99
Subjects formulated by the pupils	4	22	74	100

Source: DLF and DPI (1981).

problems that are the subject of my research now and in another context. The problem is that while pedagogic *research* resting on a social analysis can illuminate some conditions, some relationships and some consequences for action, pedagogic *practice* may also well be reduced to externally determined conceptions among both teachers and pupils, reduced to formal interaction and to ritual control with an educational product. Without direct participation in a living school, it is very seldom that pedagogic research can be coined to form a usable pedagogy. This is a form of conclusion.

If work and education can, however, become a process that embraces conception (concerning change of the physical conditions, the implementation of changes and the evaluation of the utility of the changes, and where the participants work towards reducing external determination in relation to conceptions, in relation to action and in relation to the control of the output), will the school then be capable of changing society? Here I must still answer no. But if I am faced with the statement, 'In the end, the production conditions determine the school's development', then I must immediately agree. On that level the interpretations from political economic analysis will never reach further than to self-fulfilling prophecies. The core of the matter is that the school is a part of society, so important a part that its designation as an ideological state apparatus has gained ground in the newer Maxist theory. The ideological state apparatus is dominated by the ideology of the ruling class; other ideologies are suppressed. Translated into everyday language, this means that different interests break with the dominating interest's conceptions with regard to society, with regard to life's norms, rituals, forms of practice and habits. The relationship is not causal but dialectal.

In Denmark the teacher as such is in no way bound in the legal sense to any certain interpretation of the contents of education; not to any definite form or method. The children, on the other hand, are forced into the situation.

Who is allied with whom?

Neither teachers nor pupils are homogeneous groups, and external determination or suppression is to be found in may forms and to many degrees. But the *attitude* of the agents is not necessarily that of the dominating ideology. Here we can see the strategic problem for those interested in reform; how do we get relatively autonomous agents to assume a democratic responsibility and thus to work against external determination, suppression and meaningless activities? As shown, in a part-system of an organisation it is possible to analyse the tendencies in the agents' visions and conduct by examining power layer by layer – the agents' *interest, access, resources* and *actions*. This was my model's third dimension.

When several people together engage in an acitivity on the basis of agreements in interest, access and the use of resources, then, as I see it, they comprise a faction. If the people themselves have a comprehensive view of the relationship of the four variables to a matter, or complex of matters, one can talk about a conscious faction formation. It is this comprehension of the four variables within the faction itself that determines whether one can talk about a conscious or an unconscious forming of a faction.

With the introduction of the four variables and the concept of factions, the analysis of an organisation such as the school can be not only refined, but also used to direct a research group's intervention in an action-research project. A teacher group is heterogeneous; it contains possible factions, but not all factions are necessarily engaged by emancipatory interests, or are exercisers of liberating actions. By working with researcher roles, working with decision areas and types and carrying out the concrete analysis of the power layers and possible factions within a situation, it is possible for teachers to reach forward to support those factions that have a democratic perspective and an emancipatory interest and practice. Disparity and the overcoming of discrepancies form the starting point in learning processes; and recognition of this is one of the conditions for the learning process to be developed into a democratising one in the widest sense. In a corresponding way, the result of a learning process is not a longer-lasting harmony, but the discovery of new obstacles or the attaining of a new free-space with the challenges that this involves.

By taking seriously the pupils' right to be consulted, and through research and theoretical and practical support to those factions desiring a radical re-shaping of the school with little externally determined control of the work in school, a democratic perspective can be stregthened. Naturally, even with such considerations, progressive schools cannot change the whole of society. The point is that it is possible to reduce the dominance, to create breathing space in which changed social relations and methods of gaining experience can, perhaps, be tranformed to other spheres – spheres in which they can be used more directly in the work for greater social equity and solidarity.

For this reason, I am now working with and carrying out research in the theory formation and educational practice of progressive teachers' factions, i.e. with the following three theses that it is possible to develop democratic and unifying educational and work situations:

(1) when participants or factions of participants with different interests can sum up a conception and enter into agreement concerning what is to be done, and how one can achieve the realisation of the conception;
(2) when participants or factions of participants co-ordinate actions around agreements regarding the fulfilment of the aim, regardless of whether the actions are literary, manual, musical or political; and

(3) when the participants' or factions of participants' product and
its utility are evaluated both in relation to the individual's and
the faction's interests, resources, access and activity, in relation
to the agreements entered into and in relation to the new
possibilities.

References

DLF and DPI (1981) *The Teachers' Working Environment in the Council
School.* Copenhagen.

Danish Ministry of Education (1976) *Statement of Folkeskole Objectives.*
Copenhagen.

(1977) The Act on the Folkeskole. Copenhagen.

Jensen, Knud (1978) 'Skolen efter Skolen' in I. Goldback and S. Henriksen
(eds.), *Pedagogic Perspective*. Copenhagen, Gyldendal.

Marx, Karl (1976) *Capital Volume 1*. Harmondsworth, Penguin.

Acknowledgement

I am grateful to Stephen Walker for his painstaking work on the
draft translation of this chapter.

General Index

assessment 156, 160; *see also* credentials
Australia 76, 168

behaviour codes 97-8, 101n11, 104
black people 53, 118-45; 184;
    employment prospects 118, 142, 184;
    state policy on 118-26, 127-42, 144-5;
    see also Maoris
B/TEC courses 155, 164
Bullock Committee 61

Callaghan, James 32, 59
Caribbean Times 119
Centre for Contemporary Cultural
    Studies 122, 171
child labour 193; *see also* work
    experience
City & Guilds courses 155, 158
class: and dependence 98, 104; and
    employment 86, 94, 95-6, 98-9, 168,
    171-2, 184; attitudes 15-16, 17, 23, 98
'classification' 152-5, 159-65
clerical work 75, 77-8, 83
clothes, as work requirement 80
conservatism, radical 56, 139
Construction Industry Training Board
    73
contraception 101n11
control, state 7, 25, 47; *see also under*
    MSC

counselling 59, 158, 183
credentials/qualifications 71, 110, 156,
    158, 168, 182-3, 184; as handicap
    178-9; in France 157-8; in NZ 168-70,
    173-80
cultural reproduction *see* reproduction
    theory
culture(s) 171; and class 23, 94, 181;
    black 127, 130; British 130; youth 4,
    94-5, 97-8, 171, 180, 181, 183, (and
    gender) 94-8, 108-9, 110-11

Denmark 187-210
dependence 61, 64, 98, 104, 109, 111
disabilities 136
'dole schools' *see* JICs
domestic servants 15-16

education: and gender stereotyping 79;
    and racism 142-4; and work 32, 40,
    46; 55-6, 64, 142, 143, (in NZ) 167-71,
    173-86; 'classification' and 'framing'
    in 152-5, 159-65; 'compensatory' 136;
    control of 7-8, 51 (*see also under*
    MSC); democratisation 187, 195,
    211-12; effects of unemployment on
    3, 5-6, 110; funding 36; general 62-3,
    159; 'Great Debate' on 32, 33, 51;
    history of 14, 191-2; ideology 25, 38,
    41-2, 61, 74, 188-93, 210; in Denmark

213

188–210; in France 157; political
58–60; selection in 29, 71; 'work' 187,
191–2, 194–207; *see also* FE *and*
schools
'Empire Settlement' campaign 13
employers 58, 61, 78; selection strategies
71, 178–9, 184
employment 60, 64, 70, 76, 86; social
relations of 68, 77, 81, 83, 84; *see also*
labour market(s), unemployment
and work
equal opportunities policies 138, 140

factory work 100
'feminised' work 81, 83
feminism 95, 96
'framing' 152–5, 159–65
France 153, 155–8, 160, 164
FE (Further Education) 37, 47–56, 83;
and class 86; competition 85;
'conscription' 52–3; divisions in 52,
61, 158–9; MSC and 37, 49, 51, 53–4,
87–8; relative autonomy 87–8; *see also*
training

gender stereotyping and roles 33, 50,
92–3, 94–8, 99, 100–11; *see also* sexual
division of labour *and under* JICs
Germany 69
girls: in JICs 13, 14, 15–16, 21;
restrictions on behaviour 97–8, 108–9;
unemployment 9–10, 97, 184; *see also*
gender stereotyping, sexual division
of labour *and* women

hairdressing 76, 83
housing 104, 105

identity 2–3, 4, 56
industry 50, 58–60, 100; schools and 32,
40

Jenkins, Roy 128–9
JICs (Junior Instruction Centres)
10–23; and gender divisions 13, 14,
15–16, 21; curriculum 13, 14–15,
16–17, 25; effects 22–3; ideology 22;
opposition to 19; sanctions 18, 20, 22

labour market(s) 67; divisions in 52, 67,
68–9, 70, 73–4, 170–1, 173, 178–9

(*see also* sexual division of labour);
entry into 61–2, 71–2, 87, 184; in NZ
170, 180–1; internal 68, 74–7, 86;
intervention into 185; regional 88;
young people's position in 52, 67,
69–73, 80, 86, 180–1
labour movement 19
legitimation crisis 3, 5–6, 183
leisure 10, 11

MSC (Manpower Services
Commission) 47, 48, 51, 69–70; and
black people 118, 124, 130, 134–6,
137–8, 141; and control of education
7, 51, 53,.58–9, 61; and FE *see under*
FE; and political education 58–60;
and TVEI 30, 31, 33; assessment
guidelines 74; content of schemes
24–5, 56–7, 58–60, 62, 74, 87;
'occupational training families' 55,
79; use of old ideas 10–11, 23; *see also*
New Training Initiative *and* YTS
Maoris 173–4, 184; language 169
marriage 92, 101, 103–4, 109
mobility 13, 16
Morrison, Peter 58
mugging 131–2
multiculturalism 143

New Training Initiative 48, 153, 155–8;
see also YTS
New Zealand 167–71, 173–86

OTFs ('occupational training
families') 55, 79
Official Information Act (NZ) 167
OECD (Organization for European
Co-operation and Development) 70

physical training 16–17, 21, 80
political education 58–60
pregnancy 101; *see also* marriage
profiling 26, 37, 38, 41, 59, 74, 158, 160
police 122, 125, 127, 132
population 18, 43, 46, 53
positive action 138
pupils' rights 211

qualifications *see* credentials

race: research on 124–5, 126–7; *see also*

Author Index

Index